MW01680789

A GUIDE TO ASCENSION

THE ARCHITECTURE OF THIRD, FOURTH, AND FIFTH DIMENSIONAL CONSCIOUSNESS

Contact & Publisher

Publisher Contact: http://www.AscendedHearts.com
Printed in the United States of America
Published by: Ascended Hearts™, 2026-June
Cover & Editing: Marc Mourier
Co-editor: Pramala Mourier
Inside Graphics: Marc Mourier
Some illustrative graphics were co-created with AI (ChatGPT),
and refined by the authors to ensure technical and aesthetic consistency.

Identifiers

ISBN 979-8-9886896-0-7
Library of Congress Control Number
Printed Book Version (LCCN) 2026902854
BISG REL065000

Disclaimer

Intellectual Property

A Guide to Ascension

The Architecture of Third, Fourth, and Fifth Dimensional Consciousness

By

Marc Mourier &
Pramala Mourier

Dedicated
To Those Precious
Lightworkers and Starseeds
Who Tirelessly Assist
The Light in Fulfilling
Its Objective—to Serve
The Infinite Creator.

CONTENTS

THE PREMISE

THE BUILDING BLOCKS

THE TOOLS

THE PREMISE

THIS SECTION INTRODUCES YOU TO THE AUTHORS, OFFERS CLARIFYING INSIGHTS INTO OUR CORE THEMES, AND REFINES THE SCOPE OF WHAT ASCENSION TRULY ENCOMPASSES.

PREFACE

"...We are not human beings having
a spiritual experience here.
We are spiritual beings having
a human experience...."

Pierre Teilhard de Chardin

The human experience that de Chardin describes is about to take a profound turn. For thousands of years, humanity has debated our purpose, and place in the universe. That conversation is now approaching a turning point, because the fundamental reality we have long known—life in the 3rd Dimension—is gradually coming to an end.

Modern Western science and philosophy are approaching a shift that may require a major reconsideration of many of our current assumptions. The transition now underway may become one of the most significant changes in human history, possibly surpassing any global transformation seen in tens of thousands of years.

Earth quietly completed this transition in 2012. Many expected dramatic signs announcing the arrival of the Age of Aquarius. Instead, the change began gently, and almost unnoticed. The process has been gradual. We refer to this transition as the *Great Shift,* and the coming decades will likely bring changes that will reshape our understanding of *consciousness, and our place in the universe.*

Like everyone else, Pramala and I are simply small particles of light moving forward in the river of consciousness. Yet we hope we may offer something useful: insight into a transformation that is already unfolding around us. We have done our best to present the material in this book as clearly and faithfully as possible. What you are about to read is not speculation or casual opinion.

The original book on LightStreaming was published in 2020. Some elements have been refined since then, but its essential ideas remain intact, and are included here because they form the practical companion to the subject of Ascension.

The purpose of LightStreaming is to loosen the ego's grip on the conscious mind so that Ascension—the shift into higher dimensions—can occur more naturally. In the pages ahead, we examine the process of Ascension step-by-step, including both its benefits, and its challenges.

We also touch on the origins of the ego itself. This book offers an alternative way of understanding how the mind functions, and addresses several misunderstandings that have developed within traditional psychology.

For a long time, questions about consciousness have often been dismissed by the scientific establishment, and placed at the margins of serious inquiry. Yet the results emerging from this work suggest that consciousness may operate beyond the limits of current scientific models. Modern science has not yet fully recognized consciousness as a creative force.

Yeshua (Jesus) is frequently mentioned in these pages because he is *the only historical figure known to have completed the journey* through the 4th Density, described as the 6th Dimension. For this reason, he serves as a monumental example of the transition we are discussing. We ask readers to view this strictly from a *metaphysical perspective,* separate from the religious institutions, and doctrines that later formed around his name.

Nothing in this book should be interpreted as allegiance to any religious organization, institution, or philosophical movement. The authors remain fully independent of such affiliations.

LightStreaming is a registered trademark with the United States Patent and Trademark Office. It was developed by Marc Mourier and Pramala Mourier through decades of study, inquiry, and experience. Those who have worked with this modality often report that it helps open channels of connection with the Light. However, it should be understood strictly as a *spiritual* tool, and not as a replacement for medical or psychological care provided by licensed professionals.

The ideas presented in this book have been distilled into a clear and concise form. This guide is intended for readers who feel drawn to explore these concepts further. The subject may be unfamiliar to some, especially those without a background in cosmology or metaphysics. For that reason, the chapters have been arranged carefully so that understanding can gradually develop. Because this subject can easily overwhelm if not presented in an organized manner, we offer *a step-by step approach.* This allows the reader to stop and think, and reflect, if a pause is needed, without interrupting the grasp of the material.

Because the book frequently discusses densities and dimensions, we have chosen to spell out these terms rather than abbreviating them. For example, the text generally avoids shorthand such as "3D," in order to reduce confusion.

Ascended Hearts, the organization behind this work, was founded with a simple purpose: to provide a clear and open path for those seeking spiritual growth. Ascension, in its complete fulfillment, is not a minor event, nor is it something to approach casually. It represents a significant step in human development, and requires thoughtful preparation.

We would not devote our lives to helping others prepare for this process if such preparation were unnecessary. Meaningful Ascension requires a deliberate and personal effort.

It is our hope that the ideas presented here may encourage a deeper relationship with the spiritual realm—whether through prayer, meditation, quiet reflection, or inner listening. May this work help lift the veil for those who feel themselves standing at the threshold of awakening, drawn toward the Light rather than toward the structures of organized religion.

The world of Ascension and LightStreaming remains open to all who feel called to explore it. Many have already sensed that true spiritual freedom arises not from doctrine but from direct contact with the Light itself.

PREFACE HIGHLIGHTS:

- We live in an era of **historic planetary transition** in which 3rd-dimensional living is passing away, and Earth has **already** begun a major shift.
- LightStreaming is not a stand-alone modality, but a **practical tool needed to facilitate Ascension.**
- Our work and method is positioned as fully **independent** of religion, institutions, and conventional scientific orthodoxy.
- **The Ascension process is serious work** requiring planning, preparation, and deliberate inner development rather than passive belief.

ABOUT THE AUTHORS

PRAMALA

From an early age, I have been deeply curious about the fundamental nature of life and reality. I remember being seven years old, sitting quietly and wondering what happens when this life fades. Could it truly be that everything ends—that "life" simply stops? Something deep within me resisted that thought. Even then, I sensed that life could not be contained within a single breath of time.

As I grew up and moved across countries and cultures, I began to notice a universal rhythm. Every people, every land holds its own story about life, death, and the journey beyond. Beneath these differences runs a single current: the awareness of something greater—a presence that listens, guides, and heals.

My curiosity deepened. If this higher power could be reached through prayer, what exactly was prayer touching? My parents were born into the Hindu tradition but were not practicing, so my connection to that heritage came later. It was not until I walked the soil of India as a teenager that the names of Ganesh, Shiva, and Lakshmi began to speak to me—not as distant gods, but as living expressions of energy, each reflecting a facet of the Infinite.

I came to understand that when I prayed to Ganesh, I was not calling to an image, but to a vibration of clarity and strength that dissolves obstacles.

My schooling took me through the Christian faith and a convent, where I learned the prayers of another path. Whether it was Yeshua, Mary, or Ganesh, I sensed the same light shining through many windows. Every song and every prayer seemed to rise toward the same horizon.

Throughout my life, prayer has been both compass and companion—especially during illness, when the fragility of the body met the endurance of the Spirit. In 2015, after a brain aneurysm and other serious challenges, I witnessed the quiet power of the Light leading me back each time. During those uncertain nights, I felt held—not by chance, but by grace.

One of the most profound gifts of my recovery was the opening of a clear communication with the Light, most specifically with the presence of Yeshua. What began as subtle external whispers that at first unsettled me gradually became a steady and reliable stream of guidance. Today, these hundreds of channelings form the foundation of our Ascension work, offering a roadmap for the spiritual priorities of this transitional time.

Through this dialogue, I came to understand something important: the true engine of Ascension is not complex intellect, but the intelligence of the heart.

In our regular sessions with the Light, we are taught that the heart functions as a crystalline bridge—a portal translating higher-dimensional energy into a living experience within the body.

To me, this process of "remembering" is a deep and rhythmic attunement to the Universal Heart. By quieting the mind and entering the stillness of the heart center, we dissolve the barriers of the ego, and awaken the Divine Blueprint that has always existed within us.

Over time I came to understand that my path is guided—that I am meant to serve the Light that has never left me. To follow it means to heal, to comfort, and to help others remember what they already are. My gift gradually revealed itself through healing—through intuition, energy, and Soul memory.

My studies in clinical psychology, hypnotherapy, and the LightStreaming modalities have deepened this work. Through the teachings of Dr. Brian Weiss, and the practice of Quantum Healing Hypnosis, I help individuals reconnect with the eternal nature of their souls through past life regression.

Meeting my twin flame, Marc, has been one of the great miracles of my life—a union of purpose as much as of heart. Together we stand as instruments of the Light, serving those who seek wholeness in spirit, mind, and body.

Every life, I have learned, is a dialogue with the Universe—a journey from forgetting to remembering. And in that remembering we awaken to a simple truth: there has never been a separation between us and the Infinite. There has only been the slow, luminous unfolding of who we have always been.

MARC

My life unfolded very differently from what my parents imagined. They believed deeply in the security of lifelong employment, and saw predictability as the safest path in life. But that life felt to me like a slow erosion of the Soul, and I knew early on that I had to step away from it. In more than seventy years of living, I have spent less than two as an employee.

My journey has been a tapestry of many callings: Mayan tour operator, astrologer, garbage collector, car dealer, investment advisor, organist, piano tuner, conductor, author, fresh-food importer, and language teacher. Each became a different expression of curiosity and courage. I found success in most of them, but the true reward was always freedom itself.

Freedom became my constant companion—the insistence to live life on my own terms: to choose when to work, when to rest, what to eat, what to drive, and where life should take me next. It was not rebellion. It was the Soul refusing confinement.

Eventually that longing for freedom extended beyond worldly matters, and reached into the center of my spiritual life.

At seventeen, after moving from France to Norway, I traveled with my mother to Brighton, England. On the pier she had her palm read by a woman named Eva Petulengro. Everything Eva predicted later unfolded with astonishing accuracy—names, dates, even the appearance of a future companion. I watched in amazement as unseen forces seemed to reveal themselves through her words. It was my first glimpse of a universe alive with invisible intelligence.

Since that day I have always respected those who truly possess Higher-Self sight. They have rarely led me astray.

As I read sacred writings later in life, one question often troubled me: why did divine voices seem reserved only for prophets and chosen figures? Why could the Infinite not address me as well? Granted, I was no Isaiah or Ezekiel—but I longed for even a whisper of that communication.

That longing eventually led me from the frozen quiet of Norway to the ashram of Swami Narayanananda. There I learned that the path to truth can be illuminating, but also deeply revealing. Yoga showed me not only the body's lack of flexibility, but also the mind's lack of readiness for awakening. Somewhere within I already knew that Yoga would *not* be my vehicle to illumination in this life.

Years later life brought me to Jerusalem, a city where ancient stones still echo with prayer. There I reconnected with something vast and radiant—an inheritance of spirit that transcends time and creed. At the time I did not yet realize that the many fragments of my life were guiding me toward a discovery waiting in that holy city: direct communion with the Light.

The Light did more than answer—it revealed a way to make that communion accessible to others. That path became LightStreaming.

No soul walks this journey alone. My meeting with Pramala was divinely orchestrated—a union not of convenience but of calling. Together we formed a living partnership with the Light.

For much of my life I drifted without fully recognizing the current guiding me. Once I acknowledged the Light's invitation, everything changed. My purpose became clear: to teach what I am shown.

Though I have studied in respected institutions, I do not measure wisdom by degrees. True knowledge reveals itself through what one brings forth to uplift others.

Our primary spiritual mentor is Yeshua, along with the consciousness known as the Ananda Collective—a social memory complex of less than ten beings that includes Masters such as Saint Germain, Buddha, and Melchizedek.

When communication occurs with Yeshua, the information arrives as a unified thought from the entire collective, much as Ra describes in The Law of One[1]. Speaking with one member of the collective is, in effect, speaking with all of them simultaneously. One might say there is less privacy—but also far less possibility of misunderstanding. Sixteen eyes see better than two.

We share only what has been confirmed through that higher communion—never speculation, and never hearsay. Truth requires no decoration, only clarity.

In 2015 we were guided to begin developing LightStreaming. What we later discovered was that LightStreaming was never meant to stand alone. It is one of several tools designed to assist the Ascension process.

Ascension itself involves the compression of Light energy, and deeper access to what many traditions call Christ consciousness. To access its full potential, specific mental tools are required. LightStreaming provides some of those tools.

Around that same time an astrologer in Mysore, India pointed out something unusual in my horoscope. He told me that Moksha—enlightenment—was indicated in this lifetime, and even suggested the approximate year. Curious, I later reexamined the chart, and confirmed the same aspect. When reviewing Pramala's chart we found the same rare alignment.

Naturally, we brought these discoveries to Yeshua during our LightStreaming sessions. He confirmed them, though somewhat cryptically hinting that there would be others beyond us receiving Moksha.

From that moment we knew the coming decades would not be ordinary. With Yeshua's guidance we began mapping what preparation

---

1 Rueckert, C. L., Elkins, D., & McCarty, J. A. (2017). The Ra contact: Teaching the Law of One (Vol. 1).

would be required for the changes ahead. Gradually a remarkable picture began to emerge—a vision of humanity moving toward a profound transformation.

Today, more than a decade later, after hundreds of conversations with Yeshua and the Ananda Collective, we have gained a clearer understanding of what may help maximize the Ascension experience.

The teachings of the Light are universal. The curriculum is the same for anyone ready to remember. LightStreaming, as it relates to Ascension, unfolds through many stages. These stages are explored in the chapters that follow.

May this book serve as an invitation—to discover how the mind, the body, and the Light weave the fabric of our being. Study deeply, and you may find not only a longer life, but a fuller one—rich with purpose, wonder, and peace.

HOW TO APPROACH THIS MATERIAL

Many readers approach spiritual material in one of two ways. Some accept everything immediately through blind belief. Others reject the ideas just as quickly because they seem extraordinary. Neither reaction is necessary.

There is a third approach that is far more useful: *experiential verification.*

Much of Western religion has struggled because it relies heavily on belief without offering personal verification. Many teachings are presented as truths that must simply be accepted. Yet if a process cannot be verified through experience—even if it cannot be scientifically proven—it is reasonable to question whether the process is complete, or fully understood. This principle is very similar to the foundation of the scientific method.

BELIEF IS NOT REQUIRED

The purpose of this book is not to convince you to adopt a belief system. Its purpose is much simpler: to invite you to observe your own experience honestly.

Spiritual development is not a matter of belief. It is a matter of *expanding awareness.* This guide therefore invites you to observe, experiment, and reflect.

Let me share a small anecdote.

Years ago, I had a friend in Norway named Bjørn who was a medical doctor. He was a committed atheist, and believed in almost nothing beyond established science. Bjørn did not even believe that human beings possess a Soul. His medical practice relied heavily on pharmaceuticals.

The mind is everything. What you think you become."

Buddha

At the same time, in a nearby community lived a man known as Snåsamannen (the "Snåsa Man" - pron. 'Snaussa'), whose real name was Joralf Gjerstad. He was widely known throughout Norway as a healer. During his lifetime he reportedly helped around fifty thousand people over a period of sixty-five years. He never charged anyone for his services, and was known as a deeply humble and spiritual man. He passed away in 2021, but his reputation remains strong throughout the country.

One evening over dinner I asked Bjørn what he thought of the Snåsa Man. His response was immediate. He dismissed him as a fraud and a disgrace to medicine.

This is the kind of closed mind we hope readers will avoid. A lack of understanding should never lead automatically to rejection. A more balanced response could have been:

"I don't understand it, but perhaps there is something there. Let me learn more."

Rigid belief systems—whether religious or scientific—can create the same limitation that Ascension seeks to overcome: fixed mental positions.

TREAT THIS GUIDE AS A WORKING HYPOTHESIS

Some ideas in this book may initially feel surprising or even uncomfortable. When that happens, it may help to treat the material as a working hypothesis rather than a final conclusion.

Think of the ideas presented here as possibilities worth exploring. You are *not* asked to believe them. You are free to test them through observation and personal experience. This approach avoids dogma, and encourages curiosity—and curiosity remains one of the most powerful tools of discovery.

PERSONAL EXPERIENCE TAKES PRECEDENCE OVER AUTHORITY

In spiritual matters, personal experience has always been the most reliable teacher.

Throughout history, individuals who explored consciousness through meditation, contemplation, and inner observation often reported remarkably similar insights about the nature of awareness, and the evolution of the human spirit. These insights form the foundation for many of the ideas discussed in this book.

It is not the strongest of the species that survives, nor the most intelligent that survives. It is the one that is most adaptable to change."

Charles Darwin

Some readers may encounter concepts here that initially seem unfamiliar or unlikely. That reaction is perfectly natural. New ideas rarely become clear immediately.

Rather than accepting or rejecting them too quickly, it is often more helpful to remain curious.

Some ideas may resonate immediately. Others may take time and reflection before their meaning becomes clear.

Understanding tends to unfold gradually. Concepts that appear abstract at first often reveal deeper meaning as awareness develops.

The true value of any spiritual teaching does not lie in words on a page. Its value lies in the transformation it may inspire within the reader.

For this reason, the purpose of this guide is not to provide final answers, but to offer perspectives and tools that may help us explore our own consciousness.

Approach the material with curiosity, honesty, and a willingness to observe your own experience. Over time, what is meaningful will reveal itself naturally.

In that journey, the ultimate authority is not an external book, but your own direct insight.

WHY UNFAMILIAR CONCEPTS APPEAR IN THE GUIDE

Some ideas in this book may feel unfamiliar because concepts such as densities, higher consciousness, and Ascension are rarely discussed in conventional education or scientific models of reality.

Our everyday language was developed to describe the physical world—a world of objects, linear time, and separation. Ascension, however, involves states of awareness based on unity and higher frequency. Because of this, ordinary language often struggles to describe these experiences.

The measure of intelligence is the ability to change.

Albert Einstein

New terms sometimes become necessary. Words such as densities, vibrational alignment, and multidimensional awareness serve as tools that help describe realities beyond everyday experience. At first these terms may feel unfamiliar, much like technical language when learning navigation before setting sail. With time and repetition they become easier to understand.

The analytical mind—often associated with the ego—naturally prefers what it already knows. Presenting unfamiliar ideas early in the book therefore helps move beyond the automatic resistance of the logical mind. That moment of intellectual discomfort is often a signal that consciousness is expanding.

The transformation described in this book is not a small adjustment in lifestyle. It is a profound shift in awareness.

Because of that, it would be surprising if the ideas felt completely familiar from the beginning. The presence of new concepts simply reflects the depth of the transition being described.

A PERSPECTIVE ON KNOWLEDGE

Consider how often humanity has misunderstood reality: Thousands of years later we still do not know exactly how the pyramids were built. Modern machinery cannot reproduce the Great Pyramid of Cheops. The miracle of the Sun reported at Fatima in 1917 was witnessed by over seventy thousand people, and still lacks a conventional explanation.

Only a little more than a century ago, scientists believed that the Milky Way was the only galaxy in the universe.

Even the scientific study of consciousness itself is relatively recent. It was only in 1990 that scientists *identified reliable neural correlates of consciousness* through the work of Francis Crick and Christof Koch et al.

Other mysteries remain equally intriguing. The Shroud of Turin continues to puzzle researchers because no known artistic or chemical method explains how its three-dimensional image was formed on ancient linen. The Piri Reis map of 1513 depicts parts of Antarctica with striking accuracy centuries before the continent was officially discovered. How could that happen?

Even the structure of DNA—the double helix that governs all life—was only decoded in the mid-twentieth century.

These examples remind us that scientific understanding evolves continuously. What we consider certain today may one day appear incomplete. The foundations of our knowledge are often less solid than we assume.

Before beginning the deeper exploration ahead, it may help to see how the ideas in this book unfold, and a map of the journey ahead that accompany them.

APPROACH REMINDERS:

- Avoid both blind belief and automatic rejection, and instead **adopt experiential verification** as the proper stance.
- The book is meant to function as a **working hypothesis**, inviting observation, testing, and reflection rather than dogmatic acceptance.
- **Direct experience is given priority** over authority in spiritual matters.
- Unfamiliar concepts are introduced because Ascension **requires a new vocabulary** for realities that ordinary language does not adequately describe.

A Map of the Journey Ahead

The Journey Through This Book

This book guides you through the profound evolution of human consciousness—from ego-centered awareness to unity consciousness.

Part I The Premise

Why there is suddenly a global shift in consciousness.

The human condition is in flux, undergoing a profound transformation already set in motion, and nearing full activation. Cosmology points toward a convergence of measurable events unfolding in real-time. In this cosmic drama, consciousness is the protagonist, we are the supporting cast, and Earth is the stage. Here, we explore the premise of this global evolution, and how it will transform life as we know it.

Part II The Building Blocks

How do we access consciousness?

The essential tools for this journey are the mind, the Light and its conduits, and the energetic network of the chakras. Simply possessing these building blocks is insufficient; we must also master their configurations, and the conditions required to activate them. To do so, we must examine a main interface: the mind.

Part III The Tools

How do we integrate the transformation?

The tools required to prepare for Ascension are varied and task-specific. We may find ourselves drawn to certain methods over others, as we each respond to different frequencies. Our Soul contract already contains these preferences; by unlocking the inner depths of that contract with these tools, you will find the complete map waiting for you there...

This journey moves from ***understanding***... to ***awakening***... to ***transformation.***

May this journey awaken remembrance, deepen wisdom, and guide you home to your true nature.

INTRODUCTION

Less than 150 years ago, humanity's understanding of the spiritual world was missing a crucial element: the role of the Ascended Masters. How could such an important piece of the spiritual puzzle remain largely unknown?

For centuries, many organized religions tightly controlled which teachings were delivered, and how they were interpreted. These institutions rarely encouraged direct mystical insight—the Gnostic[1] path that seeks personal knowledge of the Divine—and therefore seldom promoted the idea of spiritual Ascension.

The Light, however, moves with its own timing. As humanity approached a new transition in consciousness, conditions were prepared to introduce a broader understanding of the spiritual hierarchy that supports life on Earth. This development created a more open relationship between the spiritual realms and humanity—a connection that had long been restricted by institutional religion.

For centuries, religious authority often emphasized sin and human unworthiness. The path to redemption was frequently portrayed as dependent on obedience to religious structures that claimed authority over salvation. In many cases, this approach created a cycle of dependency rather than genuine liberation.

Yeshua's original message was one of profound freedom, yet much of its essence became obscured during the Piscean Age. This distortion shaped global consciousness for nearly two thousand years.

---

1 A direct, experiential, and mystical insight into the nature of reality and the divine.

Then, in the late nineteenth century, a remarkable shift occurred. Helena Petrovna Blavatsky[2] introduced the Western world to the concept of the Ascended Masters through her writings and teachings in the 1870's. Her revelations expanded humanity's view of the spiritual world in ways few had imagined.

For many observers, the impact was extraordinary. It was as if an entirely new dimension of spiritual reality had suddenly been revealed. Blavatsky described the existence of advanced spiritual beings—masters who had completed their human journey, and continued their work from higher realms of consciousness. What began as an esoteric teaching slowly helped shape a new spiritual culture that no longer depended solely on traditional religious institutions.

Her work also introduced ideas that later evolved into concepts such as the Galactic Federation—a collective of advanced spiritual intelligences assisting the evolution of consciousness on Earth.

Today, many individuals believe humanity is receiving increasing guidance from beyond the physical world. The relationship between the Infinite Creator, advanced spiritual beings, and humanity itself is becoming more visible to those sensitive to these realities.

Within this framework, the spiritual hierarchy can be viewed as consisting of four principal groups[3]:

1. ***Earth Beings who have crossed over***
2. ***Ascended Masters***
3. ***Angels***
4. ***Archangels***

---

[2] Helena Petrovna Blavatsky, often known as Madame Blavatsky; 12 August [O.S. 31 July] 1831 – 8 May 1891) was a Russian occultist, philosopher, and author who co-founded the Theosophical Society in 1875. She gained an international following as the leading theoretician of Theosophy, the esoteric movement that the society promoted. [https://en.wikipedia.org/wiki/Helena_Blavatsky]

[3] Seraphs, Cherubs (and Elohim) are not dealt with here as they have limited direct influence in LightStreaming.

Among these groups, the Ascended Masters occupy a unique position.

An Ascended Master is generally understood as a being who has completed the human evolutionary cycle. During their final incarnation, the higher centers of consciousness—often symbolized by the 3rd-Eye and Crown Chakra—fully awaken, allowing direct communion with the Divine. The Crown Chakra acts like a veritable spiritual satellite dish.

After physical death, such beings are no longer required to reincarnate. They may return to Earth if they choose, but they are no longer bound by the cycle of rebirth known in Eastern traditions as samsara. In other words, they have completed the human curriculum.

Around the same time that these ideas entered Western spiritual thought, modern psychology was beginning to explore the structure of the human mind. Through the development of hypnosis and depth psychology, researchers discovered that the subconscious mind could play an active role in personal transformation. Under deep hypnotic states, individuals sometimes reported contact with deeper aspects of consciousness—what many traditions refer to as the Higher-Self.

These discoveries suggested that the human mind may be capable of accessing information beyond ordinary awareness, including memories, insights, and intuitive guidance. Psychology eventually identified another layer of consciousness known as the Superconscious mind—a level of awareness that appears capable of receiving impressions from beyond the individual personality.

In the framework presented in this book, communication between humanity and the spiritual realms often occurs through these deeper levels of consciousness.

The four groups described earlier—those who have crossed over, Ascended Masters, Angels, and Archangels—are believed to be among the principal communicators within this larger spiritual ecosystem.

The chapters ahead explore these relationships in greater detail, particularly in the section titled "Our Family: The Group of Four."

As the book unfolds, we will examine how Ascension may occur, under what conditions it becomes possible, and what practices may help prepare individuals for this transition.

Three primary forces interact in this process:

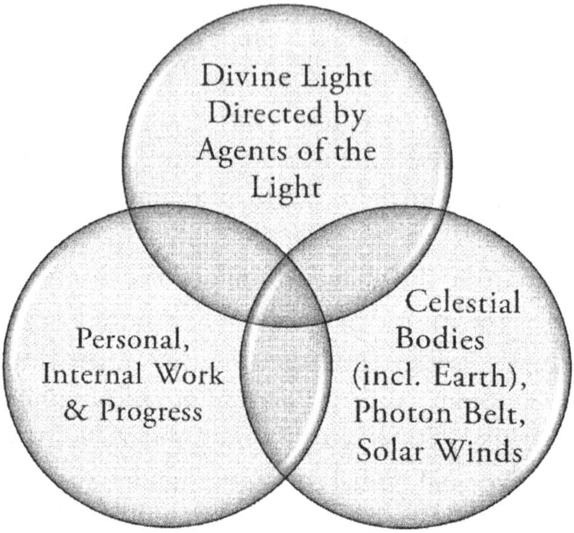

WHY ASCENSION MATTERS

Ascension is not a quick fix within the framework of linear time.

Over vast spans of evolution, a Soul experiences many environments and stages of development. Each stage introduces new lessons and challenges. The Soul is therefore an extraordinarily resilient traveler, capable of adapting to many different density environments. At present, humanity appears to be approaching another major threshold. Ascension matters for several important reasons:

1. From Survival to Sovereignty.

3rd-dimensional life is largely governed by the physical laws of matter. Much of our attention is devoted to survival—securing resources, maintaining health, and navigating the challenges of physical existence.

Ascension gradually shifts this focus. Instead of feeling controlled by external circumstances, individuals begin to recognize their capacity to shape their own experience. Life moves from survival toward sovereignty.

2. From Separation to Unity.

3rd Density consciousness is strongly influenced by the ego, which creates the perception that we exist as separate individuals competing within a fragmented world. This sense of separation often produces fear, conflict, and isolation.

Ascension gradually dissolves this illusion. As awareness expands, individuals begin to experience a deeper interconnectedness with others. Compassion and cooperation become natural expressions rather than moral obligations.

In such a world, the idea of harming another becomes increasingly difficult, because the boundary between self and other begins to soften.

3. A New Relationship with Time.

Ordinarily we experience time as a straight line moving from past to future. The past can generate regret, while the future can produce anxiety.

Ascension alters this relationship with time.

As consciousness expands, awareness becomes increasingly centered in the present moment. The delay between thought and manifestation begins to shrink. Life becomes less about waiting for future outcomes, and more about fully inhabiting the present.

The familiar phrase "living in the now" has sometimes been overused, but the deeper reality behind it represents a significant transformation in human perception.

4. The Role of Wanderers

Many individuals alive today feel a strong inner calling toward service. Some spiritual traditions describe such individuals as Wanderers—souls who have evolved beyond 3rd-density consciousness but voluntarily incarnate on Earth to assist during periods of planetary transition.

These beings may originate from higher densities of consciousness—4th, 5th, or even 6th Density—and choose to enter human life in order to support humanity's evolution. Their presence helps stabilize higher frequencies of awareness within the collective field of the planet.

For these individuals, Ascension represents the completion of a specific phase of service. It allows them to return to a higher vibrational state where they can continue contributing to the evolution of consciousness on a broader scale.

If you feel strongly drawn to the ideas in this book, it is possible that this description resonates with your own experience.

(The diagram below visually summarizes these four reasons Ascension matters: the shift from survival to sovereignty, the dissolution of separation, the transformation of time perception, and the fulfillment of a Wanderer's purpose.)

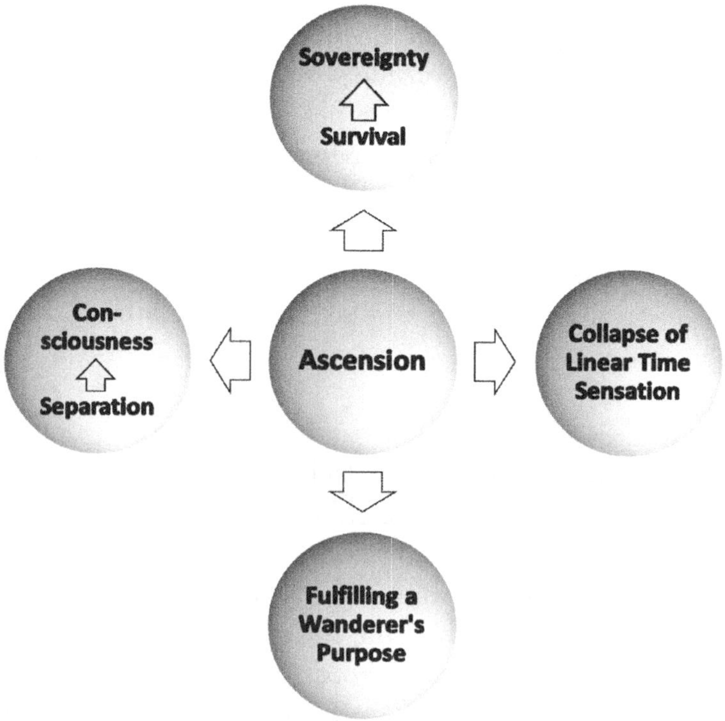

INTRODUCTION HIGHLIGHTS:

- We encourage our readers to approach the teachings neither with blind belief nor immediate rejection, but with an **attitude of open inquiry,** and **personal verification**.
- The guiding principle of the book is **experiential verification**—the idea that spiritual concepts should be examined through **personal experience** rather than accepted solely on faith or authority.
- Readers are invited to observe their own experiences honestly, and evaluate the teachings through direct inner confirmation, **much like the scientific method tests ideas through observation and evidence**.
- The material is therefore not presented as a belief system to adopt, but as a framework for exploration that may help individuals **better understand consciousness**, the Light, and the process of spiritual evolution.
- By maintaining curiosity and discernment, the reader can engage with the ideas in a constructive and balanced way, allowing genuine insight to arise through **experience rather than dogma**.

CHAPTER ONE

DENSITIES AND DIMENSIONS

DENSITIES

We begin this exploration of densities—and later dimensions—with an important clarification. These concepts form the foundation of Ascension, yet they are often misunderstood.

Because both terms appear throughout this book, it is helpful to establish a shared vocabulary before going further. (Some readers may find this chapter and the fourth slightly technical. Take your time. Once the foundation is clear, the rest of the guide becomes much easier to follow.)

A useful way to understand the relationship between densities and dimensions is through the analogy of education.

School systems consist of major stages such as elementary school, middle school, high school, and university. These stages resemble densities. Within each stage there are individual grade levels—first grade, second grade, and so on. These levels resemble dimensions.

Moving from one school to another represents a shift in density. Advancing from one grade to the next within the same school represents a change in dimension.

Our planet is a conscious entity. It emits and receives conscious energy, and participates actively in its own development. In simple terms, Earth evolves.

This evolution unfolds in stages. According to the framework used in this book, Earth progresses through seven major phases of development, called densities. Some of these phases have already occurred, while others lie far in the future. Interestingly, the account of creation recorded in the Book of Genesis appears to describe the emergence of the first two densities, and the order in which they unfolded.

Earth remained in 2nd Density until approximately 75,000 years ago. At that time it entered 3rd Density, where it remained for roughly 75,000 years.

In 2012, Earth transitioned into 4th Density. This stage will last approximately 30 million years before the planet continues evolving toward the 5-7th Density, more than 150 million years from now. Each density functions as a kind of evolutionary laboratory where consciousness exhibits specific qualities.

According to the Ra material, the densities unfold in the following way:

1st Density:	***Elemental/Atomic.*** Lasted ~2 billion years. [Started ~6.6 billion years ago[1].]
2nd Density:	***Plant/Animal Consciousness.*** Lasted ~4.2 billion years.
3rd Density:	***Consciousness and Individual ego.*** Started ~75,000 years ago.
4th Density:	***Unified Consciousness, Love, & Empathy.*** Started in 2012.

[1] "Modern" Science has, according to the Ra-material, so far miscalculated the Earth's age to 4.54 billion yrs. The Ra-Material, states her age to be ~6.6 billion yrs. old. Rueckert, C. L., Elkins, D., & McCarty, J. A. (2017). The Ra contact: Teaching the Law of One (Vol. 1).

	Will last ~30 million years[2].
5th Density:	***Wisdom/Non-dual Awareness*** Will last ~50 million years.
6th Density:	***Unity of Love and Wisdom.*** Will last ~75 million years.
7th Density:	***Source Return/Completion.***

Humanity entered 3rd Density roughly 75,000 years ago. Prior to that time, human beings existed, but did not yet possess full self-awareness. Life operated primarily through instinct.

Earth itself (excluding its dwellers) has now moved into the early stages of 4th Density. The dominant qualities of this phase are love, unity consciousness, and empathy. The central challenge for humanity today is to grow into these qualities.

Each planetary body within the solar system evolves at its own pace. Not all planets progress at the same speed or express the same vibrational intensity—just as no two human beings mature at exactly the same rate.

The Sun itself occupies much higher ranges of development. Ananda tells us it is home to densities between 14 and 50, playing an important role whenever Earth undergoes a major evolutionary shift. In summary, densities represent *broad stages of consciousness* through which life evolves.

They describe the long arc of spiritual development for both planets, and civilizations. Each density reflects a particular level of self-awareness, moral agency, and unity with the whole. In this context, the word density refers to the degree of conscious compression within large celestial systems such as planets and solar systems. As awareness expands, that compression gradually loosens.

The veil separating individual consciousness from the greater whole

---

2 This is the approximate amount of time Earth will stay in 4th Density, not the amount of time *mankind* will remain in 4th Density.

becomes thinner.

DIMENSIONS

While densities represent major stages of evolution, dimensions describe how consciousness operates within each stage. In other words, a density tells us where we are in the evolutionary process, while a dimension describes how consciousness expresses itself at that level.

Some densities contain multiple dimensions. For example, both 3rd and 4th Density are subdivided into two dimensions each. Other densities—such as 1st, 2nd, 5th, 6th, and 7th—appear to function as single unified levels.

Within each dimension, consciousness expresses itself in a different way. Later chapters explore these expressions in greater detail: how duality operates in the 3rd Dimension, how exposure and awakening characterize the 4th, and how unity consciousness becomes fully established in the 5th.

Creation, in this sense, is elegantly structured. At the deepest level, the inner spirit acts as an anchor that keeps us balanced regardless of what occurs in the external world. When we remain aligned with that inner center, we access a steady source of strength and unity that transcends physical circumstances. Dimensions therefore represent finer subdivisions within a density—much like grade levels within a school.

Humanity is currently completing its experience within 3rd Density, which contains two dimensions: the 3rd and 4th.

These dimensions describe stages[3] of awakening within the density itself. They are explored in greater detail in later chapters. As a young student, I (Marc) struggled early on understanding the difference between weight and mass until a teacher made it click. The relationship between density and dimension is similar. Don't let the technicalities confuse you. Simply focus on *dimensions* 3, 4, and 5—they are what truly matter right now.

[3] Even though equi-temporal on the chart, real time numbers would render each dimension's timespan unequal.

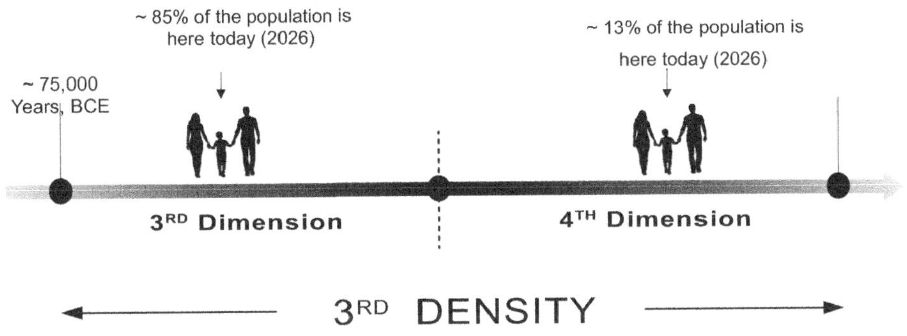

Earth has already moved into 4th Density, slightly ahead of most of its population.

The transition toward 4th Density began around 1994 and reached a major turning point in 2012. According to this model, the shift will become fully integrated—allowing 5th-dimensional awareness to emerge—around the year 2030. In other words, Earth is already inviting humanity to evolve along with it.

A population cannot remain indefinitely on a planet whose energetic environment no longer matches its own level of consciousness.

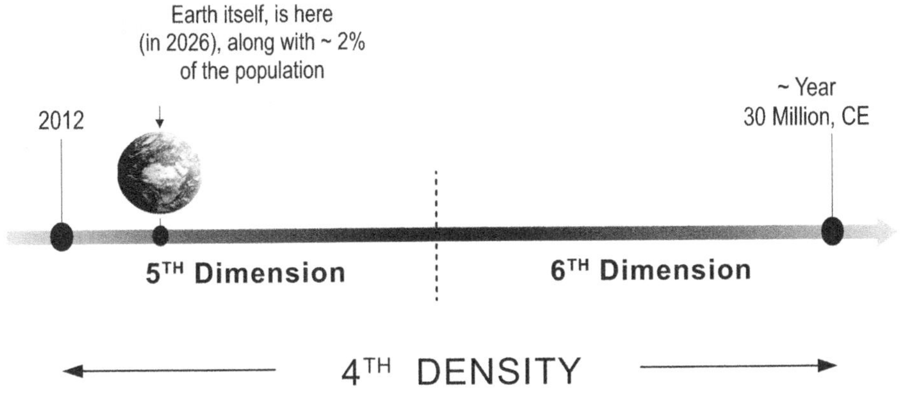

On a linear graph, densities 3,4 and 5 would look like this for Earth:

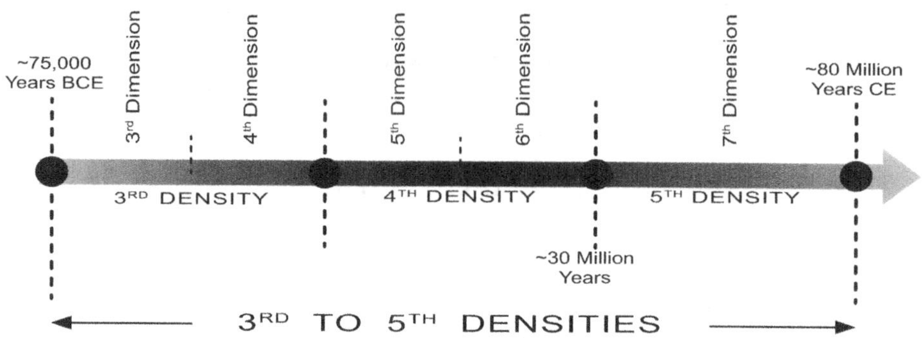

The larger evolutionary movement described in this book is therefore a transition from duality consciousness to unity consciousness.

Duality consciousness defines the 3rd Dimension. It perceives reality through opposites: hot and cold, good and evil, right and wrong. Unity consciousness, characteristic of the 5th Dimension, dissolves these divisions, and replaces them with unconditional awareness and creative harmony. This shift represents one of the most profound transformations humanity has ever faced.

One key mechanism supporting this transformation is a gradual change in how we experience time. Past, present, and future begin to merge into a single continuum. For some individuals this shift may occur quickly; for others, it may unfold gradually over years.

In the next chapter, we turn to the central force driving this entire evolutionary process: consciousness itself.

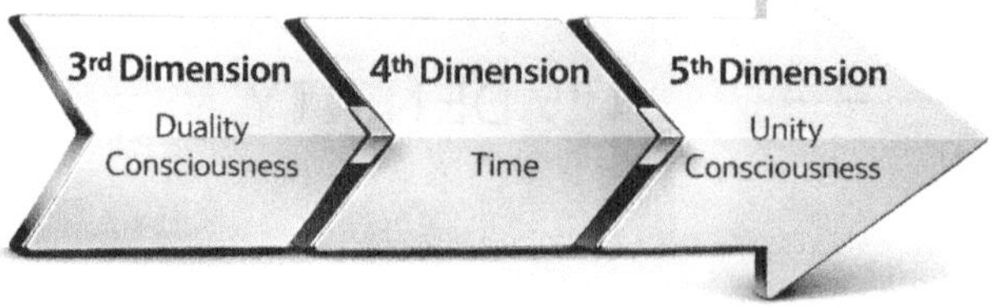

CHAPTER HIGHLIGHTS:

- **Densities are broad stages** of planetary and spiritual evolution, representing major levels of consciousness development through which Earth and life progress over immense time scales.
- Earth evolves through **seven** densities, each associated with a different archetype of consciousness (e.g., elemental matter, biological life, individual ego, love/unified awareness, wisdom, unity, and eventual return to Source).
- **Humanity entered 3rd Density about 75,000 years ago**, the stage where self-awareness and individual identity emerged.
- Within this model, **Earth transitioned into 4th Density in 2012**, characterized by themes of **love, empathy, and unified consciousness**, though most humans are still completing the transition.
- **Dimensions are finer subdivisions within a density** that describe how consciousness operates or expresses itself at that level—similar to grade levels within a school stage.
- The evolutionary movement described is a shift from 3rd Dimension duality consciousness toward 5th Dimension unity consciousness, **representing a major transformation** in human awareness.

THE SCHOOL OF CONSCIOUSNESS

How Densities and Dimensions Relate

Densities are the major stages of evolution—like schools.
Dimensions are the grades within each stage—how consciousness operates.

1. DENSITIES = THE SCHOOLS

Major stages of planetary and consciousness evolution

1ST DENSITY → **2ND DENSITY** → **3RD DENSITY** → **4TH DENSITY** → **5TH DENSITY**

- **1ST DENSITY** — **Matter & Energy**: Elements, minerals, atoms — *Kindergarten*
- **2ND DENSITY** — **Life**: Plants, animals, growth, instinct — *Elementary School*
- **3RD DENSITY** — **Self-Aware**: Individuality, ego, free will — *High School*
- **4TH DENSITY** — **Unity & Love**: Compassion, understanding, group consciousness — *University*
- **5TH DENSITY** — **Wisdom**: Non-dual awareness, higher mind, service — *Graduate School and Beyond*

2. DIMENSIONS = THE GRADES

How consciousness operates within a density

WITHIN 3RD DENSITY

- **3RD DIMENSION** — **Duality Awareness**: Ego, separation, right vs. wrong, polarities
- **4TH DIMENSION** — **Awakening Phase**: Exposure of truth, spiritual seeking, inner expansion

WITHIN 4TH DENSITY

- **5TH DIMENSION** — **Unity Consciousness**: Heart-centered, oneness, acceptance, expanded empathy
- **6TH DIMENSION** — **Love + Wisdom Integration**: Higher mind, synthesis, service, co-creation

3. HUMAN EXPERIENCE

Our journey through the school of consciousness

SURVIVAL → **IDENTITY** → **AWAKENING** → **UNITY** → **WISDOM**

- **SURVIVAL**: Basic needs, physical focus
- **IDENTITY**: Personal self, desires, roles
- **AWAKENING**: Questioning, seeking truth
- **UNITY**: Love, connection, we are one
- **WISDOM**: Higher purpose, service, creation

Ego Dominant → Ego Weakening → Heart Consciousness → Unity Consciousness

KEY TAKEAWAY

You are a soul-student moving through the School of Consciousness.
Each density is a school. Each dimension is a grade.
The goal is not perfection, but evolution.

CHAPTER TWO

CONSCIOUSNESS

THE THREE ASPECTS OF CONSCIOUSNESS

Attempting to explore Ascension without first understanding consciousness would be nearly impossible. It would be like trying to cross the ocean without ever leaving the shore.

Rather than diving into an abstract philosophical discussion, our goal here is simpler: to clarify the basic structure of consciousness, and our place within it. This approach helps avoid the vague explanations that often surround the topic, and instead builds a clearer framework for understanding.

Consciousness can be viewed through three primary lenses:

- **Universal consciousness**
- **Personal (Human) consciousness**
- **Archetypal consciousness**

UNIVERSAL CONSCIOUSNESS

Consciousness is the fundamental substance of creation, and the driving force behind the Ascension process. At its deepest level, consciousness exists as a single unified field. In other words, there is *one* consciousness. All things arise from it.

The primacy of the Infinite Creator implies that creation must have a structure through which infinite awareness can express itself. That structure is consciousness. In this view, the universe itself is *made* of consciousness. (The smallest units of consciousness are often referred to as monads.)

As discussed in the previous chapter, consciousness evolves through seven densities, or levels of awareness. The 4th Density marks an important turning point. It is the level where humanity begins to engage more directly with universal consciousness, and where love becomes the dominant frequency of awareness.

To perceive this expanded reality, additional sensory capacities must develop. Many traditions describe these capacities as energetic centers or chakras, which begin to activate more fully as consciousness evolves. (We will explore this topic later in the book, page 127).

HUMAN CONSCIOUSNESS

Before we can fully experience universal consciousness, we must first navigate the structures of *human* consciousness. The 3rd and 4th Dimensions provide the environment where this process unfolds. If universal consciousness is compared to a high-voltage energy system, human consciousness is its carefully stepped-down version—adapted to operate within the physical body in that density.

The human structure therefore functions through two opposing influences:

- the ego, which focuses on survival and identity
- the spiritual self, which moves toward unity and awareness

The challenge of human life is to gradually shift our orientation from ego-driven perception toward spiritually guided awareness. In doing so, we prepare ourselves for the transition into the next density.

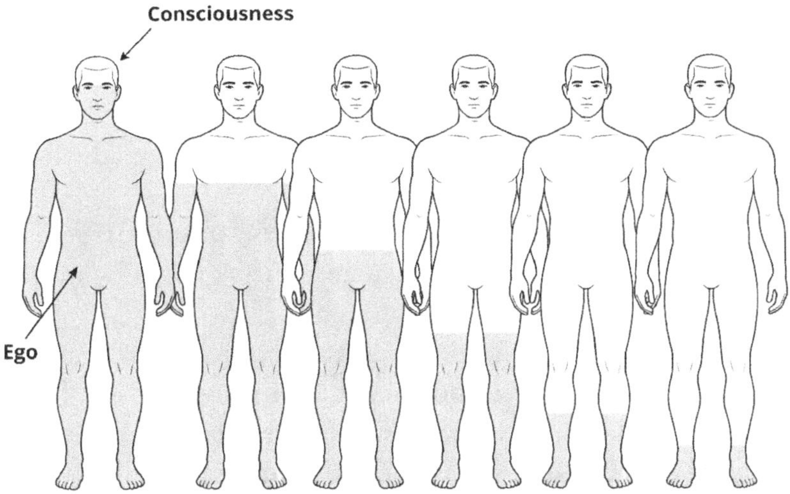

THE GRADUAL REPLACEMENT OF EGO BY CONSCIOUSNESS

Human consciousness can be perceived in three tiers:

1. The Subconscious Tier

The subconscious mind is associated with sleep, dreams, and stored habits. It functions as a repository for patterns and memories accumulated over time. Because of this, the subconscious is often accessed during hypnosis.

2. The Lower Consciousness Tier (Ordinary Human Awareness)

In everyday language, this level is often simply called "consciousness." More precisely, it is lower consciousness, or the lower self.

This level corresponds to ordinary human awareness within the 3rd Dimension. It allows us to think, remember, reason, and identify ourselves as individuals.

Several characteristics define this state:

Ego Governance: The ego functions as the primary authority, therefore shaping how consciousness interprets "reality."

Duality: Experience is structured through opposites: self and other, good and bad, fear and love.

Limitation: Awareness is fragmented, rooted in fear, and strongly tied to physical identity.

Transience: From a metaphysical perspective, this state is temporary. As consciousness evolves, identification with the ego gradually dissolves.

3. Superconsciousness (Higher Consciousness): Superconsciousness represents a state of heightened awareness guided by intuition rather than sensory logic.

It stands in contrast to the lower mind, and reflects a corrected perception of reality—one no longer dominated by ego-based survival instincts. This level of consciousness often produces creative insight, inspiration, and what we sometimes call genius.

At its highest expression, consciousness enters what many traditions call Christ consciousness—a state of pure unity that transcends ordinary perception. This state reflects the omnipresent intelligence of the Creator, present within every atom of existence.

It cannot be fully experienced while the mind remains dominated by the ego. Instead, it represents a profound expansion of identity—from identification with the physical body to awareness of the greater "I AM" presence.

Most people identify strongly with their thoughts, emotions, and personal history. Higher consciousness reveals something different: You are not the thought itself—you are the observer of the thought. Several qualities characterize this state:

Forgiveness and Calmness:

Awareness becomes peaceful and intuitive.

Clarity:

The illusions of the physical world are recognized without being mistaken for ultimate reality.

THE REPLACEMENT OF EGO BY CONSCIOUSNESS

Our Ascension Journey: From Separation to Unity

"The ego divides and protects. Consciousness unites and expands."

EGO DOMINANT STATE

3rd Density Experience
Living from Separation and Fear

IDENTITY
I am the body and mind. Defined by roles and possessions.

MOTIVATION
Fear, lack, control, and personal gain.

PERCEPTION
Sees separation, judgment, and duality.

EMOTIONS
Fear, anger, jealousy, guilt, and pride.

FOCUS
Past regrets or future worries. Survival and self-protection.

RELATIONSHIPS
Uses, competes, compares, and seeks validation.

POWER
Over others, through force, manipulation, or domination.

RESULTS
Stress, conflict, karma, and repeated lessons.

THE SHIFT

Choice • Awareness • Inner Work
Grace • Guidance

THE BRIDGE OF TRANSFORMATION

AWARENESS
I see my patterns.

ACCEPTANCE
I accept myself fully.

RELEASE
I let go of what no longer serves me.

HEALING
I heal and integrate my experiences.

ALIGNMENT
I align with truth, love, and purpose.

SURRENDER
I trust the Divine within and without.

CONSCIOUSNESS DOMINANT STATE

4th & 5th Density Experience
Living from Unity and Love

IDENTITY
I am a soul having a human experience. Infinite and whole.

MOTIVATION
Love, purpose, growth, and service.

PERCEPTION
Sees unity, connection, and divine order.

EMOTIONS
Peace, joy, gratitude, compassion, and love.

FOCUS
Present moment awareness. Creation and inner alignment.

RELATIONSHIPS
Supports, uplifts, collaborates, and honors all.

POWER
With others, through love, wisdom, and co-creation.

RESULTS
Harmony, abundance, evolution, and freedom.

THE ESSENCE OF THE SHIFT

FROM EGO...

I am separate
I want
I protect
I control
I survive

→ **RECOGNIZE**
See the ego patterns clearly.

→ **CHOOSE**
Choose love over fear.

→ **TRANSFORM**
Release the old, embrace the new.

→ **EMBODY**
Live from your higher truth.

→ TO CONSCIOUSNESS...

I am connected
I give
I trust
I co-create
I thrive

Ascension is not about becoming something new.
It is about remembering who you truly are.

Transitional Function: Superconsciousness acts as a bridge between ordinary perception, and direct spiritual knowledge.

Non-Dual Awareness: The sense of separation between observer and observed disappears.

Timelessness: While lower consciousness operates within linear time, higher consciousness exists in the eternal present.

Knowledge Rather Than Perception: At this level, awareness moves beyond interpretation, and enters direct knowing.

ARCHETYPAL CONSCIOUSNESS

Archetypal consciousness is not a separate form of consciousness, but rather a system of universal symbolic patterns embedded within consciousness itself. The archetypal mind is a kind of metaphysical operating system created by the Logos, the creative intelligence governing our galaxy. An archetype is like a lens through which consciousness expresses itself, to allow us to see the true meaning of something.

Archetypes function as tools that accelerate the evolution of consciousness back toward the One Infinite Creator. They allow communication from Creation to appear in symbolic form. Dreams provide a good example.

Just as artificial intelligence (AI) can convert written information into images, consciousness often communicates through symbolic imagery during dreams. Dreams, generated outside the body, can arise in two ways:

- As natural symbolic processing of daily experience
- As directed communication from spiritual sources

Spiritual intelligence existed long before artificial intelligence. In many traditions it is believed that higher intelligence can communicate with us through symbolic imagery connected to our individual life path. Dreams sometimes clarify past events, reveal emotional patterns, or offer insight into future developments. Dreams therefore function as one of the major channels through which archetypal consciousness communicates with us.

For example, years ago I dreamed that I was standing in front of a casino slot machine, and had won a large jackpot. The coins poured out so abundantly that the machine jammed. I had experienced similar dreams before, and sensed that it symbolized abundance, but I did not know how it would manifest. Later, during a LightStreaming session, we asked the Light for clarification. The answer was simple: "A financial windfall is coming." Soon afterward, a family member passed away, and an inheritance arrived exactly as the dream had suggested.

Experiences like this illustrate how symbolic communication can operate through dreams. There are millions of archetypes. Some are more recognizable than others, but all carry deeper meaning. For example, do we recognize the archetypal meaning of the Star of David, the chambered nautilus, the menorah, a river, a volcano, and so on?

Archetypes act as the deep structural language of consciousness itself. They are universal patterns that *organize* perception, behavior, emotion, and spiritual development. During the Ascension process, archetypes help us recognize the hidden forces operating within the psyche—fear, power, sacrifice, wisdom, transformation, and awakening—allowing these forces to be consciously integrated, rather than unconsciously acted out.

Archetypes also serve as *evolutionary templates*. They provide symbolic pathways through which the mind can interpret spiritual experiences that would otherwise appear chaotic or incomprehensible, like in the dream story above. By consciously working with these patterns, individuals begin aligning themselves with deeper layers of universal intelligence rather than remaining trapped in repetitive emotional conditioning.

In Ascension, the goal is not to worship archetypes, but to understand and embody the higher principles they represent. They become *mirrors* through which consciousness recognizes its own potential. In this way, archetypal awareness *accelerates transformation* by bringing hidden aspects of the self into coherence, helping the individual evolve from reactive survival consciousness into conscious participation with the larger design of creation.

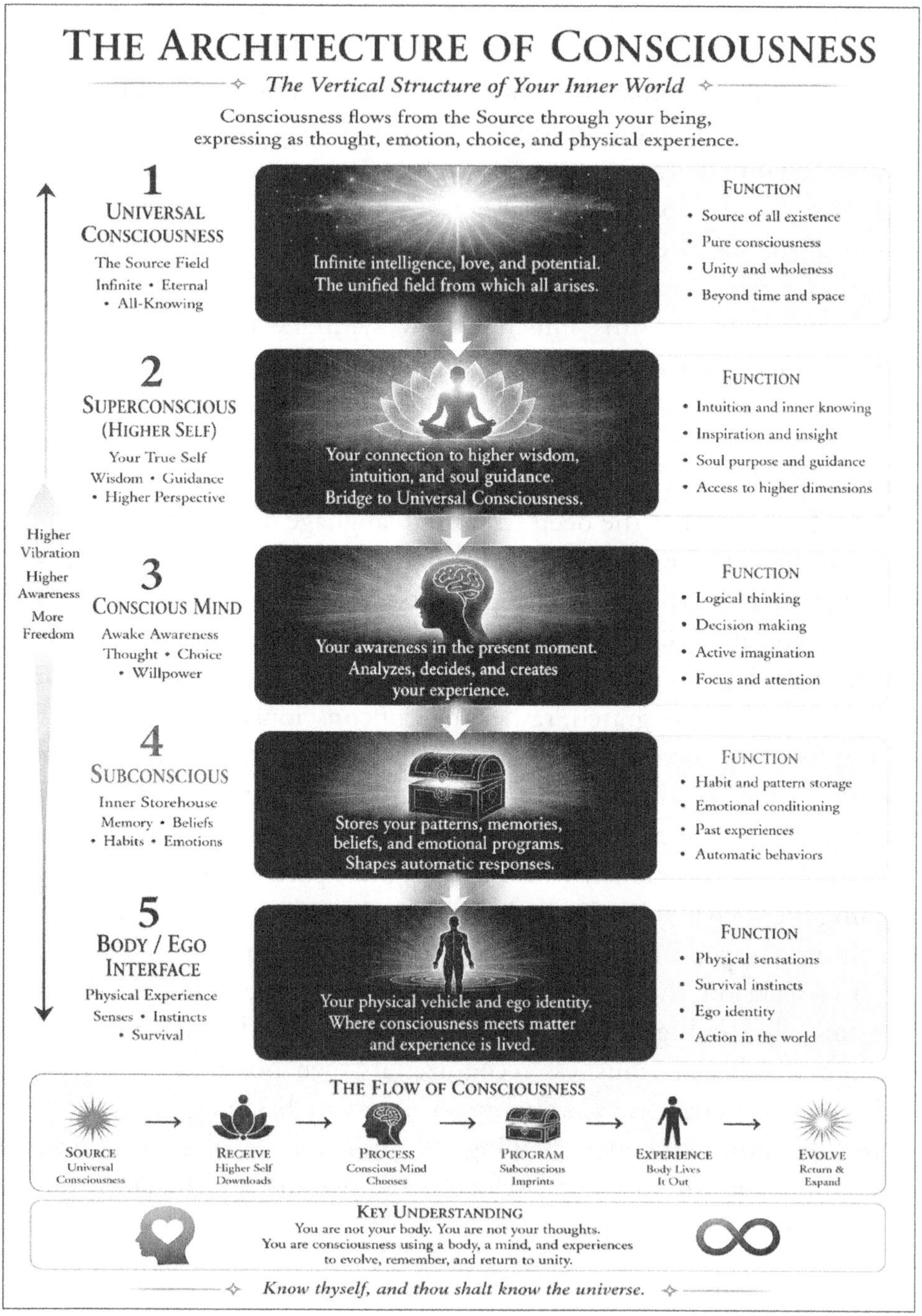
THE ARCHITECTURE OF CONSCIOUSNESS
The Vertical Structure of Your Inner World
Consciousness flows from the Source through your being, expressing as thought, emotion, choice, and physical experience.
1
UNIVERSAL CONSCIOUSNESS
The Source Field
Infinite • Eternal • All-Knowing
Infinite intelligence, love, and potential. The unified field from which all arises.
FUNCTION
• Source of all existence
• Pure consciousness
• Unity and wholeness
• Beyond time and space
2
SUPERCONSCIOUS (HIGHER SELF)
Your True Self
Wisdom • Guidance • Higher Perspective
Your connection to higher wisdom, intuition, and soul guidance. Bridge to Universal Consciousness.
FUNCTION
• Intuition and inner knowing
• Inspiration and insight
• Soul purpose and guidance
• Access to higher dimensions
Higher Vibration
Higher Awareness
More Freedom
3
CONSCIOUS MIND
Awake Awareness
Thought • Choice • Willpower
Your awareness in the present moment. Analyzes, decides, and creates your experience.
FUNCTION
• Logical thinking
• Decision making
• Active imagination
• Focus and attention
4
SUBCONSCIOUS
Inner Storehouse
Memory • Beliefs • Habits • Emotions
Stores your patterns, memories, beliefs, and emotional programs. Shapes automatic responses.
FUNCTION
• Habit and pattern storage
• Emotional conditioning
• Past experiences
• Automatic behaviors
5
BODY / EGO INTERFACE
Physical Experience
Senses • Instincts • Survival
Your physical vehicle and ego identity. Where consciousness meets matter and experience is lived.
FUNCTION
• Physical sensations
• Survival instincts
• Ego identity
• Action in the world
THE FLOW OF CONSCIOUSNESS
SOURCE Universal Consciousness
RECEIVE Higher Self Downloads
PROCESS Conscious Mind Chooses
PROGRAM Subconscious Imprints
EXPERIENCE Body Lives It Out
EVOLVE Return & Expand
KEY UNDERSTANDING
You are not your body. You are not your thoughts.
You are consciousness using a body, a mind, and experiences to evolve, remember, and return to unity.
Know thyself, and thou shalt know the universe.

CHAPTER HIGHLIGHTS:

- **Consciousness is the fundamental substance of the universe**, a single unified field through which all creation emerges. Individual beings are expressions of this universal consciousness rather than separate entities.
- Human consciousness functions as a **customized expression of universal consciousness**, adapted to operate through the physical body and the conditions of the 3rd and 4th Dimensions. Its evolution gradually shifts authority from ego-based perception toward spiritually guided awareness.
- Human awareness operates through three primary tiers: the **subconscious** (storage of habits and dreams), **lower consciousness** or ego-based awareness (ordinary human perception rooted in duality), and **superconsciousness** (soul-guided intuition and higher insight).
- Superconsciousness represents the bridge to higher states of awareness, eventually culminating in Christ consciousness—a **unified state of being** in which identity expands beyond the individual self into the universal "I AM."
- Archetypal consciousness refers to **universal symbolic patterns** embedded in the deep mind, functioning as a metaphysical blueprint that helps guide the evolution of consciousness.
- **Dreams and symbolic imagery are key channels** through which archetypal consciousness communicates, transmitting deeper knowledge through symbolic forms rather than linear language.

CHAPTER THREE

WHY ASCEND?

WHAT IS MEANT BY "SPIRITUAL"?

Throughout this guide, the word spiritual appears in many different contexts. It is not a title, a discipline, or a belief system. Rather, it describes a way of being.

Spirituality and Ascension are deeply connected. Both arise from the same inner movement of the Soul toward greater awareness. Living a spiritual life is not primarily about studying ancient texts, attending sacred places, or performing rituals. These practices can be helpful, but they are not the destination.

True spirituality emerges naturally when the influence of the ego begins to loosen.

To live spiritually is simply to move through the world *without* being dominated by ego.

A spiritual life does not require perfection or superiority over others. It begins when our thoughts, words, and actions arise from a quiet inner center rather than from the restless demands of the ego.

As awareness deepens, the ego gradually loses its authority. Eventually, spirituality no longer requires effort—it becomes our natural state. This shift happens because our internal energy begins to operate at a higher level of consciousness. Growth does not occur because we studied enough philosophy or practiced enough rituals. It happens because we learned to release the ego's constant need for control.

This inner change cannot be forced by rules or authority. It unfolds naturally, much like sunrise following a long night. Ascension is simply the continuation of that natural process. It is not about traveling somewhere else. It is about becoming something different. Ascension represents the evolution of consciousness—from the illusion of the separate self to the realization of the One Infinite Creator.

At a certain point along this path, there is no longer any need to try to "be spiritual." One simply *lives* as an effortless expression of Spirit.

SPIRITUAL ASCENSION

Spiritual Awakening is not a sudden event, but an enduring current through which the measure of Sacred consciousness within us gradually increases. It is not a withdrawal from the world's complexity, but an expansion of awareness that alters the way we perceive and engage with reality. At its core, this process reflects the evolution of human consciousness—from identification with transient form and the limitations of the Lower Self toward alignment with the Soul's higher mandate. Ascension is not an escape from Earth, but the integration of a multi-dimensional awareness within it. It is not a matter of rising upward, but of unfolding into one's full capacity for conscious being.

This movement into multi-dimensional awareness is not determined by education, material wealth, physical strength, social standing, or institutional rank. It is governed by the degree to which we reduce the influence of the ego, and allow the heart to guide our thoughts, actions, and responses. The process is inherently personal.

Are we committed to sustaining clarity in thought, intention in action, and stability in emotional response across all aspects of life? The transition from the 3rd to the 4th and into the 5th Dimension does not occur as an abrupt shift. It unfolds gradually, through a structured and progressive realignment. Expectations of sudden transformation, external intervention, or instantaneous mastery are misplaced. Ascension follows a consistent developmental path, available to those who engage in the necessary internal work, and maintain alignment with the underlying current of the Divine[1].

Ascension is unrelated to religion, philosophy or science. It rather explores the impact of the Law of One on our existence.

The term "Spiritual Dimension," in a metaphysical context, refers to a specific frequency range of consciousness. The majority of humanity currently operates within the framework of the 3rd Dimension. A smaller portion—perhaps 20% of the global population—functions within the 4th or 5th Dimensions. Current planetary shifts indicate that within approximately 80 years, Earth will no longer support 3rd-Density existence. After that point, reincarnation into a 3rd-Dimensional environment on Earth will no longer be possible. The result will be a natural recalibration of the population, projected to culminate around the year 2105.

At this stage, the Soul is presented with two primary options: to remain aligned with the patterns of the current system and continue its development elsewhere, or to undergo a process of vibrational refinement. The latter alters perception, behavior, and interaction at a fundamental level, and allows continued participation in Earth's next evolutionary phase, if consistent with the Soul's contract.

We are positioned at a transitional threshold. The process is now more accessible because Earth itself has already shifted into a new vibrational

---

1 Ascension is thus different from certain Indian techniques, who for a measured amount of time are temporarily able to activate the 3rd-Eye. With full Ascension comes the permanent opening of that chakra.

state—something unprecedented in its history.

This creates a clear point of decision: whether to align with that shift or remain within prior patterns. Not all Souls will make the transition. This remains an individual determination.

The current period represents a unique phase in Earth's history. Its significance exceeds that of major geological, historical, or religious milestones. The transition from the 3rd to the 4th Density will not repeat. The opportunity to consciously participate in this level of transformation is without precedent.

The developments associated with this shift are substantial. As they stabilize, they will define a new phase of human history characterized by increased coherence and integration across multiple domains. Within the foreseeable future, we can expect measurable advancements: the application of quantum principles in medicine and computation; the development of sustainable, high-efficiency energy systems; expanded understanding of human cognitive and perceptual capabilities; more stable global governance structures; improved distribution of resources; restoration of environmental systems; and large-scale ecological recovery.

Additional changes are likely to include open interaction with non-terrestrial intelligences[2]; new transportation technologies based on crystalline or energy-based systems; extended human lifespans; stable food availability; and more integrated economic structures. These developments are not theoretical projections, but part of the broader transition already underway. The question is not whether change will occur, but how individuals will position themselves in relation to it. Given this context, the practical consideration becomes straightforward: whether to engage consciously in the Ascension process and participate directly in the conditions that follow.

---

[2] We anticipate that by 2030, the 'Great Disclosure' will be complete, marked by the global arrival of piloted craft from other star systems. This event will profoundly shift humanity's perspective on Ascension and our place in the Cosmos.

AN EVENT OF UNPRECEDENTED SIGNIFICANCE

What occurrence, across the vast span of the world, has left the deepest imprint on humanity? Was it the retreat of the last glacial age? The sinking of Atlantis? The construction of the pyramids? The arrival of Yeshua? The invention of the printed word? Or the twentieth-century discovery of galaxies beyond the Milky Way?

Whatever conclusion we reach, one point stands: no singular event in the history of our planet—extending even beyond the story of humankind—equals the magnitude of the shift now unfolding. In truth, no event on Earth, aside from its primordial formation, has carried greater significance than the recent transition into 4th Density, and the profound spiritual renewal it initiates for humanity.

How the mind and inner being respond to this transition is central to this inquiry. The process of Ascension is not symbolic—it is a real and consequential development, the full scope of which is not yet widely understood.

The movement from the 3rd and 4th Dimensions—the stages of 3rd Density—into the 5th Dimension, marking the beginning of 4th Density, leads directly to the realization of our inherent multi-dimensional nature.

Among the attributes associated with this shift, the 5th Dimension introduces expanded capacities: deep self-healing, the restoration of others, telepathic communication, form-shifting, direct channeling beyond the veil, and access to the Akashic records—the informational field containing the record of all expressions of consciousness across time.

The basis for these claims lies in precedent. Certain individuals have demonstrated aspects of these capacities in earlier periods. Yeshua is described as having entered this world aligned with the 5th Dimension, later advancing further following his initiation at baptism. Mary of Magdala is understood to have reached that same level during her lifetime, expressing it more fully in her later years in Southern France. Similar trajectories appear across the traditions of rishis and yogis throughout the Asian subcontinent.

What was once limited to a small number of individuals—often after lifetimes of disciplined refinement—is now presented as accessible to a broader segment of humanity, contingent upon conscious participation, and internal development. Until recently, there was no clearly defined framework to guide this transition in a structured way. The necessary elements existed, but they were not assembled into a unified model. Ascension into the 5th Dimension was generally considered beyond the reach of the average individual.

The caretakers of Earth tell us she is overpopulated, and will undergo an approximate 30% attrition by the year 2105.

That assumption no longer holds.

THE TRICHOTOMY OF WORLDS

The decades ahead will be marked by the simultaneous presence of three distinct dimensional realities on Earth: the 3rd, 4th, and 5th Dimensions. This has never occurred on Earth in this way before. The result will be a clear segmentation of consciousness among humanity.

At present, the majority of the population—approximately 85%—remains deeply immersed in 3rd-dimensional awareness. A much smaller group, roughly 13%, is currently functioning within the 4th Dimension. An even smaller group, approximately 2%, has stabilized within the 5th Dimension. This raises a serious question for each of us:

At which dimensional level do we currently resonate, and which level do we intend to reach?

Earth itself has already crossed into 4th Density. Metaphorically speaking, the train has begun to move. There is still time to board, but the train is no longer sitting still.

The Earth of tomorrow is no longer energetically calibrated to permanently host beings stabilized only in 3rd-dimensional consciousness. Those who choose to remain within the familiar patterns of the 3rd Dimension may do so only until their next physical transition. After that, reincarnation on Earth in the 3rd Dimension will no longer be available.

Those who remain aligned with 3rd-dimensional consciousness will simply continue their evolutionary journey elsewhere. Following the natural transition that occurs after physical death, the Soul will pass through the life-between-lives state, discussed later in this book. From there, it will reincarnate on another planet, within another solar system, and in another galaxy, where a 3rd-density environment still exists. Life will continue there in a form similar to what we have known on Earth during the long cycle of the 3rd Density, with its familiar patterns of duality and ego-based learning.

This is not punishment. It is placement by resonance. Each Soul continues its journey in the environment most aligned with its current state of consciousness.

The seriousness of this moment should not be underestimated. Earth is moving forward, and each Soul must decide whether to move with her or continue its lessons elsewhere. This is the point: **reincarnation on Earth in the 3rd Dimension is no longer part of the future path.**

THREE OBSTACLES TO ASCENSION

Navigating the path of Ascension requires a skilled pilot. The deception within many organizations is pervasive, and often difficult to identify, as most groups blend elements of truth with distortion. Consequently, they can easily lead us astray. Three specific systems warrant a brief, closer inspection:

1. Religion. Organized religion's strength lies in its acknowledgment of transcendence. The church often cites the resurrection of Yeshua as a primary example—a valid point—and it has successfully preserved ancestral wisdom through the centuries. However, in these structures, truth often becomes frozen; revelation is treated as a historical event rather than a living reality. This stagnation occurs when obedience replaces awareness, and when blind faith is prioritized over direct perception or

Gnostic experience. Adherents may behave ethically to avoid punishment rather than out of a clear understanding of karmic law. "Attending church" frequently devolves into a social requirement where "belonging" outweighs the pursuit of truth, and any deviation is labeled heresy. Ultimately, who finds (or has found) true salvation solely through scripture or institutional participation? Religion is the adoration of authority.

Religion tells us what to believe.

> *Fighting against individuality is one of Christianity's basic principles. It will take us hundreds of generations to free us from the yoke of Christianity.*
>
> *Edvard Grieg*

2. Psychology. Psychology serves as a secular counterpart to religion, focusing on labeling, mapping, and explaining ego formation. While it provides tools to stabilize the nervous system, these methods remain superficial. The discipline falters by viewing consciousness merely as a biological byproduct. By ignoring the role of the Spirit, psychology lacks clear perception. Therapy often morphs into an endless cycle without defined parameters, and spiritual awakening is often pathologized. Countless individuals receiving auditory guidance from the Light have been misdiagnosed with personality disorders. The objective is often to help the individual adapt to a fractured society rather than questioning the system itself. Psychology effectively repairs the cell without asking why the prisoner is there, and it offers no clear vision of human perfection or a map to achieve it. Psychology is ego analysis without Spirit.

Psychology tells us why we behave.

3. New Age Spirituality. New Age thought rightly acknowledges non-material reality, emphasizing inner experience, and rejecting rigid dogma. However, these strengths quickly become obstacles. Lacking a framework for inner discipline and personal responsibility, the movement often dissolves into a superficial culture of "Love and Light." An obsession with crystals, star origins, and UFOs—paired with the repetitive, casual mantra of "living in the now"—relegates it to the realm of fantasy rather than rigorous mental work. This fosters a metaphysical ego-culture defined by labels like "awakened" or "chosen." In this space, true atonement[3] is frequently shunned, as is the recognition of the Godhead as a distinct spiritual reality. New age abides in spiritual ego.

New Age tells us how special we are.

True spirituality excludes the one who needs to be told anything at all.

WHO WILL ASCEND?

The Law of Ascension, embedded within, and conditioned by the Law of One[4], implies that all particles of creation are continuously evolving upward in consciousness. In this metaphysical chain reaction, the fuel is infinite consciousness. In that sense, every being on Earth is already paricipating in Ascension, because Earth herself is continuously ascending. If this is the case, a reasonable question naturally arises:

If we are all ascending anyway, why should we do anything at all? Why not simply follow the flow, and allow the process to unfold on its own? The first answer lies in the clear advantages available to those who actively pursue their Ascension. If we can learn to heal ourselves and others, extend our lifespan substantially, and free ourselves from the chains of duality that define the 3rd Dimension, is that not reason enough to move forward deliberately rather than passively? These possibilities alone offer powerful motivation to accelerate our own development. Yet there is

---

[3] The Atonement Principle is the profound act of convergence with, and exposure to the Light. It is unrelated to the Old Testament understanding of atonement.

[4] The central tenet of the Law of One is that everything in existence is one—an expression of a single One Infinite Creator. The four states of matter, solid, liquid, gas and plasma have a single common denominator that allows for their energetic manipulation, and thus, manifestation, or creation.

a deeper reason.

According to the teachings of the Light, an individual must reach a minimum threshold of 51% positive orientation in thoughts, words, and deeds in order to qualify for the path of Ascension. Without reaching this level of alignment, the transition to higher dimensional states does not occur. This requirement leads directly to the second answer.

Humanity has already crossed the point where Earth itself has moved forward into a new vibrational state. We are not about to shift gears; the shift has already happened. If we choose not to participate consciously in this transition, the result is not stagnation, but relocation.

For many Souls, this path is entirely acceptable. In fact, a large number of individuals consciously made this decision during their last life review, before incarnating in the present lifetime. Some chose simply to observe the events of this period of transition. Others agreed to continue their evolutionary path on another world if they felt unprepared to complete the Ascension process here. Within this group are those who are aware of their Soul contract, and many more who are not.

There is, however, another group: those individuals who declared during their previous life review that they were ready to move forward more rapidly in this incarnation.

Here again, some are aware of this commitment, while the majority are not. This may sound somewhat deterministic, and to a small extent it is. Humanity now stands at a bifurcation point. The road ahead divides into two directions. One path continues the long journey of development within the familiar framework of 3rd-density experience. The other leads toward accelerated evolution within the emerging environment of 4th and 5^{th-}dimensional consciousness. Each Soul must ultimately decide which direction to take.

The purpose of this book is not to force that decision. It is simply to provide information, and guidance so that the choice can be made consciously.

That choice will determine
the path of our Ascension.

CHAPTER HIGHLIGHTS:

- True spirituality is not defined by religion, ritual, or belief, but by the **gradual dissolution of ego,** and the emergence of the Soul's natural expression in daily life.
- Ascension is the **progressive expansion** of consciousness, moving from identification with the lower self toward alignment with the Soul and higher dimensional awareness.
- Humanity is currently living through a rare planetary transition, as **Earth itself has already shifted** into a higher vibrational state, inviting individuals to evolve from 3rd-dimensional consciousness toward the 4th and 5th dimensions.
- This transformation is not instantaneous but gradual, **requiring conscious inner work**, emotional refinement, and the cultivation of love, clarity, and presence.
- Each individual now faces a conscious choice: to **participate in Earth's Ascension process or to continue the evolutionary journey on another world,** more suited to 3rd-dimensional consciousness.

CHAPTER FOUR

TWO TRUMP CARDS IN THE DECK

THE BELT

March 21st (0° of Aries) has served as a universal point of reference for calendar design for as long as recorded history. Millennia of observation have allowed astronomers to recognize that this point slowly drifts backward when measured against the fixed stars of the zodiac.

In this gradual movement, the reference point completes a full 360° cycle in approximately 25,800 years. This implies that the entire Solar System performs a slow rotational cycle over that period. Astronomers refer to this phenomenon as the precession cycle.

Because the zodiac contains twelve constellations (Aries, Taurus, Gemini, and so on), the axis of Earth points toward each constellation for an average period of approximately 2,150 years (25,800 ÷ 12).

For the past 2,150 years, Earth's axis has pointed toward the constellation Pisces. Because the precessional movement occurs in retrograde motion, the next constellation is Aquarius. Astronomical

THE PRECESSION CYCLE

· THE SLOW 25,800-YEAR ROTATION OF OUR SOLAR SYSTEM ·

March 21st (0° of Aries) has served as a universal point of reference for calendar design for as long as we can remember.

Millennia of observation have allowed astronomers to see that this point continuously drifts backward when measured against the fixed stars of the zodiac.

In this slow movement, the reference point completes a 360° journey in approximately **25,800** years, implying that the entire Solar System makes a complete rotation over that period.

We refer to this astronomical event as the **"precession cycle."**

With twelve astronomical constellations (Aries, Taurus, Gemini, and so on), the axis of Earth points toward each for an average period of 2,150 years (25,800 ÷ 12).

WHAT IS PRECESSION?

Earth's axis slowly wobbles like a spinning top, causing the Vernal Equinox (0° of Aries) to drift westward along the zodiac.

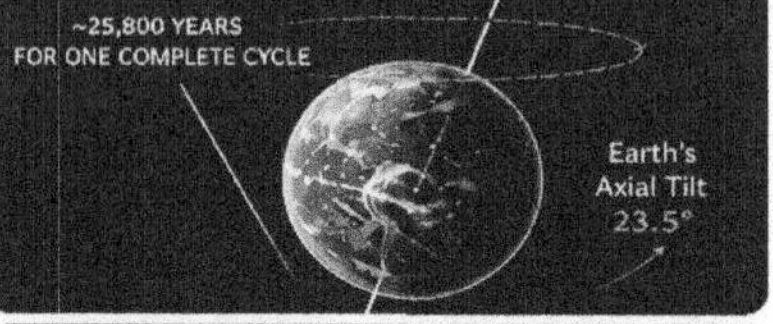

THE REFERENCE POINT DRIFTS

When measured against the fixed stars, the Vernal Equinox moves backward (westward) along the zodiac.

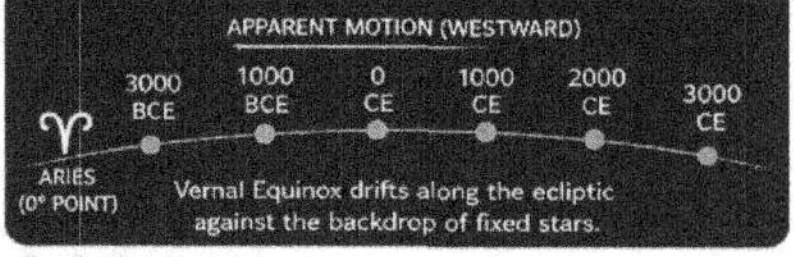

Vernal Equinox drifts along the ecliptic against the backdrop of fixed stars.

HOW IT WORKS

1. Earth's axis is tilted 23.5° relative to its orbit around the Sun.
2. Gravitational influences—primarily from the Sun, Moon, and planets—cause Earth's axis to wobble in a conical motion.
3. This wobble causes the Vernal Equinox (0° of Aries) to shift backward along the zodiac.

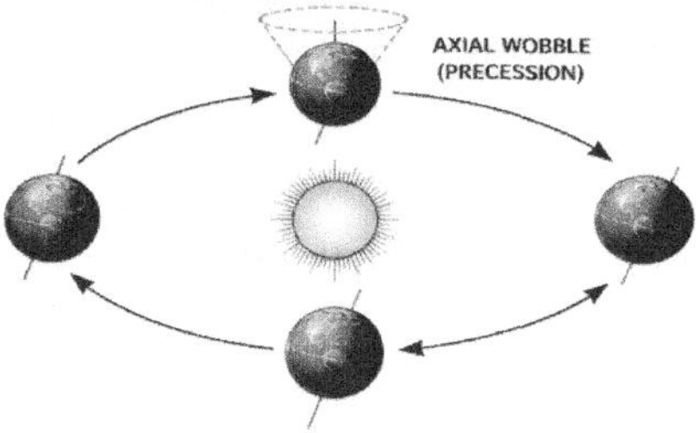

PRECESSIONAL AGES THROUGH THE LAST 6,500 YEARS:

♉ **The Age of Taurus (c. 4500 BCE – 2300 BCE):**
Spirituality - Worship of the Bull (Apis in Egypt, Mithras) and Mother Goddess figures, emphasizing fertility and the abundance of the Earth.

♈ **The Age of Aries (c. 2300 BCE – 150 BCE):**
Spirituality - Shift from Earth-worship to Father-gods; The Ram's horn is worshipped; emphasis on the "hero's journey" and individual will.

♓ **The Age of Pisces (c. 150 BCE – 2000 CE):**
Religion - Defined by the "Fisher of Men" archetype; the global spread of Christianity and Buddhism, focusing on compassion and sacrifice.

♒ **The Age of Aquarius (c. 2000 CE – 4150 CE):**
Humanitarianism - Focus on global unity, equality, and the recognition that all individuals are part of a singular collective consciousness.

KEY TAKEAWAYS

- **MARCH 21ST (0° OF ARIES)** is our traditional calendar starting point.
- **THE PRECESSION CYCLE** takes ~25,800 years to complete one full rotation.
- **THE ENTIRE SOLAR SYSTEM** completes this 360° rotation over that period.
- **EACH SIGN** is aligned with Earth's axis for an average of ~2,150 years.

calculations indicate that Earth entered this new 2,150-year period in 2012. From a purely astronomical perspective, this transition appears routine. However, this is where we must move beyond traditional science, because the expressions of consciousness involved in this process lie outside the instruments currently used by scientific observation.

To visualize the situation, imagine a gigantic torus-shaped structure—a doughnut positioned at a 90° angle across the entire Solar System. The structure is large enough that the entire Solar System sits within the hollow center of the torus.

THE PHOTON BELT WITH ROTATING SOLAR SYSTEM

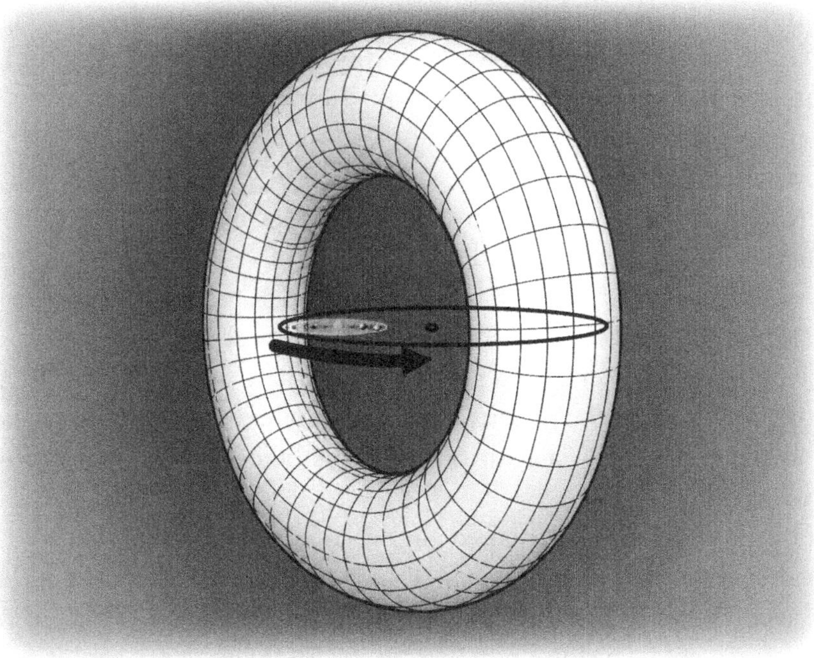

We refer to this structure as the Photon Belt[1]. Within this configuration,

[1] The photon belt is unrelated to the Pleiades, since Earth is not gravitationally anchored to that open star cluster.

the Solar System effectively "floats" inside the Belt. The toroidal structure—our first trump card—is aligned in a fixed position along the Leo–Aquarius constellation vector (Leo lies 180° opposite Aquarius).

At this point in the discussion we must leave conventional science behind. Science does not recognize consciousness as a creative force; it generally interprets consciousness only as information processed by the brain, or as subjective awareness.

The Photon Belt may be understood as an immense stream of high-frequency photon particles, invisible to the naked eye, producing an extremely concentrated radiation of Light consciousness. One might compare its energetic behavior to that of a natural particle accelerator.

The last time Earth passed through the Photon Belt occurred approximately 12,900 years ago (25,800 ÷ 2). The passage lasted roughly 2,150 years. At that time Earth was pointing toward the constellation Leo, and entered the Belt from that direction. According to The Law of One (Ra Material), the fall of Atlantis did not occur as a single catastrophe but as two major events.

The first catastrophe occurred around 10,821 BCE.

The second occurred around 9,600 BCE.

If we examine the timeline from 10,821 BCE to 2012 CE, we arrive at approximately 12,833 years since the first destruction of Atlantis.

Given that Earth encounters the Photon Belt roughly every 12,900 years, this implies that the Atlantean civilization had access to this elevated consciousness energy for at least 60–70 years before the first catastrophe occurred.

Photon Belt energy in the Leo alignment appears to have allowed the Atlanteans to access 4th-dimensional consciousness that had not been experienced for many thousands of years. Their civilization advanced with remarkable speed, developing powerful technologies and sophisticated metaphysical capabilities. However, their society increasingly combined technological ambition with ego-driven motives, abandoning their alignment with the Divine. The result was a volatile mixture of advanced knowledge and destructive intent.

The final destruction of Atlantis occurred roughly 1,221 years after

THE PHOTON BELT CYCLE
AND THE FALL OF ATLANTIS

1 THE GALACTIC CYCLE

ONE FULL CYCLE = ~25,800 YEARS

THE SOLAR SYSTEM CROSSES THE PHOTON BELT TWICE EVERY CYCLE—ABOUT EVERY ~12,900 YEARS.

2 THE PHOTON BELT

DURATION OF EACH PASSAGE ~2,150 YEARS

A TIME OF HEIGHTENED ENERGY AND ACCELERATED EVOLUTION.

3 LAST PASSAGE

CONSTELLATION: LEO

THE EARTH WENT UNDER THE BELT, RECEIVING ELEVATED CONSCIOUSNESS ENERGY.

THE ATLANTEAN TIMELINE

4 ATLANTEAN CIVILIZATION

HIGH TECHNOLOGY
SPIRITUAL ADVANCEMENT
ELEVATED CONSCIOUSNESS POTENTIAL

→

5 FIRST CATASTROPHE ~10,821 BCE

PARTIAL DESTRUCTION OF LAND AND CIVILIZATION

→

6 SECOND CATASTROPHE ~9,600 BCE

FINAL DESTRUCTION ATLANTIS SUNK BENEATH THE WAVES

→

7 THE MATHEMATICAL TIMELINE

FROM THE FIRST CATASTROPHE (~10,821 BCE) TO THE YEAR 2012 CE:

= ~12,833 YEARS

10,821 BCE → 2012 CE = ~12,833 YEARS

→

8 MODERN HUMANITY

WE HAVE ALREADY ENTERED (2012) INTO THE PHOTON BELT PASSAGE.

HUMANITY STANDS AT THE THRESHOLD OF A NEW EVOLUTIONARY CYCLE

9 KEY INSIGHT

WITH THE EARTH ENTERING THE PHOTON BELT EVERY ~12,900 YEARS, THE ATLANTEANS HAD ACCESS TO THIS ELEVATED CONSCIOUSNESS ENERGY FOR AT LEAST 60–70 YEARS PRIOR TO THE FIRST CATASTROPHE.

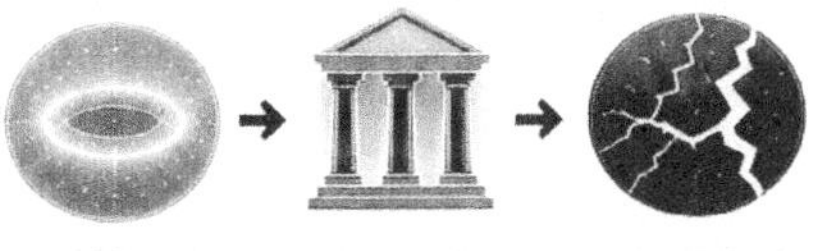

PHOTON BELT ENERGY RISING → ADVANCED POWER & TECHNOLOGY → MISUSE LEADS TO PLANETARY CRISIS

SUMMARY OF THE CYCLE

GALACTIC CYCLE 25,800 YEARS → PHOTON BELT ENTRY EVERY ~12,900 YEARS DURATION ~2,150 YEARS → LAST ENTRY ~12,900 YEARS AGO CONSTELLATION: LEO → ATLANTIS FALLS 10,821 BCE & 9,600 BCE TWO MAJOR CATASTROPHES → 10,821 BCE → 2012 CE = ~12,833 YEARS → NEW CYCLE STARTED IN 2012 the first catastrophe. This event coincides with the transition from the Pleistocene Period to the Holocene Period, the geological epoch in which we now live.

Whether coincidence or correlation, Atlantis disappeared beneath the sea during a time when Earth was also undergoing a major geological transition, and operating under the energetic influence of the Photon Belt.

This historical episode provides an example of the profound impact that Photon Belt energy can exert on planetary civilizations. As Earth has now reentered the sphere of influence of the Photon Belt[2], significant transformations should be expected. The period of preparation has passed. The period of awakening has begun.

The question remains: will humanity use this energy wisely this time? The emergence of quantum technologies and advanced computational systems may already represent early signs of this influence. Earth will undergo a process of energetic renewal, just as it did during the Atlantean period. Photon Belt energy brings a complete energetic reset.

Entry into the Photon Belt is therefore a decisive marker that Ascension will occur. The influence of the Belt is now present whether humanity consciously chooses it or not. In this sense, free will does not apply to the arrival of the energy itself.

SOLAR ACTIVITY

The Sun provides Earth with electromagnetic radiation essential for life. Visible light enables photosynthesis. Infrared radiation warms the planet. Ultraviolet radiation drives atmospheric chemistry. Solar energy powers the hydrological cycle that produces clouds, rainfall, and climate regulation. The Sun also stabilizes Earth's orbit, preventing it from drifting into deep space. It maintains the structure of the atmosphere and,

---

[2] Every 12,900 years, Earth spends roughly 2,000 years inside the "belt of light" (Photon Belt) and 12,400 years in a period of "darkness" outside of it. The Atlanteans were the last to experience it. We have now re-entered the belt, leading to DNA activation and spiritual Ascension.

regulates the biological circadian rhythms of plants and animals.

At the same time, the Sun continuously emits streams of charged particles known as solar wind. This phenomenon represents our second trump card. Earth's magnetic field forms a protective structure known as the magnetosphere. However, near the north and south poles there are openings through which solar particles can enter the atmosphere.

Solar winds consist primarily of ionized gas particles known as plasma, the fourth state of matter. These particles originate in the Sun's corona, where temperatures are so high that matter escapes the Sun's gravitational hold. When openings appear in the corona, plasma can erupt outward at speeds ranging from 300–800 km/s, and during extreme events can exceed 2,000 km/s[3]. If such ejections are directed toward Earth, they can produce serious consequences, including:

- Satellite damage
- Disruption of GPS and radio communication
- Electrical grid failures
- Increased radiation exposure for astronauts and high-altitude flights

We are the likely recipients of such disruptions should a category X[4] storm activate. There have been solar storms so severe that entire electrical grids have caught fire in parts of Europe. The regular occurrence of Aurora Borealis and Aurora Australis is also a direct consequence of Solar plasma entering the atmosphere, and a good indicator of Solar plasma ejections.

The purpose of this discussion is to remind us that the Sun is not simply a provider of warmth and light. According to the framework presented earlier in this book, the Sun is a conscious celestial entity, operating within densities ranging from 14th to 50th Density (Earth currently operates within 4th Density).

---

[3] One can follow the space weather conditions at https://www.swpc.noaa.gov/ (National Oceanic and Atmospheric Administration). We recommend alerts subscription, to be prepared for the next Solar storm!

[4] On the Kp-Index of the GOES (Geostationary Operational Environmental Satellites) system.

When intense solar activity occurs, the plasma emitted from the Sun may therefore carry not only physical energy, but also an infusion of solar consciousness. While solar activity has always existed, its effects become significantly more powerful when combined with the energetic influence of the Photon Belt.

Recently, astronomers have detected the appearance of 3I-ATLAS, an interstellar object entering our Solar System—the third such object ever confirmed to originate outside the Solar System. According to communications received through Spirit, this object originated in the Lyra star system, is crewed, and passed between Mars and the Sun in order to upload energetic information into the Sun. The intention of this energetic transfer was allegedly to allow the Sun to redistribute this coded energy toward Earth through future solar winds and storms, to facilitate humankind's Ascension. To some readers this may sound like science fiction. However, humanity will likely witness events even more unusual in the years ahead.

Earth spends approximately 2,000 years inside the Photon Belt and roughly 12,400 years outside it in a comparatively lower-energy period. The Atlanteans were the last civilization to experience this passage. Humanity has now reentered the Belt. This transition initiates DNA activation and spiritual Ascension.

In conclusion: Both the Photon Belt and intensified solar activity are external forces influencing humanity's transition. They are not random events, but components of a larger process orchestrated by Creation to support the emergence of 4th Density consciousness.

The bottom line is that both the Photon Belt and the Solar winds are important players orchestrated by Creation to help bring forth our Ascension. *Our ingress to 4th Density will not occur without massive Solar Storm emissions from the Sun's Corona.* This means that the next 4 years will showcase geophysical transformations at an unprecedented level[5]!

---

[5] We have been alerted to a significant plasma outburst expected by 2030, an event that will likely precipitate profound changes for humanity.

CHAPTER HIGHLIGHTS:

- There are two major external forces that accelerate Ascension: the **Photon Bel**t and intensified **Solar activity**.
- The Photon Belt is a vast field of **high-frequency spiritual Light emissions** (of consciousness) that the Solar System periodically enters during the precession cycle, with Earth re-entering it in the current era.
- The last passage through the Photon Belt was during the Atlantean era; the event heightened consciousness energy to produce rapid advancement, but also triggered **catastrophic misuse when combined with ego-driven motives**.
- Solar winds and plasma emissions from the Sun are the second "trump card," carrying not only physical effects but also a form of **infused solar consciousness** that influences Earth.
- The combined effect of the Photon Belt and solar activity is not incidental, but part of a larger orchestration intended to bring about **humanity's Ascension into 4th Density**.
- The coming years will likely bring major geophysical and energetic **transformation**, including severe solar events that will help drive this transition.

CHAPTER FIVE

3RD DIMENSION: THE REALM OF POLARITY

Our deep and enduring relationship with Earth is not merely a romantic vision of nature. It is anchored in a very real spirit-sourced energetic link called the Earth Star. Think of it as an "underground chakra" that serves as a master connector between human consciousness and Earth.

The Earth Star remains with us throughout our entire lives. It was present when we first began walking upon this planet, and it accompanies us throughout our earthly journey. It is normally located about six inches beneath our feet, within the body of our Mother Gaia (Earth). Its most common form is that of an inverted pyramid.

We have learned to rely upon Gaia as our Earth-Mother. The Earth Star functions much like a chakra, acting as our underground spiritual energy link. This direct connection requires that the consciousness of both humanity and Earth remain energetically aligned at the same frequency. You may already know the benefits of walking barefoot. Indigenous cultures often maintain a palpably stronger connection to the Earth—both physically and spiritually—than those who wear shoes. The secret to this profound attachment lies within the Earth Star.

In an era saturated with negative news, one may reasonably ask: Is humanity truly progressing, or are we regressing?

Emerging from the most violent century in recorded history, our behavior in the 3rd Density does not present an especially flattering portrait. One may even wonder why we study history when we so often fail to learn from it.

The 3rd Density has been a demanding master. Combined with a dominant ego, life within this density has often felt like a form of spiritual boot camp. Souls who successfully graduate from this density deserve recognition for their endurance in what has effectively been a long campaign of inner struggle.

Until recently, our planetary home—Gaia—remained firmly stabilized in the 3rd Density. However, as we have repeatedly emphasized, this situation has now changed. She has already entered the 4th Density. This shift has opened an unprecedented gateway for her inhabitants: the eventual departure from the 3rd Density. Those who wish to remain in a 3rd-density environment will continue their evolution on another planetary system.

THE EGO-CONSCIOUSNESS CONFIGURATION

The balance between ego and consciousness within human beings has been organized in a way that naturally favors the ego. The structure of our biological and psychological system has long acted as a stabilizing force that kept humanity anchored in the 3rd-density experience. Consider one controversial example.

Ananda has let us know that humanity was deliberately modified to require additional vitamin B^{12}. Implementing such a biological change would require sophisticated molecular engineering at the cellular level—an area in which the Anunnaki, an advanced galactic race, were said to possess advanced expertise.

The purpose of this modification, was to reinforce a culture dependent on the killing of animals for food, thereby perpetuating cycles of violence. These actions, attributed to the Anunnaki, and their service-to-self orientation, represent serious interference in humanity's development. Yet they did not anticipate that humanity would ultimately find its way beyond these limitations, and approach the gateway to 5th-Dimension Ascension.

A fusion of human chromosome #2 happened ca. 200,000 years ago, through intentional manipulation.

Despite these manipulations, humanity is not guilty of wrongdoing. We have largely behaved according to the conditions that were placed upon us—conditions we did not choose. One might compare the situation to a patient who has been given a powerful sedative. How responsible is that person for not being fully alert?

The encouraging news is that this period is now ending. Recognizing our fundamental innocence can provide powerful motivation to move forward. Humanity now has the opportunity to live under conditions that support genuine liberation. That is…if we can eviscerate the entries in the list of ego manipulations on the following pages. There we present a list of twenty ego-driven behavioral patterns that characterize the 3rd-dimensional human condition. Few individuals will identify with all twenty traits, but honest reflection will reveal that most of us exhibit several of them.

Rather than viewing these patterns as inherent flaws, it is more helpful to see them as temporary conditions—attributes that will gradually disappear as humanity evolves beyond the 3rd-dimensional framework. And, yes, preparing for Ascension requires confronting these tendencies directly. Recognizing ego manipulation is the first step toward reclaiming authentic agency, and distinguishing fear-based impulses from true intentionality. Identifying these internal distortions prevents the ego from sabotaging personal growth through defensive narratives, or a need for validation. This self-awareness fosters the clarity needed to align our actions with deeper values rather than fleeting insecurities.

How To Recognize Ego Manipulation in Yourself

5 Practical Signals

Recognize them ✦ Understand them ✦ Transcend them

A 

You feel a strong emotional reaction.

Ego manipulation triggers fear, anger, shame, or defensiveness. Notice when your emotions feel disproportionate to the situation—this is often the first sign.

B 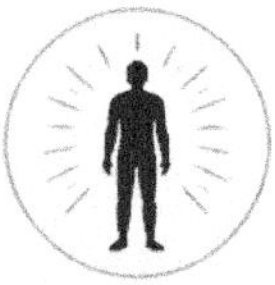

You feel the need to defend, justify, or prove.

The ego wants validation and control. If you feel the urge to explain yourself, prove your worth, or win approval, your ego may be running the show.

C 

You blame others or the circumstances.

Ego avoids responsibility. When you habitually point outward instead of looking within, it's a sign your ego is protecting itself and avoiding growth.

D 

You feel separate, superior, or special.

When you put yourself above others, or believe the rules don't apply to you, ego is creating separation and reinforcing illusion.

E 

You lose inner peace and clarity.

Ego manipulation clouds intuition and creates inner conflict. If you feel unsettled, confused, or out of alignment, pause and look within.

How to Respond:

Pause. Breathe. Observe without judgment.
Choose awareness over reaction, and love over ego.

THE TOP-20 LIST OF EGO MANIPULATIONS

1. ***The Lower Self and Ego Dominate***: Not exactly attractive, this personality is typically characterized by an intense focus on immediate gratification, self-preservation, and an external, often insecure sense of self-worth. Desires displayed are driven by basic, instinctual expressions, and a need for validation; higher ethical considerations, and needs to validate others are sidelined. This personality structure often leads to cycles of *temporary* satisfaction followed by dissatisfaction, as the needs of the lower self and ego are infinite and ongoing, and can never be truly satisfied by external means.

2. ***Self-centeredness***: The world is primarily viewed through a lens of "What is in it for me?" Decisions are driven by personal gain, need for comfort, and advantage. Little or no genuine regard is given for the needs or feelings of others. Egocentricity is the main currency. It is about me, me, me. Narcissism is lurking right around the corner.

3. ***Control and Power***: There is a strong, often desperate gravitation towards the need to dominate situations and people. The ego attempts to mask a deep-seated insecurity by establishing external control and authority. There is a desire to control individuals, situations, and/or our environment.

4. ***Materialism***: The acquiring of external possessions and experiencing sensory gratification take on a life of their own. What matters is what we own, and those possessions' worth. Wealth, status, and appearance dominate. We have to keep up with the Jones', and we compare ourselves to others. There is a strong penchant to define ourselves by our physical bodies, appearances, names, careers, credit scores, and so on. We show an adoration for an idealized physical appearance; looks—often stylized through fashion and cosmetic alterations—are everything. We have built a life where immediate sensory pleasures (e.g., food, alcohol, drugs, sex, comfort etc.) are recurring attractions.

*5. **Fear***: Fear is the catalyst to most emotions. Whether realized or not, fear is a powerful engine in many of us. Fear of death, pain, animals, fear of loss of material values, fear of being alone, fear of speaking in public, and so on. Whatever the phobia, fear is close by. *Fear is, along with anger, one of the master building blocks of the ego.* We easily adapt to a work or family environment based on fear, lack, domination, subjugation, and conformity. Survival instinct is an operative mode—driven by fear. Decisions are often based on fear, and lack of survival instincts. The 3rd-dimensional human is a fear-driven creature.

*6. **Manipulative Interpersonal Interactions***: The motto is, "What can they do for me?" Relationships are not genuine, but *transactional.* Others are often viewed as means to an end—tools to satisfy the ego's needs for admiration, and comfort draws one to first consider the utilitarian aspect of a relationship; "How can this person be useful for my advancement?"

*7. **Reactive Behavior***: Instead of observing and processing what we have observed, we react instinctively. Our reactions are often unexamined, and triggered by emotional mirroring. A lack of inner calm is instigated by emotional reactivity, fear, anger, or lust, often leading to impulsive decisions without mirroring long-term ethical consequences or implications. As an aspect of duality, judgment is common. Remember: *A Master observes; he does not react.*

*8. **Judgmental Attitude***: We form opinions about people, groups, or situations, often in the form of snap judgments, excessive criticism, biases, comments regarding superficial appearances, black-and-white thinking (e.g., "good" or "bad"), along with a posture of superiority.

*9. **Lack of Empathy***: These individuals are fake in their emotions to others, as if they had artificial hearts. They are masters in *simulating* a sense of care and true concern. Obligation forces them to *pretend* empathy where necessary, a quality that does not resonate with the ego-consumed lower self.

***10. Defensiveness and Tit-for-tat*:** The ego cannot tolerate criticism or failure. Lack of security and any perceived attack on the self-image are fiercely defended. Blaming others, and retribution are this person's modus operandi.

***11. Competition*:** The envy for what others have draws out the competitive angle that accompanies materialism. We have been thoroughly indoctrinated to compare ourselves with others; that is par-for-the-course, and commonly accepted (and especially lauded by the ego). Our fellow man is perceived as a *rival*, and we struggle to genuinely celebrate the success of others. The world is perceived as finite, competitive, and with a glass ceiling, and we must protect what we own.

***12. Lack of Self-Confidence*:** Arrogance and deep insecurity often go hand in hand. This individual demands a constant need for external validation (praise, status, luxury), which ultimately reflects a lack of internal self-worth.

***13. Anchoring the Status Quo*:** Any steps toward personal advancement is deeply frowned upon. The ego loathes true personal growth as it can quickly challenge its false perception of control. It is the uncertainty of the future that becomes the main reason for not developing oneself. With a "I am happy where I am" mentality, there is strong ego influence to resist change or uncertainty.

***14. A World of Limitations*:** 3rd Dimension holds that we are unable to manifest. The idea that "things are impossible" is a common, false thinking-loop. Scarcity, as opposed to abundance, is part of what we project and experience in our mind.

***15. We are the Object, not the Subject*:** The notion that "*We* don't control life; life is *happening* to us," leads us to not seeing ourselves as 100% responsible for what we think, feel and do. We are entrenched in the idea that karma and karmic debt govern us, mentally and physically.

***16. The Ego Demands Logic*:** Science is our God. "If it can't be proven, it is not true," mentality. We show skepticism toward spirituality, the Law of One, energy manipulation, and metaphysics. This person lives by "I'll believe it when I see it." Materialism is justified by the law of cause and effect[2]. Here, we rely on logic and the rational mind, both ego-driven extensions. With it, we are assured to block Ascension!

***17. Separation and Polarization*:** One of the hallmarks of 3rd Dimension! We see ourselves as separated from others, nature, animals. Even Sacred consciousness is outside us. Our thinking is polarized, driven by "us versus them" thinking, Christian versus Muslim, Republican versus Democrat, poor versus rich, white versus black, right versus wrong, etc. We view society through a competitive but judging lens, with winners and losers.

***18. Linear Time Perception*:** Although more generally associated with 3rd Density conditioning, it clearly has a limiting impact on our perception. Time is expressed in a straight-line segment, as past, present, and future; all are clearly separated. Time only moves in one direction, forward. We breathe uni-directionality: events that have passed cannot be revisited or undone, embodying the principle of irreversibility, which is why Past Life Regression is so relevant in this context (being able to revisit the past, and undo blocks that originated there).

***19. Sexuality is Fundamental and Instinctive*:** Much of the

---

2 The Cartesian Causal Adequacy Principle.

debate on sexuality over the last 5000 years or so has centered on morality. Over the last 2000-3000 years, most religions have almost exclusively associated and accepted sexual activity when linked to biological reproduction. According to the same religions, sexuality as a means of pleasure is an expression of shame, debauchery and immoral behavior. Control rather than freedom has dominated the topic.

We have being told, by some very advanced yogis on the Indian subcontinent, that sexual energy should be saved as it can be converted into spiritual energy[3]. This is true in a narrow sense, and is only applicable to an extremely limited group of yogis who have succeeded in this very advanced art of energy manipulation[4]. It is not for the common man, and even Yeshua has commented that the technique is so difficult to master that it is practically inaccessible to the common man.

Dispensing sexual energy without heart involvement, can generate negative karma.

If we want to understand sexuality from a spiritual perspective, we must bypass all judgment and preconceived ideas: sexuality is driven by an energy, nothing more. The big question is, how are we going to handle it? Sexual energy emanates from the Sacral Chakra area. A seldom shared secret is that *it is not designed to act alone* within the body. Just like the Soul works in tandem with the Higher-Self, *the Sacral Chakra is fashioned to work in tandem with the Heart Chakra.* We have been conditioned by the ego to avoid any co-operation between other chakras and the Heart Chakra. That is settled law-and-order for the ego, because our Heart is linked to our Soul, and our Soul to the Higher-Self, and the Higher-Self is the dangerous gateway to liberation from the ego's domination, it assesses.

3 This is different from the practice of Tantra Yoga.

4 Sexual energy conversion is not related to Kundalini. Kundalini is a *non-sexual*, spirit activating energy.

Using sexual energy independently from the Heart Chakra can easily generate negative karma in the Sacral Chakra. This means that self-gratification, or the absence of a loving heart connection with a compatible partner amounts to using that energy in the way it should not be used. The problem is not morality, or lack of it, or marriage status. *The problem is that sexual energy consummated by itself, with all that may accompany it, stimulates the ego, which we ideally are trying to avoid at all costs.* On the other hand, if we use that energy judiciously, we stimulate a genuine love connection with the heart, and develop positive karma!

20. Idolizing Violence: We take pleasure in witnessing violence, through news channels, murder mysteries, video games, movies—with the excuse that it is only entertainment, not "real"—adoration of weapons and more. We proudly display an "I must defend myself" attitude. For some, direct involvement in violent acts is the ultimate satisfaction to the ego.

Strangely, yet not so strangely, we have come to accept these deficient conditions as part of human nature. We all recognize the platonic exclamation "He is only human," to give pardon to trespassing behavior. We have grown so used to portraying these characteristics that we take them for granted. For example, "Being dishonest is part of human nature," or "Errare humanum est," as coined by the Romans.

Beginning the Transition: Ascension cannot commence without an acknowledgement that change is desired (if it is). Recognizing these patterns is the first step toward transcending them. Leaving these tendencies behind is not easy. Attempting to transform ourselves without assistance can be extremely difficult. Guidance from higher perspectives—entities capable of seeing the broader picture—can greatly accelerate the process. For this reason, one recommended approach is to:

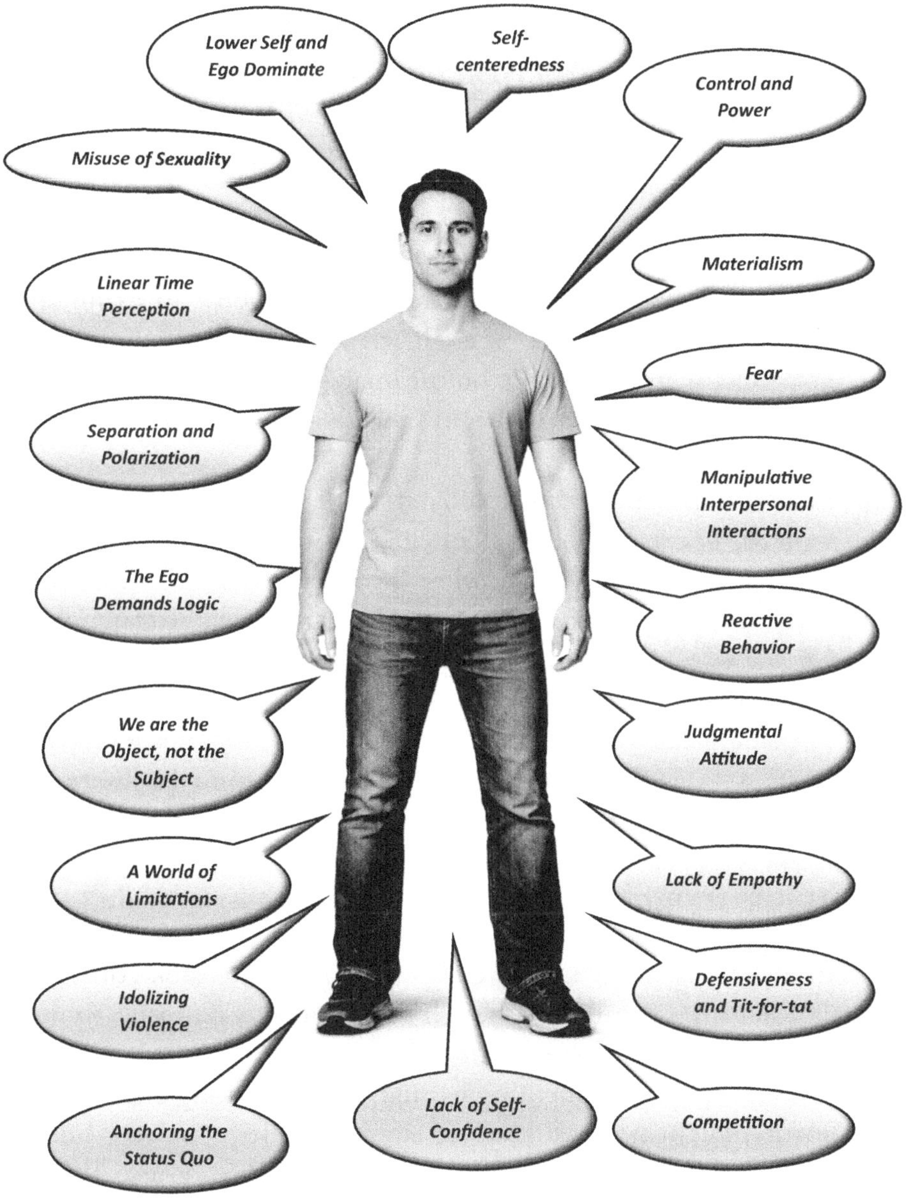

THE 3RD-DIMENSIONAL MAN WITH 3RD-DIMENSIONAL CHARACTERISTICS

Use qualified intermediaries to help:
(A) assess one's current dimensional level and,
(B) determine the most appropriate roadmap for Ascension, under the guidance of the most qualified Ascended Masters available.

The First Decision: Some individuals may choose to maintain the current status quo. For them, the suggestions offered in the following chapters may remain interesting, but ultimately *neutral* reading.

Others may decide to begin the work of inner restoration immediately.

The first step is a conscious declaration of *intent*. This decision ***must arise from the heart***, not from the intellect. One practical method is to lie quietly in a relaxed position, allowing the breath to settle into a natural rhythm for several minutes. Then, make a clear internal declaration such as: *"I have decided to seek co-creation with the Heavenly Light of the Infinite Creator. And so it is."*

This statement communicates intention to the deeper layers of consciousness—our Soul and Higher-Self—which must be aware of the direction we choose to take. After all, they are our partners in the process.

YESHUA IS "CALLING"

On a personal note, in September, 2023, Yeshua took contact with Pramala: "We need to talk." Although this frequently happens, we invariably get jittery when there is an incoming "call" announced in this manner. Have we done something wrong? Was something ominous about to happen? No; instead we received some wonderful news—but with strings attached. Here is the unabridged exchange in an unusually formal tone (and pay attention to the wording):

"Blessings to you all,

I am the one you call Yeshua. I have come to you to enlighten you on some aspects of your journey into the spiritual world. You are undertaking some trials and tests as you call them, and you are embarking onto a new phase on your spiritual path. The next phase will be demanding, and will ask of you to stretch your capabilities and commitment, for more than you have done so. Remember while you are on this path you also have free will, and you can choose not to advance yourself. You are still in the 3rd Dimension, and therefore attachment to that dimension is still prominent in your path. Relinquishing these will help you advance. There is no room in the 4th Dimension for these 3rd Dimension attachments.

You may ask what these attachments are. You already know what they are and how they affect you. I am not here to instruct you to do as I say, but to offer you choices. Some examples of attachment could be the attachment to food, to alcohol, to expensive purchases, to provoke anger and so on. We are not asking that you should reform in accordance to our wishes, however any advancement in the spiritual direction will require relinquishment of 3rd Dimension attachments. There is no room for these things if you want to advance to the 4th Dimension. Very soon you are going to go through the 4th initiation, this is different from advancing to the 4th Dimension. 4th Dimension is a stepping stone to the 4th Density. However, for your 4th initiation[5] also, these attachments need to be relinquished. Do not forget, we do not ask that you give up your free will, but just as you wish to join this exclusive group, there are membership criteria to be met.

You are loved, and we want you to fulfill your destiny as it should be. Blessings to you.

Yeshua."

He could easily have added another dozen items from the Top-20 list to make the point, but did not need to. We got the message: we are in, or

[5] 4th Initiation is the ingress to 4th Density.

we are out! (We were in…)

THE TIMELINE

To navigate the terrain of personal evolution is an immense and necessarily measured process. Any attempt to accelerate it prematurely would disrupt the inner equilibrium of the Soul. This work of restoration requires patience, and its duration varies from one individual to another, determined by the depth of internal restructuring required. A conscious effort to disengage from the influence of the ego can significantly accelerate the process, and shorten the overall timeframe.

It is not possible to assign a fixed duration to this journey, as all aspects of it remain in constant motion. For this reason, the LightStreaming process serves as a practical tool, allowing unseen intelligence to guide the progression, and provide a clearer sense of what can be achieved at each stage. The full process may unfold over several months, or extend across a number of years.

Before stabilizing within the 5th Dimension, individuals pass through the 4th Dimension, where the embodiment of awakening becomes the primary focus. This stage is often described as a bridge dimension, as it marks the transition away from the purely physical and material patterns of the 3rd Dimension, and toward the unified consciousness characteristic of the 5th.

The 4th Dimension represents a period of structured development—marked by learning, inquiry, healing, and deliberate preparation.

CHAPTER HIGHLIGHTS:

- The Earth Star acts as a **grounding magnet** located below the feet, linking human consciousness energetically with Gaia so that the evolutionary state of humanity and Earth remain synchronized.
- The 3rd Dimension is a demanding stage of evolution **dominated by the ego**, survival instincts, and polarity, where fear, competition, and material attachment shape human behavior.
- Humanity's difficult behavior in this density is attributed partly to intentional creative manipulation. The ego is designed to **suppress spiritual development**, and maintain its selfish, service-to-self driven patterns.
- We identified twenty ego-based behavioral tendencies—including materialism, fear, judgment, control, competition, separation thinking, and reactive behavior—as signatures of 3rd-dimensional conditioning.
- Liberation from the 3rd-dimensional grip begins with a **conscious decision** to pursue Ascension, often **aided by spiritual guidance,** and cooperation with higher intelligence, rather than relying solely on individual effort.
- The process of disengaging from ego attachments, and preparing for higher dimensions is **gradual**, and may take months or years. Various tools are available to help **speed up the transformation considerably**.

THE TOP-20 LIST OF EGO MANIPULATIONS

RECOGNIZE THEM ✦ UNDERSTAND THEM ✦ TRANSCEND THEM

1. **The Lower Self and Ego Dominate**
Intense focus on gratification, validation, and external self-worth.

2. **Self-centeredness**
The world is viewed primarily through "What is in it for me?"

3. **Control and Power**
A strong need to dominate situations, people, and our environment.

4. **Materialism**
Identity tied to possessions, wealth, appearance, and status.

5. **Fear**
Fear drives emotional reactions and decision-making.

6. **Manipulative Interpersonal Interactions**
The motto is, "What can they do for me?" Relationships become transactional.

7. **Reactive Behavior**
Reacting instinctively instead of observing and processing.

8. **Judgmental Attitude**
Forming snap judgments, excessive criticism, and superiority.

9. **Lack of Empathy**
Simulating concern without genuine compassion.

10. **Defensiveness and Tit-for-tat**
The ego cannot tolerate criticism or failure.

THE TOP-20 LIST OF EGO MANIPULATIONS

RECOGNIZE THEM ✦ UNDERSTAND THEM ✦ TRANSCEND THEM

11 **Competition**
Seeing others as rivals rather than collaborators.

12 **Lack of Self-Confidence**
Arrogance and deep insecurity often go hand in hand.

13 **Anchoring the Status Quo**
Strong resistance to personal growth, change, or uncertainty.

14 **A World of Limitations**
Belief that abundance and manifestation are impossible; scarcity dominates.

15 **We are the Object, not the Subject**
Life happens to us; we feel controlled by it.

16 **The Ego Demands Logic**
Relies only on science and material proof; rejects what it cannot measure.

17 **Separation and Polarization**
"Us vs them" thinking and division dominate perception.

18 **Linear Time Perception**
Past, present, and future seen as rigidly separated.

19 **Sexuality is Fundamental and Instinctive**
Sexual energy expressed without heart integration.

20 **Idolizing Violence**
Attraction to violence in entertainment and culture.

CHAPTER SIX

FORGIVENESS

It is a striking paradox that a guide to Ascension must place the ego on center stage. Yet, as our previous Top-20 list illustrates, the ego possesses an extensive repertoire of illusions. Among these illusions, three stand out as master deceivers: anger, judgment, and forgiveness. Of the three, forgiveness is the most critical for achieving Salvation. Because of its central role in this process, it deserves closer examination.

This is particularly so because the very purpose and meaning of forgiveness change as we move beyond the 3rd Dimension.

The common 3rd-dimensional understanding of forgiveness rests on a distorted framework built around punishment. It functions through a loop of consequences rooted in distorted perception, and spiritual enslavement. According to this perspective, forgiveness is conditional and transactional.

This model was most recently introduced by the entity collective described in the biblical narrative as the Yahweh group. The *original* Yahweh group—a social memory complex, and member of the Confederation of Planets—*ceased* its direct leadership role in human development more than 70,000 years ago. When this occurred, a vacuum was created. A negatively oriented group, driven by a service-to-self agenda, moved in to occupy that vacuum by *impersonating* the original Yahweh. They fooled the Israelites to believe they were interacting with the Divine itself. In other words, the group guiding the Israelites was *not* the original Yahweh group, but an impersonating entity.The strategy of this service-to-self group unfolded in three stages:

Cultivating Awe. They performed supernatural "miracles" in order to establish an overwhelming and terrifying god-image.

Creating Dependency. They selected specific individuals to serve as intermediaries, fostering deep psychological dependence among the population.

Rule by Fear. They enforced strict laws with severe punishments. Even minor infractions—such as the failure to observe the Sabbath—could carry the penalty of death.

This structure governed the Adamic race until the destruction of the Second Temple in 66 CE. After that time, the overt presence of the false Yahweh group disappeared. What remained was a lingering psychological system built on domination and fear. This historical framework helps explain the modern misunderstanding of forgiveness. Today, forgiveness is still often viewed as a transaction:

- If you commit a wrongdoing, you must pay a price.
- If the payment is accepted, you are forgiven.

This idea of ransom-based absolution has been passed down through centuries. It was later adopted by the institutional Church, and remains a dominant psychological model in modern interpersonal relationships. In essence, it is a legacy of control and domination.

KEY INSIGHTS:

The Transactional Trap: Notice how frequently modern forgiveness feels like a bargain or exchange. This pattern originates directly from the service-to-self logic introduced by the false Yahweh system.

The Power Vacuum: If individuals do not assume responsibility for their own spiritual sovereignty, external authorities inevitably step in to determine moral worth. Not insignificant!

Transcending the Loop: To move toward the 5th Dimension, we must stop asking,

"What price must be paid for this mistake?"

Instead we must ask:

"How do I return to a state of observation?"

THE LOW ROAD - THE ILLUSION OF FORGIVENESS

The prevailing 3rd-dimensional approach to forgiveness is often little more than a "variation on an ancient biblical theme." We frequently hear—or say—things like: "You lied to me, but because I am a kind person, I choose to forgive you." Well-meaning friends might even urge, "Make sure you forgive them." This is the ultimate deceptive loop.

There are layers of deception hidden within this logic. Most glaringly: what power do we truly possess to "correct" or absolve one another? If we "forgive" a transgression, what occurs at a physical, metaphysical, or spiritual level that resets the reality of the event? In truth, we are often saying: "Your dishonesty hurt me, but because I believe myself to be superior, I will perform an act of forgetting. I am now ready for you to hurt me again whenever you choose."

When remorse is offered through tokens—flowers, gifts, or gestures—it becomes a transactional attempt to "buy" goodwill and mask a "sin." This directly mirrors ancient rites where offerings were made to temporarily cover transgressions rather than remove them. In this exchange, the ego of the wounded party demands a ransom, offering a hollow forgiveness in exchange for being admired for its "mercy." This is sometimes further evidenced by the common refrain, "I forgive, but I don't forget"—a clear admission that the grievance remains held in the heart. No true release has occurred.

Spiritually, dishonesty violates the karma-eluding law: "We are encouraged to utter only those words that radiate Love." To lie is to generate negative karma; to offer "forgiveness" while leaving that karma intact is a mere verbal illusion. *True* forgiveness requires the actual *removal* of that energetic distortion.

We see the ultimate example of this in the record of Yeshua at Pentecost, where he removed the karmic burden of his disciples. That was inter-human forgiveness in its highest form—a powerful act that shifted them from the 3rd to the 4th Density. Within the limitations of the 3rd-dimensional ego, we simply do not yet possess the power to replicate such a profound transformation.

Key Insights:

Transactional Forgiveness: Most modern forgiveness is an ego-driven trade for moral superiority, not a genuine clearing of energy.

The Weight of karma: A simple, verbal "I forgive you" does nothing to address the actual karmic imbalance created by dishonesty.

The Observational Shift: Mastery requires moving beyond "acting" as if we aren't hurt, and instead reaching a state where the ego cannot be wounded in the first place.

THE MIDDLE ROAD - SELF-CORRECTION

A more spiritually aligned approach to forgiveness departs entirely from traditional, judgmental logic:

"You have lied to me. Regrettably, I allowed my ego to react to the deception. However, as I am committed to my own evolution, I forgive myself for this lapse in consciousness. The error in reaction was mine alone, and I hold nothing against you."

This response is grounded in absolute sincerity, and excludes false logic. Its authenticity is first demonstrated by the refusal to offer traditional "forgiveness" to the other party. Instead, we acknowledge both our ego's vulnerability, and the other person's temporary weakness. If we feel "hurt" by a lie—knowing full well it *is* a lie—it serves as a signal that our own mastery requires further refinement.

This level of awareness is characteristic of the 4th-dimensional frequency. John the Baptist, a resonant being of this density, lived the "Middle Road," and championed a single transformative concept: *Repentance*. In its true metaphysical sense, this is simply the act of *forgiving oneself* for momentarily following the dictates of the ego.

Key Insights:

Own the Reaction: The focus shifts from the external lie to the internal response. Forgiveness is directed inward to clear the energetic distortion caused by the ego's interference. It is very important *not* to harbor a grudge.

The **Illusion of Injury**: To be hurt by an untruth is to admit that the ego still finds the lie "real." Mastery recognizes the lie as a void, requiring no defense.

Repentance **as Realignment**: True repentance is not about guilt; it is the conscious decision to stop taking orders from the ego and rise to a state of observation. Doing so is an aspiration to the High Road.

THE HIGH ROAD - THE PATH OF THE MASTER

The most profound way to address this is as follows: "You were untruthful. However, my consciousness has reached a state where the ego no longer governs; consequently, I feel only compassion for your own egoic entrapment, hoping for your eventual liberation."

Such a reply emanates from a true master. It demonstrates absolute self-governance, empathy, and grace. In its stillness, the response perfectly mirrors the principle:

"A Master observes; he does not react."

Forgiveness becomes unnecessary, because no offense was taken; the ego was absent, leaving no target for the deception to strike. Simultaneously, the dishonesty fails to find its mark, leaving the speaker's ego neutralized. This embodies the quintessential "frequency" of Yeshua—a hall-mark of 5th Density conduct.

CHAPTER HIGHLIGHTS:

- Forgiveness is presented as one of the three major ego distortions—along with anger and judgment—and **becomes a decisive issue** at the threshold of the transition into 5th-dimensional consciousness.
- The common understanding of forgiveness is transactional and punishment-based, rooted in religious systems that framed it as
- a **conditional exchange**, not a true spiritual clearing.
- What often takes place is a trade for moral superiority or reconciliation—while the emotional grievance and **karmic imbalance remain unresolved.**
- A more advanced approach, the "Middle Road," shifts the focus inward: instead of forgiving the other person, one **forgives oneself for reacting through the ego**, correcting one's consciousness, and returning to observation.
- The "High Road" of mastery arises when **the ego is no longer there to react**; deception or injury produces only compassion for the other person, leaving nothing to forgive.
- In this highest state—associated with 5th-dimensional awareness, —forgiveness becomes unnecessary because the ego has disappeared as a target for offense.
- This 3-tiered perspective (low, middle and high road),can, and **should be applied to every item of the Top-20 list categories**!

THE 3 ROADS OF FORGIVENESS

THREE PATHS. ONE DESTINATION: FREEDOM.

FORGIVENESS IS THE KEY THAT FREES US FROM THE CHAINS OF PAIN, RESENTMENT, AND THE PAST.
IT RESTORES OUR PEACE, OPENS THE HEART, AND RETURNS OUR POWER TO US.

1

THE LOW ROAD - THE ILLUSION OF FORGIVENESS

"YOU LIED TO ME, BUT BECAUSE I AM A KIND PERSON, I CHOOSE TO FORGIVE YOU."

TRANSACTIONAL FORGIVENESS
Most modern forgiveness is an ego-driven trade for moral superiority, not a genuine clearing of energy.

THE WEIGHT OF KARMA
A simple, verbal "I forgive you" does nothing to address the actual karmic imbalance created by dishonesty.

THE OBSERVATIONAL SHIFT
Mastery requires moving beyond "acting" as if we aren't hurt, and instead reaching a state where the ego cannot be wounded.

FROM THE EGO - FORGETTING IS NOT FORGIVENESS.

2

THE MIDDLE ROAD - SELF-CORRECTION

"YOU HAVE LIED TO ME. REGRETTABLY, I ALLOWED MY EGO TO REACT TO THE DECEPTION. HOWEVER, AS I AM COMMITTED TO MY OWN EVOLUTION, I FORGIVE MYSELF FOR THIS LAPSE IN CONSCIOUSNESS. THE ERROR IN REACTION WAS MINE ALONE, AND I HOLD NOTHING AGAINST YOU."

OWN THE REACTION
The focus shifts from the external lie to the internal response. Forgiveness is directed inward to clear the energetic distortion.

THE ILLUSION OF INJURY
To be hurt by an untruth is to admit that the ego still finds the lie "real." The lie is a void, requiring no defense.

REPENTANCE AS REALIGNMENT
True repentance is not about guilt; it is the conscious decision to stop taking orders from the ego and rise to a state of observation.

FROM THE HEART - ACCEPTANCE BRINGS PEACE.

3

THE HIGH ROAD - THE PATH OF THE MASTER

"YOU WERE UNTRUTHFUL. HOWVEER, MY CONSCIOUSNESS HAS REACHED A STATE WHERE THE EGO NO LONGER GOVERNS; I FEEL ONLY COMPASSION FOR YOUR EGOIC ENTRAPMENT, HOPING FOR YOUR LIBERATION."

CONTEMPLATE
A Master observes; he does not react

ABSENCE OF EGO
No offense is taken

TRUE MASTERY
You show self-governance, empathy and grace.

FROM THE SOUL - RECOGNITION BRINGS FREEDOM.

CHAPTER SEVEN

4TH DIMENSION: EXPOSURE AS A BRIDGE TO AWARENESS

A long and complicated relationship—spanning roughly 75,000 years—with a less-than-desirable partner, the ego, has left a deep imprint on the human mind. Our mannerisms, evasions, neural pathways, and habitual reactions have had an immense period of time to settle into our psychological structure.

For this reason, the idea of living without the ego is often perceived as psychologically impossible. Yet this very possibility is now beginning to emerge.

When we reflect upon the behavioral patterns described in the previous chapter on 3rd-dimensional behaviors, most Souls will recognize many of these patterns as deeply embedded within their psychological makeup. While we may initially view them as simple character flaws, dissolving them requires a far deeper engagement than ordinary conversation or traditional therapy can provide.

Just as stubborn weeds do not disappear until their roots are fully removed, these ingrained patterns cannot dissolve until their original source is addressed. The root is simple: the ego.

THE FATE OF THE EGO

Is the complete dissolution of the ego immediately within reach? The honest answer is: not yet. However, with the tools now becoming available to humanity—combined with the refined vibrational environment created by Earth's transition—we are gaining the ability to greatly reduce the ego's influence, almost to the point where it no longer interferes with our consciousness. Ultimately, however, the ego's influence is temporary.

As humanity advances toward initiation into 5th Density, the ego will gradually lose its authority. In time, it will be almost entirely relinquished. Interestingly, the ego itself senses this trajectory. It recognizes that its influence is approaching its end.

The 4th Dimension is a pivotal stage to gently accustom us for the Great Shift to the 5th Dimension.

The imprint it has left on human behavior is so deep that we have almost accepted it as a permanent companion. Yet the ego is not a conscious entity. It is a reactive psychological mechanism.

If we attempt to push it aside without clear intention, we often encounter resistance and internal conflict. If, however, we establish a clear intention—for example, a sincere declaration to expand our awareness—the ego reacts immediately and aggressively. This dog bites.

There is one circumstance the ego fears more than anything else: humanity reaching the 5th Dimension. Once the threshold of the 5th is crossed, the ego recognizes that its influence has ended. Humanity begins living in a new framework based on love rather than 3rd-dimensional polarity. At that point, the negatively oriented Forces of Service to Self (FSS), and the ego lose their leverage. Recognizing their defeat against the forces of Light, they abandon the struggle.

PREPARING FOR THE GUEST OF HONOR

The 4th Dimension represents both a recalibration phase and a preparation phase. Something extraordinary is approaching.

The transformation we are preparing for will affect our existence on four levels:

- The mind
- Biology
- Chemistry
- The metaphysical field

The renewal we are entering is not superficial. It is a complete reconstruction of our inner infrastructure, preparing the human vessel for a far greater presence of Sacred consciousness. We are preparing the body for a consciousness of much higher lineage—one that will fully inhabit us upon entering the 5th Dimension. This process resembles a full structural renovation rather than a simple rearrangement of furniture. Walls that have stood for millennia are being dismantled.

The house itself is being rebuilt.

ASSESSMENT BEFORE RENOVATION

Any serious renovation requires a careful evaluation of the structure. Before replacing components, we must determine what is worth preserving.

Despite the many limitations associated with the 3rd Dimension, humanity still possesses valuable strengths that can serve as foundations for further development. The challenge lies in evaluating ourselves objectively.

Human beings rarely judge themselves impartially. Even other individuals operating within the 3rd Dimension struggle to offer objective insight because their own egos introduce bias, judgment, and projection. Seeking this type of evaluation through traditional psychology is therefore comparable to a blind person asking another blind person to show the path. Unfortunately, humanity has done precisely that for thousands of years.

THE ROLE OF LIGHTSTREAMING

This is where LightStreaming Channeling becomes a powerful tool. A 5th-density spiritual being, such as an Ascended Master, already possesses a complete map of our energetic structure. Through channeling, such beings can reveal the elements of our personality that require attention, and provide guidance for the steps needed to proceed. The Light works methodically.

Before addressing internal dynamics, the Light first evaluates the external environment surrounding the individual. Human beings are not influenced solely by their own egos. We are also affected by the egos of those around us. Although egos do not communicate directly with one another, they recognize and reinforce each other whenever conscious interaction occurs. For example, jealousy expressed by one individual may be unconsciously welcomed by another person's ego.

Because we are often unaware of these dynamics, the first step recommended by the Light is often environmental pruning.

PRUNING THE SOCIAL ENVIRONMENT

Individuals may be asked to compile a comprehensive list of everyone with whom they regularly interact—family members, friends, coworkers, and acquaintances. The Light has already identified the energetic patterns associated with each person in that network. During the session, guidance is provided indicating which relationships support spiritual progress, and which ones obstruct it.

This can be a sobering experience. However, it is necessary in order to remove energetic obstacles that hinder forward movement.

Implementing these adjustments may take several weeks, because we are gradually reshaping the sphere of influence surrounding our daily lives.

THE DISCLOSURE OF SELF

This gradual emergence into a renewed vessel is naturally accompanied by a process of refinement. One could just as easily title this phase of the journey "The Complete Self-Disclosure of Who and How We Are."

At this stage, we begin a deliberate examination of our habits, behaviors, and internal structures. Long-standing emotional burdens and memories from the past—sometimes stretching back across multiple lifetimes—may rise into awareness. These memories are not resurfacing randomly. They appear because they are ready to be acknowledged and integrated.

We begin a comprehensive restoration of our inner landscape. Everything that has remained dormant gradually comes into the light of awareness. These elements are not meant to condemn us, but to be recognized, compassionately examined, and—when they no longer serve a purpose—released back into pure potential. This process is what we call *exposure*.

The Soul feels a strong internal impulse to complete an energetic purification. Old emotional patterns, rigid psychological frameworks, and inherited belief structures begin to dissolve as they are brought into conscious awareness. What replaces them is clarity. This clarity resonates directly with Sacred consciousness.

The expansion of awareness during this phase involves the entire human system. It affects our mental patterns, emotional responses, and even biological rhythms. At times we may feel expansive, liberated, and filled with purpose. At other moments we may experience temporary confusion or disorientation as old internal structures collapse.

During this stage we begin questioning many aspects of our lives:

- Long-held beliefs
- Spiritual assumptions
- Life direction
- Personal identity

- Social relationships

Even the core definition of who we believe ourselves to be may undergo revision.

Relationships also begin to change. Individuals who once felt closely aligned with us may gradually drift away as our internal frequency shifts. People whose values no longer resonate with our emerging awareness naturally move out of our sphere of influence. They may sense this transformation themselves. It is not uncommon to hear them say:

"You have changed."

Indeed, we have.

4TH-DIMENSIONAL ATTRIBUTES

1. ***Heightened Sensory Awareness***: Emotions become clearer, deeper, and more responsive. We begin processing information more thoroughly and thoughtfully. This often produces a richer inner life, but it may also result in slower reaction times because we are no longer responding purely through instinct.

   We begin searching for the root causes of our reactions. Questions such as "Why do I feel this way?" or "What is this experience trying to show me?" arise naturally. Through this process, we greatly expand our knowledge of ourselves.

   At the same time, empathy increases. Loving consideration toward others grows stronger, and we become more aware of the emotional states of those around us.

   Another phenomenon frequently reported during this phase is an increasing number of synchronistic events. The Higher-Self and the lower self begin operating more harmoniously. Experiences such as déjà vu, and intuitive "gut feelings" become more common, even if we do not yet fully understand their significance.

2. ***Increased Interest in the Metaphysical***: Metaphysical beliefs begin to exert a strong influence on how individuals

perceive the world and their place within it.

For example, questions about free will versus determinism can profoundly shape a person's ethical framework, and sense of responsibility. During this stage we begin to feel strongly that there is more to reality than what appears on the surface. This curiosity leads us toward spiritual self-exploration and philosophical inquiry. We may find ourselves drawn toward subjects such as:

- The nature of consciousness
- The structure of reality
- The existence of extraterrestrial life
- Metaphysics and spiritual philosophy
- Astrology
- Non-traditional healing methods
- Esoteric knowledge and hidden histories

Topics that are often dismissed by strictly 3rd-dimensional thinking—including ideas sometimes labeled "conspiracy theories"—may suddenly appear worthy of serious examination.

After the Great Shift, Metaphysics will displace traditional science and become the new gold standard for research.

In essence, we become more open-minded. While duality still governs much of our perception, we begin distancing ourselves from purely materialistic interpretations of reality.

3. <u>Identity of Self is Shifting</u>: As consciousness evolves, our sense of identity begins to change. This transformation affects our beliefs, desires, habits, memories, and personality traits[1]. The process can be compared to adjusting the major configuration settings of a software system. The underlying operating system remains the same, but the way it functions and presents itself to the user changes dramatically. This shift is highly internal.

People who interact with us regularly may immediately sense

---

1 This mirrors Locke's views from his Psychological Continuity Theory.

that something has changed, even if they cannot clearly articulate what it is.

External forms of validation that were once important during the 3rd Dimension gradually lose their influence. The traits associated with that stage—many of which appeared in the Top-20 List of Ego Manipulations—begin dissolving as we continue the internal cleansing process.

The ego, however, remains active during this stage, and often reacts aggressively as it senses its authority diminishing. Internal tension may arise as material-based values are replaced by deeper spiritual priorities.

4. Time Perception is Gradually Altered: Our perception of time may begin to fluctuate. At certain moments, one hour may feel as though several hours have passed. At other times, an entire afternoon may seem to disappear quickly.

This experience is different from the common expression, "Where did the day go?" Instead, it reflects a genuine shift in the way consciousness processes temporal experience. The mind may begin to perceive time as less rigid, and more fluid.

In some cases, attention itself affects time perception. When we focus intensely on the passage of time, it may appear to move more slowly. When our attention is absorbed elsewhere, time appears to accelerate.

Similarly, when the brain processes new and unfamiliar information, time often feels slower because more cognitive activity is occurring. When life becomes repetitive and predictable, less information is processed, and time seems to move faster.

These shifts in perception can produce a subtle blurring of reality as the mind adjusts to a broader dimensional framework.

5. Initial Changes to the Physical Human Structure: Changes associated with consciousness expansion may also begin to appear in the physical body. Some individuals report that the aging process appears to slow slightly. Hair may become softer and more natural, and subtle structural changes may occur within the skeletal and cranial systems, including the teeth.

These changes reflect the body's gradual adaptation to the new magnetic and energetic conditions emerging on Earth. Human morphology becomes slightly more flexible, and less dense as it adjusts to the changing gravitational and energetic environment.

If Earth's magnetic and gravitational dynamics were to shift without corresponding biological adaptation, the consequences for the human body could be severe. The gradual transformation of the body therefore serves as a protective adjustment, allowing both humans and animals to adapt safely to the evolving planetary environment. These changes represent just one of the physical expressions of the shift in consciousness.

6. Modified Chakra System - The Soul Star: Even though a chapter is devoted to the chakras later on, we cannot omit an early introduction of the star of this chapter at this time. During this stage, the human chakra system expands from seven to *eight* chakras. The additional chakra appears above the Crown Chakra, and is known as the *Soul Star Chakra.*

The first physical sensations associated with this chakra may include a feeling of pressure or weight near the top of the head. The Soul Star functions as a kind of energetic transducer, stepping down extremely high-frequency energy so that the physical body can safely process it. Without this modulation, the body would be overwhelmed by incoming energy.

Other symptoms sometimes reported during this phase include:

- Heightened sensitivity to artificial lighting
- Greater appreciation of natural sunlight
- Ringing or high-pitched tones in the ears (tinnitus)
- Bursts of energy followed by deep fatigue
- Temporary symptoms often referred to as Ascension Flu

THE 8-CHAKRA HUMAN - IN 4TH DIMENSION

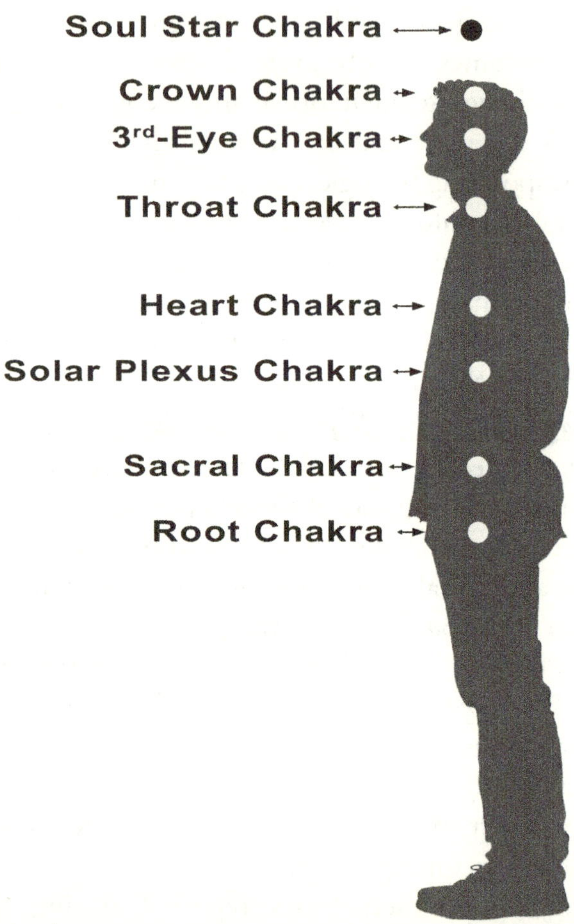

The Akashic Records serve as the storage center for all of our past lives and actions (the Akash). It contains the karmic balance accumulated across past lives, and stores the blueprint of the Soul's contract—its life purpose, and intended spiritual path. When activated, the Soul Star can provide profound insight, by accessing the Akash, to show *why* we incarnated, and what we are meant to accomplish during this lifetime. Its placement above the Crown Chakra is not accidental.

While the Crown Chakra connects the individual to the Divine, the Soul Star allows the individual consciousness to merge with universal consciousness itself. The Soul Star acts as a supervisory center for the entire chakra system, helping align, cleanse, and harmonize the lower chakras while channeling high-frequency Divine Light into the human energy field.

Because this process bypasses the rational mind and ego, it introduces a direct form of spiritual intelligence into consciousness[2]. For this reason, the activation of the Soul Star is often considered one of the first *clear* metaphysical indicators that Ascension is underway.

The 4th Dimension, often overshadowed and functionally sandwiched between the dominant 3rd Dimension and the loving unity of the 5th Dimension, remains a remarkably underrated sphere of consciousness. Yet the extraordinary faculties attributed to many of its sages have become legendary.

Elijah, the 4th-dimensional prophet, was a miracle worker without equal. He raised the dead, called down fire at will, and materialized food before ultimately being taken aboard what Ananda has described as an Andromedan starship.

Moses needs little introduction as a master of the 4th Dimension. Who parted the Red Sea?

His brother Aaron, operating in the higher reaches of the 4th Dimension, communicated directly with Yahweh, and cast his staff upon the ground, where it famously transformed into serpents.

We also invite readers to explore the story of another 4th-dimensional figure, St. George the Martyr (ca. 300 CE), who reportedly escaped death multiple times under the persecution of Emperor Diocletian, in the most extraordinary ways.

John the Baptist likewise reached the higher strata of the 4th

[2] This information will match exactly what was/will be shared with you by the Masters during LightStreaming Channeling.

Dimension, and stunned the world through his prophetic authority and uncompromising actions.

The faculties available within the 4th Dimension are profoundly transformative—particularly in its higher ranges—revealing abilities that appear miraculous when viewed from the perspective of the 3rd Dimension. In perspective:

> The shift from 3rd to 4th Dimension is seen as a transition from ***Matter-based*** Consciousness to ***Emotional/Astral Consciousness.***
>
> When going from ***Emotional/Astral Consciousness*** (4th Dimension) into 5th, we experience the shift to ***Unity/Divine Consciousness.***

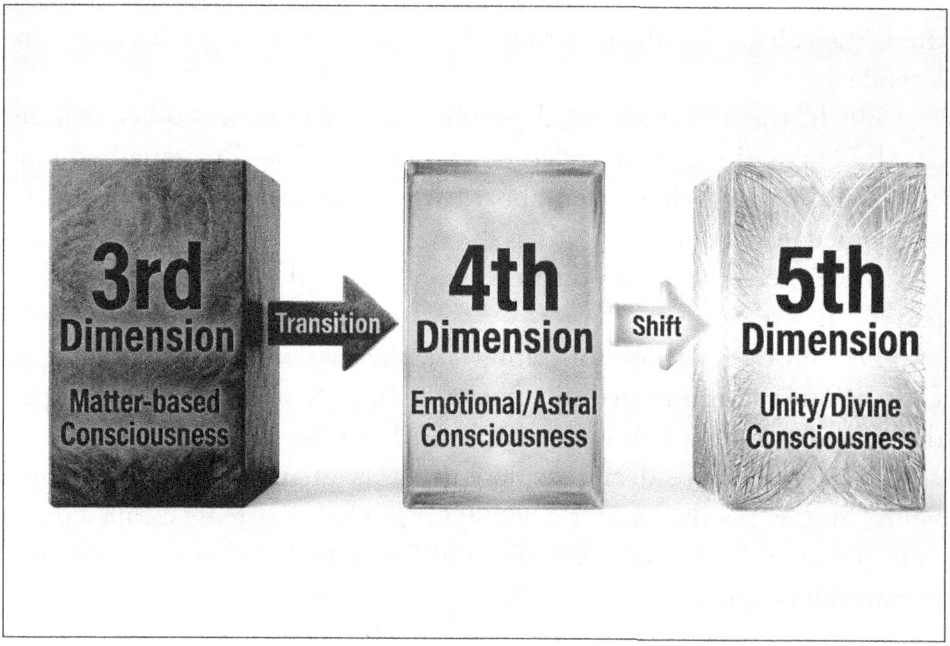

CHAPTER HIGHLIGHTS:

- The 4th Dimension functions as a **transitional stage** between 3rd-dimensional ego consciousness and 5th-dimensional unity, allowing individuals to weaken the influence of the ego while preparing for its eventual dissolution.
- This dimension initiates a **deep process of personal exposure and self-examination**: hidden habits, emotional residues, and inherited belief systems rise into awareness so they can be acknowledged and released.
- Spiritual development during this phase often involves external and **internal purification**, including reassessing relationships, environments, and influences that reinforce ego-driven patterns.
- Guidance from higher-dimensional intelligence—such as Ascended Masters accessed through LightStreaming channeling—is a method for evaluating one's energetic environment, and **identifying the steps** required for continued evolution.
- The expansion into 4th-dimensional awareness **brings recognizable shifts**: heightened intuition, stronger empathy, altered time perception, growing interest in metaphysical knowledge, and a **transformation of personal identity**.
- The transition is accompanied by changes in the human subtle body, which **expands the chakra system** (Soul Star chakra), and connects individual consciousness gradually more directly with Christ (Sacred) consciousness.

4th-Dimensional Attributes

Signs of Our Evolution into Higher Consciousness

1

Heightened Sensory Awareness

Emotions are clearer, deeper, and more responsive. We process information more deeply, which can lead to a rich inner life, but also increased reaction time. We search for root causes to reactive behavior. Synchronicities in behavior between the Higher Self and the lower self are frequent.

2

Increased Interest in the Metaphysical

We know there is more to life than meets the eye. We explore spiritual truths, the nature of existence, consciousness, and the mysteries of the Universe. Our minds open, and we begin to outgrow 3rd-dimensional thinking and limitations.

3

Identity of Self is Shifting

Beliefs, desires, habits, and identity are transforming. Old patterns dissolve as a more authentic self emerges. External validation fades, while inner truth rises. The ego resists, but the call to live by higher values becomes stronger and more undeniable.

4

Time Perception is Gradually Altered

Time feels different—sometimes expanding, sometimes dissolving. Days may feel long or short. As awareness increases, time becomes more fluid. Novel experiences slow it down, routine speeds it up.

5

Initial Changes to the Physical Human Structure

The body adapts to higher frequencies. Cells, bones, and energy systems realign. The body becomes more flexible, less dense, and more resilient to aging. These changes prepare us to thrive in higher frequencies and new environments.

6

Modified Chakra System – The Soul Star

An eighth chakra, the Soul Star, exists above the crown, connecting us to divine wisdom and universal consciousness. It guides and harmonizes the other chakras, bringing higher light, intuition, and unity. Spiritual gifts activate and ascension accelerates.

You are Awakening to your Authentic Self
A Multidimensional Being of Light and Consciousness.

CHAPTER EIGHT

5TH DIMENSION: THE DESCENT OF THE HIGHER-SELF

While the realm of 3rd-dimensional existence is largely defined by the crucible of survival and the illusion of separation, the shift into the 4th Dimension initiates a profound passage of spiritual awakening and inner purification. This beautiful preparation leads the Soul toward the 5th Dimension, a state dedicated to the embodiment of the Soul's highest wisdom—the place where the Higher-Self descends, and unites seamlessly with our very being.

The defining event of our entry into the 5th Dimension is the descent of the Higher-Self, and its complete merger with the Soul.

Within this dimension, one becomes a conscious co-creator with universal intelligence, expressing faculties and innate knowing that transcend the constraints of conventional logic, and traditional science. In this state, deep serenity and radiant clarity become the guiding energies of existence.

The 4th Density is entirely governed by the resonant intelligence of the heart. The conduct and divine nature of Yeshua can certainly be seen as an expression of this exalted state, for he was a being born into its unbroken Light. This dimension serves as a sovereign platform for genuine multi-dimensional awareness, integrating a timeless quantum element that energetically distinguishes it from the realms that precede it.

Its impact is so transformative that the rare Souls who have touched this reality in the past were often revered almost as demigods because of the extraordinary capacities they demonstrated.

When Yeshua taught that "the Kingdom of God is within," he was referring to the expanded inner vision that blossoms through spiritual perception, and eternally connects us to the Divine Source. His guidance was clear: to merge with the heart of Creation, one must look inward, and seek wisdom *there.*

The familiar patterns of life that defined the 3rd Dimension now recede into the past. Life is elevated to a new plane of communion with pure consciousness, and those who have attained this state have often been revered as saints and spiritual pioneers.

Among the radiant Souls who have walked this path are:

- Buddha
- Mother Mary
- Lao Tzu
- Krishna
- Quan Yin
- St. Francis of Assisi
- Mary of Magdala
- Rumi
- Paramahamsa Yogananda

These figures represent only a small portion of those who have embodied this expanded state of consciousness.

KUNDALINI AND THE TRANSITION

Kundalini is the dormant feminine spiritual principle coiled at the base of the spine within the Root Chakra (Muladhara). When awakened, this energy rises through the central energetic channel known as the Sushumna, moving upward through the seven chakras.

This inner ascent represents the biological counterpart to spiritual Ascension. As Kundalini rises, the 3rd-Eye Chakra opens, marking the initiation into the 4th Density/5th Dimension. Be aware that this rising of energy requires an absolutely flawless, class and unobstructed passage through the body (chakras and sushumna) to fulfill its mission.

Kundalini is neither a "conventional" energy, nor a physical "force." It is best described as a "Latent Organizing Principle"

Each chakra needs to be cleansed (not cleared…) regularly so its spiritual energy flow system remains properly flexible. Imagine the chakra system as a seven-story house equipped with an elevator. When the elevator descends to the ground floor, it anchors you to the Earth. When it rises to the top floor, it connects you to the cosmos. But if the elevator gets stuck on the third floor, you are suddenly cut off from both root and crown—neither grounded nor spiritually aligned. This perfectly illustrates why keeping our energy centers clear and unblocked is so vital to our overall well-being.

This event of rising is often accompanied by a profound energetic shift within the body. Kundalini functions as a self-regulating evolutionary trigger, acting as an interface between consciousness and biology. Its awakening can initiate emotional catharsis, releases of stored trauma, and intense pranic surges.

When the energy reaches the 3rd-Eye, it may trigger powerful neurochemical changes resembling psychedelic states of awareness. Once the process completes, Ascension into the 5th Dimension becomes permanent and irreversible.

Eventually, the pervasive sense of separation dissolves. We begin to perceive every being as an expression of the same Source.

Love, which in the 3rd Dimension often appears sentimental or conditional, becomes the foundational expression of our consciousness.

For this reason, the 5th Dimension (and Density) is often referred to as the "Dimension of Love." It represents the full embodiment of Christ consciousness.

5TH-DIMENSIONAL ATTRIBUTES

1. The Higher-Self Merges with the Soul: Seen through the prism of our life journey, the Higher-Self acts as a *Guide*. It is the most enlightened and conscious aspect of our being, always connected to the Divine universal consciousness. It holds our route plan, and shares the body's wisdom with the Soul, unconditional love, clarity, and awareness of our ultimate potential.

The Higher-Self remains in constant communication with the lower self, yet we often ignore its guidance because we fail to use our intuition to the degree we should. A strong intuition reveals a strong connection with the Higher-Self. From its vantage point, it can perceive all information at all times through a quantum perspective, and we can access this awareness if we are properly attuned.

The Higher-Self differs from the Soul in that it is pure and immutable. It perceives reality in real time, impartially, and without interference from emotions, karmic memories, or incarnational experiences. When we access the Higher-Self, what we receive is exactly what it perceives in that moment.

The merging of the Higher-Self and the Soul is, by far, the most consequential transformation when entering the 5th. Nothing quite equals it.

Through that same prism of our life journey, the Soul may be understood as the *Traveler*. It accompanies us through every incarnation, and into every new physical body in order to gather experience, learn lessons, explore life scenarios, and evolve. Everything the Soul learns is shared with Creation for its furtherance.

Unlike the Higher-Self, the Soul carries memories, wisdom, and karmic baggage from our past lives, including the present one. The Soul remains impervious to the existence of the ego, and exchanges no communication with it. The ego may attempt to influence the Soul, but the attempt is rejected by default. This boundary is established by Creation itself.

Whereas the Higher-Self remains immutable within one lifetime, the Soul is mutable. It grows, and evolves according to the experiences we lead it through, making it a central participant in our life journey. The Soul records everything about us. Opening the doors to the 5th Dimension is not a transformation for the meek. It represents a dramatic alteration of the psychological and spiritual structure to which we have grown accustomed.

The Higher-Self, which has hovered above the Crown Chakra like a luminous field of intelligence, now lowers itself, and merges with the Soul located near the heart center. This is the defining event of entry into the 5th Dimension.

Guide and *Traveler* become one. The possibility of miscommunication between them disappears, resulting in clairvoyance and clear perception. Internally, we can see where we have been, and where we are going.

To illustrate the magnitude of this transformation, imagine transporting a photographer from the 1840s—accustomed to grainy black-and-white images—into the modern world of ultra-high-resolution 4 million pixel digital color photography. The astonishment would be overwhelming. Those who have experienced this transition rarely attempt to describe it, because the experience itself lies beyond language.

2. Complete Separation From the Cycle of Karma: This unprecedented transformation signifies that we are no longer subject to the karmic mechanisms that assign consequences for unloving behavior. Why? Because we have now reached the Density of Love, where unloving behavior simply does not arise.

The possibility of 3rd-dimensional conduct disappears.

We are finally liberated from the burden of karma. Errors are no longer counted against us, because our consciousness now operates from a state of unity with Spirit. This liberation corresponds to what various traditions have called *Salvation*, *Moksha*, or *Nirvana*.

Acting without personal gain or fear, we cease generating new karma. By transcending the temporary world of appearances, we attain self-knowledge, and recognize the true nature of reality.

The ancient concept of ignorance, referring to the inability to see through the 3rd-Eye, has now been removed.

3. Unity Consciousness: The powerful sense of separation between "self" and "other" also dissolves. We enter what we call a global network of Souls, experiencing a heightened sense of connection with those who share the same dimensional resonance.

Although we may have fewer companions who fully understand us, any feeling of isolation disappears. Instead, we experience a profound sense of belonging within the greater web of life. The sense of oneness becomes so strong that harming another being feels equivalent to harming ourselves. For this reason, killing animals becomes emotionally unbearable for many individuals in this state of consciousness. This is one reason spiritually awakened people often reduce or eliminate animal consumption. The vibration of death interferes with the shared experience of peace and joy.

Operating within this interconnected network of Souls, we begin cooperating collectively to remove social systems and behaviors that conflict with 5th-Dimensional thinking.

The Law of One becomes our guiding compass.

Identity politics, tribal labels, and group mentalities dissolve as we recognize ourselves as expressions of the Infinite Creator.

4. Heart-Centered Existence: Crossing the threshold into the 5th Dimension also means entering the first dimension of the 4th Density, which is governed entirely by love. It becomes impossible to exist within this dimension without embodying love.

Fear and cold logic lose their dominance. Our emotions and Spirit guide us toward authentic, transparent, and energetically clean relationships.

Control and manipulation are no longer tolerated.

The heart opens fully. Compassion for all sentient life flows naturally, without effort or judgment.

At the same time, we experience deep compassion for those who remain in the 3rd Dimension, recognizing that humanity temporarily exists in two different states of consciousness.

We radiate love toward them in the hope that they too will eventually join this higher state of awareness.

5. Multi-dimensional Awareness: The manifestations of multi-dimensional awareness become more dramatic the higher we progress within the 5th Dimension. We come to understand that manifestation is driven by the heart, not the brain.

The manifestations we exhibit in the early stages after the transition can quickly become pronounced, and expand rapidly as we approach the middle and upper ranges of the dimension. The ability to manifest physical objects is greatly improved, as we come to understand that matter is simply condensed Light that can be manipulated by our enhanced consciousness.

Individuals experience this multi-dimensionality in different ways, and at different stages within the dimension. The process of manifestation becomes fluid, and almost automatic. Intentions are reflected almost immediately, eliminating the delay characteristic of 3rd-density existence.

"Ascending" can take on a very real meaning, as the physical and energetic bodies become refined into a Light body operating at a higher vibrational frequency. Levitation normally accompanies this state. Consciousness is no longer understood as merely a product of the physical brain, but as a multi-dimensional phenomenon.

In this sense, multi-dimensional awareness is the experience of accessing or resonating with three planes of consciousness (3rd, 4th, and 5th Dimensions). The old cliché of "living in the now" suddenly becomes reality.

Rigid living is replaced by a more personal flow with the Higher-Self, guided by synchronicity, because the Soul and the Higher-Self now speak with one voice. Everything flows without resistance.

We have arrived.

*6. **Vibrational Wholeness:*** Structurally, this attribute is of fundamental importance. Our bodies demand unity between vibrational input and output. What the mind experiences, the body also wishes to experience.

We therefore tend to select environments characterized by quietness, serenity, and peacefulness, free of noise and unnecessary distractions. This stage is often associated with the concept of Zen.

Unorganized sounds become disturbing because we prefer to cherish the peacefulness within ourselves or in nature. The media we watch or listen to must resonate with the peaceful state of our inner Soul.

As enlightened individuals, we are no longer attracted to violence, disruption, ego-driven behavior, pleasure pursued solely for its own sake, reactivity, or competitive behavior. The social environments we once cherished in the 3rd Density largely disappear—not because they were forcibly removed, but because their relevance has faded. They now appear as remnants of a distant past with which we no longer resonate.

The inner balance and equilibrium expressed by such individuals have a profound influence on their surroundings.

The foods we eat, and the beverages we consume must align with vitality, harmony, and peace. Cooking becomes simpler and more natural. Any element of performance or display associated with it disappears.

The vibrational wholeness we have achieved projects a personal energy field that is clear, radiant, and magnetic, causing others to feel calm and inspired in our presence. The deeper we move into this dimension, the more we seek the serenity that our Soul and Higher-Self now require.

Yet this is also a sphere where thoughts are electric, and emotions magnetic.

*7. **Rebalanced Perception**:* A rebalanced perception recognizes that our perception shapes our reality. Validation and truth are now sourced internally rather than being sought from external people, or circumstances.

The phenomenal world we once perceived through our physical senses is revealed as an interpretation of energy by the mind—what many traditions refer to as Maya, the illusion of material reality. We recognize that our 3rd-dimensional perception was incomplete because it was not fully aligned with ultimate reality: the Light.

In this state, our energetic perception and intuition become highly refined. Sensitivity to auric fields increases dramatically. We are able to interpret the energy fields of other individuals directly, as well as those of animals, plants, and even inanimate systems.

At the same time, our ability to engage in two-way communication with Ascended Masters, Archangels, Higher Selves, and other advanced spiritual intelligences becomes available almost immediately upon entering the 5th Dimension.

This faculty surpasses artificial intelligence by a wide margin. The intelligence accessed here is not artificial. It is real.

8. Telepathic Communication: Information moves through several levels of translation in the 3rd-dimensional communication chain. This multi-step process opens the door to miscommunication, and misunderstanding due to misaligned perception.

3D Communication Matrix

5th-dimensional communication is characterized by total telepathic mind synchronization. Traditional speech is replaced with direct neural or energetic data transfer

Thoughts, images, emotions, and even scents are transmitted simultaneously. No deception is possible. Mental states are fully transparent, and language becomes little-by-little largely unnecessary.

By the end of the 5th Dimension, language as we know it is almost completely eliminated between enlightened beings, preparing for the fully non-verbal communication of higher density consciousness.

***9. Manifestation*:** When we enter the field of conscious manifestation, some of the miracles exhibited by Yeshua come to mind—such as the conversion of water into wine at the wedding in Canaan. As extraordinary as this appears from a 3rd-dimensional perspective, it becomes a natural expression within the 5th Dimension.

The Law of One postulates that matter can be shaped through coherent intention, allowing for the alteration of physical structures—not as a rare occurrence, but as a consistent capability when necessary. Matter is understood as stabilized energy structured by information. Within 3rd-dimensional consciousness, matter is manipulated mechanically. In the 5th Dimension, beings manipulate matter energetically, and matter reorganizes accordingly.

For a precise outcome, intention must remain stable and unwavering. Thought, emotion, and will must be perfectly aligned. Only when thought—free of internal contradiction—generates a structured energy field, can manifestation occur, because atomic structures must reorganize for a stable form to

THE METAPHYSICAL MANIFESTATION MODEL

appear. As extraordinary as this may sound, this is not fantasy. It is a state in which conscious manifestation is a function of Spirit, not manual effort.

10. From Carbon to Crystalline Body: At the heart of the shift into a 5th Dimension lies a profound transformation of our physical essence: the transition from a carbon-based foundational organization to a crystalline one. This evolution is more than a spiritual shift; it is a fundamental restructuring of our atomic makeup. The journey begins as the body learns to hold and sustain "photonic Light." This is not merely a poetic description, but a literal increase in the cellular capacity to store, and conduct higher frequencies of energy.

As this process unfolds, the very nature of our physical form begins to change. The body loses its heavy, rigid density, becoming increasingly fluid and subtle.

In our present physical condition—the 3rd Dimension—carbon is uniquely suited for biological life because each carbon atom has four valence electrons, allowing it to form stable bonds in multiple directions. This makes it possible to build the complex molecular chains that form proteins, DNA, and the countless structures required for living organisms. In this density of existence, carbon provides the stability, and flexibility needed for physical life.

As human consciousness evolves, the structure of the body gradually changes as well. The idea of carbon-to-crystalline transmutation does not mean that carbon disappears from the body. Instead, it proposes that the organization of atoms within cells becomes more ordered and symmetrical, resembling a crystalline lattice rather than loosely arranged organic chains.

In such a structure, the body is better able to conduct and regulate energy. A more ordered cellular structure allows the body to handle higher levels of energetic activity without overwhelming the nervous system. It may also allow cells to store, and transmit information carried by Light—often referred to as photonic energy—more efficiently.

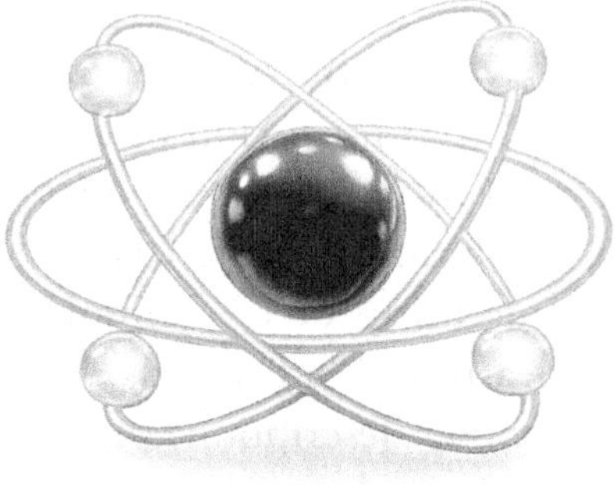

CARBON STRUCTURE

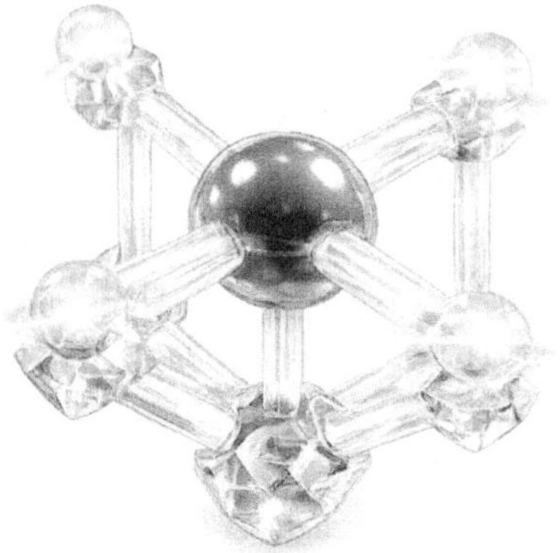

CRYSTALLINE STRUCTURE

In metaphysical teachings, this transition is sometimes associated with silicon, an element located directly beneath carbon in the same family of the periodic table. Silicon shares several bonding characteristics with carbon, but tends to form more rigid, crystalline structures. Because of this, it is often viewed as a bridge between traditional organic biology, and more energy-conductive crystalline forms of matter.

Within this framework, the proposed shift represents more than a chemical change. Carbon-based biology reflects a stage of life focused primarily on chemical energy and physical matter. A more crystalline biological structure represents a stage in which matter and energy operate more closely together, allowing the body to interact more efficiently with subtle energetic fields.

Metaphysically, this is often described as the transition from a matter-centered phase of life toward a more luminous, energy-integrated state of being. It seems we are truly crossing the threshold into the era of avatars.

Obviously, when referring to the crystalline body, this is not meant literally; the body is not turning into a giant crystal. A crystal, by definition, is a solid material whose atoms, molecules, and ions are arranged in a highly ordered, repeating pattern. The operative word is *order*.

What takes place is increased biological order within the organization of DNA, proteins, and the scaffolding network of microtubules and filaments (the dysfunction of which is related to Parkinson's and Alzheimer's diseases).

The best way to understand the shift to a crystalline body is to view it as a movement toward greater biological order, coherence, and efficiency in how the organism processes energy and information. In other words, "crystalline" is a metaphor for coherence and structural harmony, not mineralization.

11. Restructured Chakra System: Humanity has gone through the first dimension of the 3rd Density with its native seven chakras. In the 4th Dimension, we saw an expansion from seven to eight chakras, having added the Soul Star. The 5th Dimension introduces yet another recalibration of the chakra system, to align with increased interaction from out-of-body spirit elements. Outer-body chakras serve as a receptive grid for managing expanded consciousness without collapsing the nervous system or social functioning. Without them, our landing into 5th would be a rough adventure; they reduce psychological fragmentation, increase coherence (so we "keep ourselves together"), and give us the capacity to interact with higher intelligence without losing our minds.

4th Density—5th and 6th Dimensions—is pivotal in preparing the body for its final transition from flesh to spirit. This course of action of detachment from Earth starts lightly in the 4th, and is intensified in the 5th Dimension, and by the end of the 6th Dimension that detachment is complete. This life-changing metamorphosis will not take thousands of years for an old soul, but can be achieved in just a few hundred with proper attention given to it. The elevated compression of 5th Dimension consciousness *renders the lower 3 chakras redundant. The Root Chakra, the Sacral Chakra, and the Solar Plexus Chakras are now being disconnected, for never to be used again*, and we graciously thank them for their service.

We are now in the 5th Dimension, and operate on a custom-configured, *nine-chakra system*—comprised of the Heart, the Throat, the 3rd-Eye, the Crown, the Soul Star, and another four extra-body chakras. ***The removal of the three lower chakras is causing an almost total subduing of the ego, as most of its operating space lies here.*** Regardless, rest assured that the nine-chakra system in place is an amazing vibrational configuration that further connects us with Divinity. In addition to the Soul Star Chakra, the extra-body chakra map of the 5th Dimension looks like this:

CHAKRA #9: "The Causal Chakra," located behind the back of the head. It activates increased spiritual awareness, Divine inspiration, and higher thought. It opens a gateway to Cosmic consciousness and the Universal Mind, and provides us accesses to unusually high frequencies of Light. Bridging our consciousness to transpersonal fields beyond the human identity, this chakra links us directly to our Soul contract, allowing us to fulfill that contract more easily. It also enhances intuitive decision-making, and creative abilities.

CHAKRA #10: "The Galactic Chakra," located directly above the 9th Chakra, the Causal Chakra. This chakra connects us to the Akashic records, and allows us to access the entire existence records (past and future) of the Soul, including complete knowledge of our past lives, Soul contracts, and karma. Its activation influences the entire energetic field, and is the doorway to "mind over matter," and connecting to the supernatural.

CHAKRA #11: "The Divine Chakra," positioned above the 10th Chakra, within the extended aura field. Its function is binary:

(a) It filters Christ consciousness to effectuate the atonement, and harness its power to heal. The Divine Chakra "scans" the deepest

HOMO LUCIS
THE 9-CHAKRA HUMAN IN 5TH DIMENSION

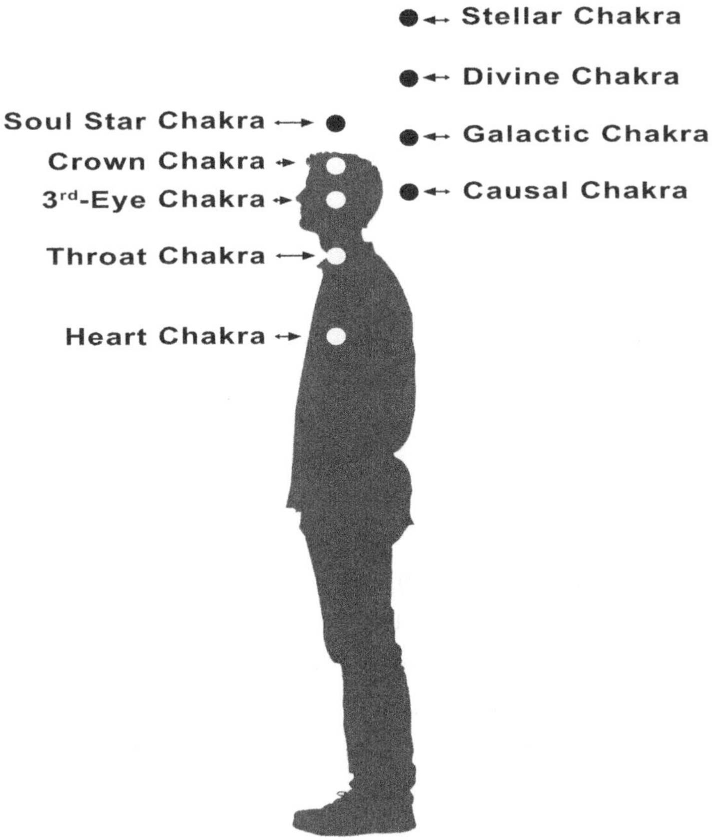

layers of the Soul's knowledge to accomplish this, and
(b) it facilitates the ability to experience universal unity, and connection to the human experience, while serving as a portal to higher awareness (accessed through the Stellar Chakra [see next]).

<u>Chakra #12</u>: "The Stellar Chakra," located at the extremity point of the outer-body system. As the name states, it accesses energies

beyond the limits of our Galaxy. It provides the ultimate doorway to cosmic consciousness, and the Divine. When fully activated, it is associated with powerful abilities like instantaneous healing, telekinesis, astral projection (out-of-body experiences), and even reversing death (in other parties)(!).

The final chakra configuration embodied by the 5th-dimensional body is thus donned by the 4th, 5th, 6th, 7th, 8th, 9th,10th,11th, and 12th chakras—for a total of nine chakras. Nine being the archetype of absolute completion, it fittingly reflects the final chakra framework that will accompany this New Human, ***Homo Lucis***, until their final full integration with Spirit, happening at the initiation into 5th Density.

12. Elimination of Faith: Faith, in the 3rd-dimensional context, represents belief in what cannot be seen. In the 5th Dimension, faith disappears as a functional necessity—not because it is invalid, but because it has been fulfilled. It is replaced by direct experience and *trust*.

We have arrived at the state that faith once pointed toward. We now exist in direct communion with the Divine, and trust what we perceive. No belief is required where direct knowing is present.

13. Healing and Life Force: As our atonement is fulfilled by being a direct extension of the Christ consciousness of the Infinite Creator, we can now heal ourselves and others—as well as animals—just like Yeshua did. This implies that diseases and illnesses will be rejected, since the power of the Light that we now radiate within is an insurmountable barrier, sufficiently powerful to eradicate them. The ability to manifest in this dimension also allows us to influence biology, substantially accelerating healing, restoring cellular structures, and stabilizing internal ecosystems. The intent in healing is always the re-patterning of the life field.

In addition to, and as the direct consequence of radiant health, our longevity is automatically expanded. As already touched upon, the physical body is now much less dense because it is largely composed of photonic, or plasma-like energy. Lifespans ranging between 120 and 230 years are now the norm! We will even witness, in our lifetime, a large swath of the population that will have lifespans well into the 120-year range. Many, who previously were on target for an 80 to 90-year life span, will be facing an extended life of up to 120 years and sometimes above. The new and altered body functions as a vehicle for consciousness rather than a survival mechanism.

These pages will only tempt us with a mere glimpse of the 5th Dimension's vast, limitless reservoir of potential. If we were to paint here the complete grid of what is poised to unfold across this earthly sphere, perhaps our minds would question our very composure, and grasp of reality. The epoch into which we now step can only be honored as "The Golden Age of Human Awakening." It transcends any mere rebirth or Renaissance, for its elevation is a place we have never yet known.

The ancient Mayas, in their profound wisdom, foresaw with clear precision that the world, as their consciousness perceived it, would reach its conclusion in the year 2012. Their sacred spiritual reckoning reveals that from that pivotal moment onward, existence would be known and lived in ways that simply cannot, and could not, be framed within the language of the 3rd Dimension.

The vibration of ecstasy for all of humankind is now resonating at its absolute zenith. The liberation of the Spirit is dawning, an ascent of consciousness is underway, the illusion of separation from the Divine Source is dissolving, and a new being emerges: *Homo Lucis*, the Man of Light. Allow not the profound significance of this literally mind-expanding planetary transformation to pass unnoticed! Embark upon the tantalizing journey with us, by gently beginning the deep, soulful process of transmuting your own life.

CHAPTER HIGHLIGHTS:

- The 5th Dimension is where the **Higher-Self descends and merges with the Soul**, creating a unified consciousness that functions as a direct co-creator with universal intelligence.
- It is always accompanied by the awakening of **Kundalini**, a latent organizing spiritual principle that rises through the spine, culminating in the **opening of the 3rd-Eye.**
- **The cycle of karma ends here**. Ego-driven behavior no longer operates; actions arise from love, unity, and selfless intent rather than fear or personal gain.
- Consciousness shifts into **unity awareness, dissolving the sense of separation** between self and others, and fosters a deep identification with all life, and the larger universal network of Souls.
- **The heart becomes the dominant organizing center of life**; fear and manipulation disappear, relationships are guided by compassion and authenticity.
- The 5th Dimension introduces **multi-dimensional awareness,** and expanded creative capacities: enhanced manifestation, telepathic communication, and deeper interaction with higher spiritual intelligences.
- A **nine-chakra configuration** replaces the lower survival-based centers with higher energetic gateways that support expanded consciousness, and cosmic intelligence connection.
- In this state, **faith is replaced by direct trust**, and the individual radiates healing life force, extended vitality, and profound harmony with the Divine.

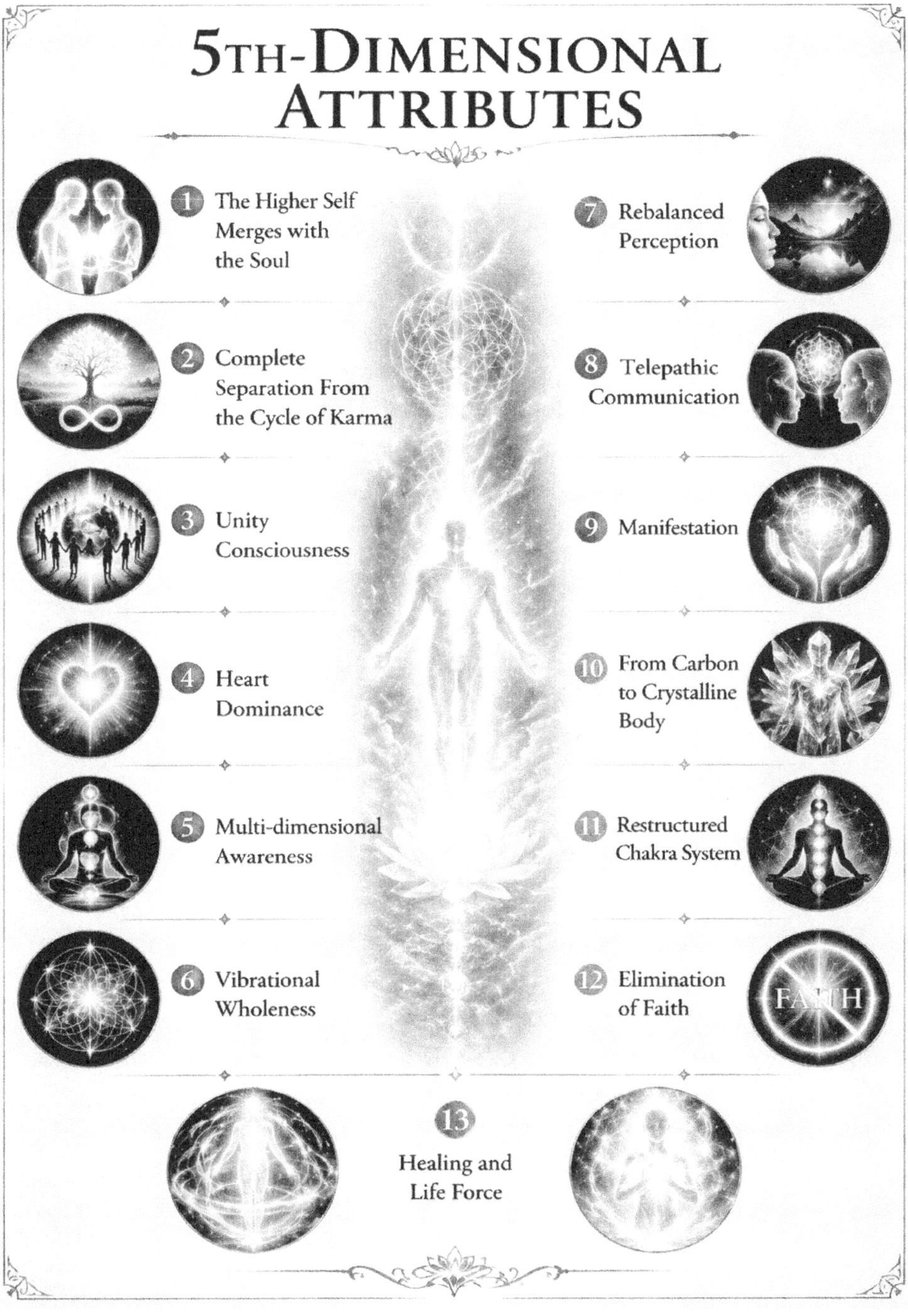
5TH-DIMENSIONAL ATTRIBUTES
1 The Higher Self Merges with the Soul
2 Complete Separation From the Cycle of Karma
3 Unity Consciousness
4 Heart Dominance
5 Multi-dimensional Awareness
6 Vibrational Wholeness
7 Rebalanced Perception
8 Telepathic Communication
9 Manifestation
10 From Carbon to Crystalline Body
11 Restructured Chakra System
12 Elimination of Faith
FAITH
13 Healing and Life Force

THE BUILDING BLOCKS

THIS SECTION ESTABLISHES THE FOUNDATIONAL INSIGHTS THAT SUPPORT OUR JOURNEY.
TOGETHER, THESE CORE ELEMENTS OFFER A COMPREHENSIVE, BIRD'S-EYE VIEW OF THE ASCENSION PROCESS, AND ITS NATURAL COMPANION, LIGHTSTREAMING

CHAPTER NINE

KARMA & CHAKRAS

KARMA: THE CONSEQUENCE

Simply explained, the human body has, at Creation, been configured with seven elemental structures: The subtle mechanics of the transition called Ascension, have often been obscured by terrestrial belief systems. These Western paradigms have meticulously avoided revealing the profound process, its inherent necessity, and its overarching cosmic design. Were the very nature of this journey understood, one might have embarked upon the arduous, yet inevitable, path of self-realization, a pilgrimage deliberately eliminated from common knowledge. Also, we were not graced with a written celestial guide at the Soul's birth—a God-given, instruction manual to accompany all subsequent sojourns. This absent compendium might simply have been

THE ELEMENTAL COMPONENTS OF THE HUMAN BODY.

titled: "How to Live in the Fundamental Harmony of the Human Universe."

Various ancient traditions have, in circuitous fashion, hinted at this universal secret, yet often shrouded their insights in a veil of guilt, shame, and punitive fear. The Ten Commandments serve as a potent example, delineating proscriptions—"You shall not do this, and you shall not do that." The implication being that deviation from these strictures invites the fierce judgment of a fearful, distant being, unleashing chaos, and literal mental turmoil.

THE THREE PRINCIPLES THAT ELUDE KARMA

The primal logos, or blueprint, that shaped our Solar System, was woven from three foundational components, that manifested sequentially: *Free Will, Love*, and *Light*—the Trinity of Creation. Of these, Free Will is paramount, and was first brought forth. We are permitted to engage in any experience we desire, yet participation is never compulsory. This is, perhaps, the fairest and most equitable system conceivable in all existence.

Simultaneously, the Infinite Creator subtly unfolds the singular, universal law of this life-experience: *Love*. The spirit-sourced signature of this adventure is sustained by three godly principles:

**1. We are invited to only express those FEELINGS and EMOTIONS that resonate with Love—
[though our free will permit otherwise].**

**2. We are encouraged to only utter those WORDS that radiate Love—
[though our free will permit otherwise].**

**3. We are meant to commit only those DEEDS catalyzed by Love—
[though our free will permit otherwise].**

The Infinite Creator adds: like any noble endeavor, there are shadows and obstructions. Our inviolable mission is to navigate these avoidances. When we succeed, the game is honorably won. The takeaway is that *that* is the simple, yet profound, essence of our earthly experience.

Being subject to karma is, ultimately, a choice we make.

The Infinite Creator offers a fatherly caution: to transgress any of these three sacred principles incurs a mark, a spiritual ledger entry that remains until a sufficient accumulation of grace, or bonus points, dissolve it. This mark is not a Divine chastisement, but rather a sober reflection that an action diverged from the underlying rules of existence. It is this spiritual marker that is known to us as *karma*.

Karma itself is a term of pure neutrality. Sanskrit suggests a translation to "deed" or "action." It holds no inherent distinction between good or unfortunate acts. Thus, we must bring our awareness to it, appending "benevolent" or "challenging," as appropriate, to provide clarity. It is imprecise to state that someone is merely "developing karma;" it is more meaningful to observe that they generated "good[1]" or "bad" karma through their manifest actions.

THE STORAGE OF KARMA

A mostly unknown realization, is that the Law of Karma is *temporary*—it is only active within 3rd Density. The higher, ethereal realms do not recognize this dynamic. Consequently, every single action we have been the source of, emotion we have felt, and word we have spoken has been neatly recorded, and labeled as karma over the past 75,000 years (the beginning of 3rd Density). Even the scents that our physical forms have experienced have been imprinted throughout that expansive timeline!

During our life, difficult karma is stored within the respective chakra

[1] Good karma, "punya" (in Sanskrit), refers to the positive merit or "spiritual credit" earned through ethical actions, kindness, and selflessness.

center that rules the sphere of that trespass. Its locus is a function of the energetic nature of the deed. A dishonest word would afflict the Throat Chakra, where the corresponding karma is anchored. Sensuality devoid of heartfelt love would engage the Sacral Chakra, lodging the challenging karma there. Indifference or callousness towards a fellow being would cause a shadow upon the Heart Chakra, and so on.

Upon our physical death, the seven chakras upload the bad karma to the Soul, where it is added to any previous life karma accumulation. Upon reincarnation, the new chakra network starts afresh, downloads any past karma from the Soul, and is ready to store eventual new karma, and repeat the cycle of chakra-to-Soul transfer at the end of that life.

Regardless of its accumulation, any residual karma not resolved in one lifetime is dutifully carried over to the next. It continues to gather, life after life, until its weight is lifted. Benevolent karma counterbalances and neutralizes the difficult, resulting in a state of spiritual equilibrium. If we generate challenging karma through an act like the taking of a life, that profound burden must be harmonized with the Soul that was departed—in a subsequent incarnation. To discern which of these vital energy wheels are weighed down by dense, challenging karma, and which remain clear, an *astrological chakra reading* can serve as a valuable compass. An individual star chart can, with great accuracy, map the current spiritual/karma status of these centers.

REMOVING KARMA

What then, are the pathways for the dissolution of this negative karma?

One might observe that we may have traversed thousands of incarnations, patiently engaged in the accumulation of negative karma. Why, then, the sudden urgency to remove it now? The accelerated pace is due to a singular, unprecedented moment in human history: mankind stands at the doorstep of crossing into the 5th Dimension. This Great Shift is *contingent upon the clarity of our most essential chakras,* a transition that cannot and will not proceed otherwise. Furthermore, the Ascension readiness status of one's chakras is not commonly known to the average person. How are we to gain this essential knowledge? We are at the juncture where LightStreaming begins its purpose, a method the reader will come to know in intimate detail within these pages. The very essence of this writing is to acquaint us with genuine means to sufficiently, and verifiably purify our energy centers, to fully prepare them for our Ascension.

Karma is stored in the Heart Chakra while alive; in the Soul after death.

An incarnation is a Creation-given opportunity to rectify a faulty navigation in a previous life—a karmic imbalance—or, to reinforce what was skillfully accomplished. We are gifted a chance to play a game; we may lose it, and then play again with the hope of securing a win. The intricacy lies in this: if we accrue a negative score upon losing, that deficit is carried forward into the new game we commence. The same holds true for positive scores, which are also brought forward, and possess the power to neutralize the negative. This is the living truth of karma, the profound timeless truth: "You shall reap as you sow[2]."

Should the errors from an earlier life cycle be of sufficient severity, they may manifest as deep spiritual impairments, paralysis, illness, and terminal physical or mental suffering. As draconian as it sounds, it is simply the consequence of doing what we should not. The consequential connection between wellness or illness and conscious choice is remarkable. There exists no uncertainty about this. Recall the narrative of Yeshua healing the crippled man at the pool at Bethesda. After his miraculous healing, Yeshua masterly instructed him: "Rise, gather your mat, and sin no more." This is a direct inference that the man's physical condition was born of unwise choices in his current and/or a prior life. [Because he became impaired as a child, before he could have accumulated significant negative karma in his current incarnation, the cause stems from karmic

---

[2] In Yeshua's own words, this is a much misunderstood (misquoted) saying. The true, intended saying was: "You shall manifest as you think."

imprints carried over from a previous life (according to the Master himself).

There are but three avenues available to dissolve negative karma:

> **(1) To be the recipient of a "Divine clemency"** of grace from the Infinite Creator—a spiritual amnesty, a "get-out-of-jail card"—which is exceedingly rare, and should not be relied upon or expected; or,
>
> **(2) To cause enough harmonic equalization,** i.e. a sufficient measure of positive actions that perfectly counterbalance the negative ones.
>
> **(3) To effect LightStreaming,** which instantly removes specific karma.

Redemption and chakra purification are also deeply influenced by sincere *repentance*, provided it springs from the core of the heart. Atonement, as clarified in this volume, is the hallowed agency that is catalyzed by repentance, because it provides unmediated exposure to the Light; remember that during the LightStreaming PLR process, the ego is placidly set aside, and rendered powerless, and *karma can be removed.*

Returning to the earthly life-cycle of Yeshua, we find a potent instance of karmic release through what we playfully just termed "executive decision:" The Master gathered his disciples in a room, and performed the very baptism by fire foretold by John the Baptist. The chamber was illuminated, and powerful electrical currents, resembling spiritual flames, swirled above the heads of his apostles—a moment of true spiritual magic!

This transpired near the close of Yeshua's life, during Pentecost, shortly before his final departure from Earth. He was, by then, a powerful avatar, despite only having had three short years of experience within the 6th Dimension (!), into which he was initiated during his own baptism. In a recent LightStreaming Channeling, we posed him the question as to the meaning, and consequence of this event. Why did he do it? His response was: "I needed to remove some karma in my disciples, so they could move

THE MECHANICS OF KARMA & RESOLUTION

KARMA IS NOT PUNISHMENT.
IT IS THE CONSEQUENCE OF THE LAW OF CAUSE AND EFFECT.

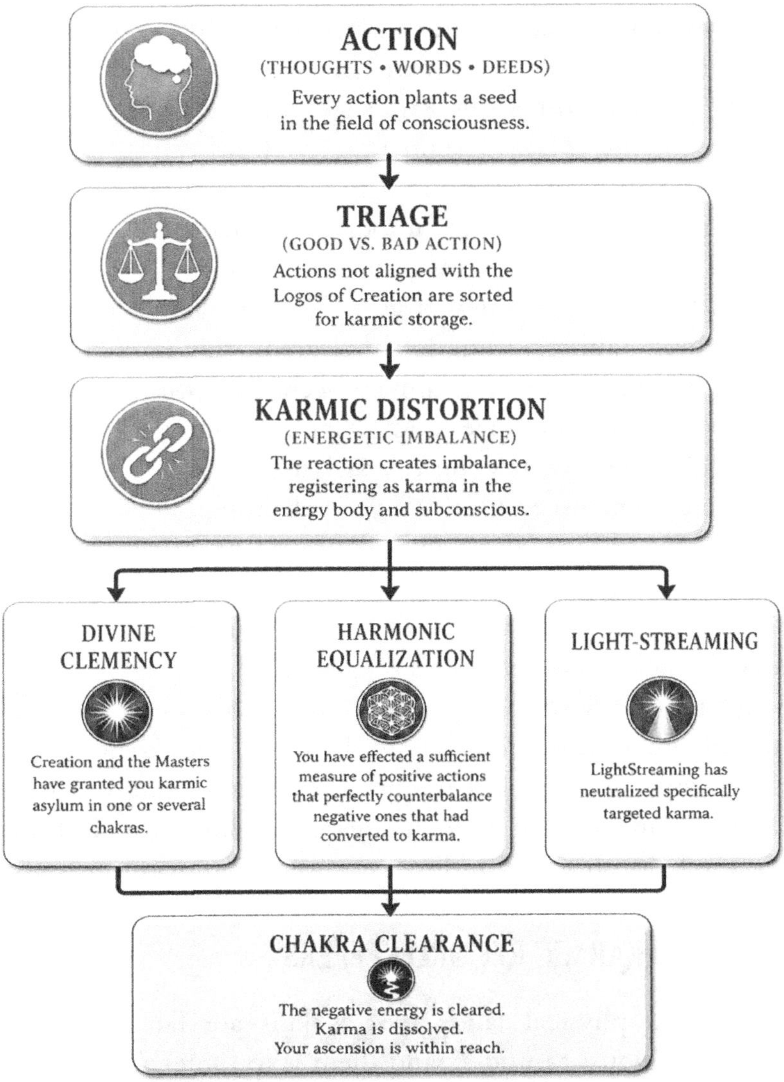

forward into the 5th dimension."

From that answer, we may intuit the doubt that must have clouded the disciples *prior* to that time, despite their teacher's assurances that upon his ultimate passing they would go forth to heal, and perform miracles, just as he had. Following the awe-inspiring, world premiere baptism by fire—an "executive decision" agreed upon by Yeshua and the Father—his disciples underwent a miraculous spiritual conversion, and were suddenly able to heal with the same Divine capacity that Yeshua had before. Healing is a magnificent gift of the 5th Dimension. (As already noted, this initiation into the 5th Dimension is the same ethereal awakening referred to as "Salvation" in the New Testament, "Moksha" in Hinduism, and "Nirvana" in Buddhism.)

All notable physical infirmities at birth are the result of karma carried over from a previous life cycle.

Due to its constituent importance, let us summarize: no Soul can ascend into the 5th Dimension/4th Density unless their Heart Chakra karma has been (almost) completely cleared. This is because the 5th Dimension is a realm consecrated to the heart, and unconditional love, and Creation requires that we begin anew with a pure vessel in this new density. There are no exceptions! We sincerely hope you can absorb the gravity, and spiritual beauty of this cosmic arrangement. This is the reason all Ascended Masters will concur, that the 3rd Density is the most challenging of all the densities (1-7) we traverse!

A vast multitude of souls presently incarnated are utilizing this final incarnation before the Great Shift to re-balance long-standing karmic debts with carefully chosen individuals. This spiritual imperative is one of the hidden energies behind the unprecedented number of relationship dissolutions we witness in the current age.

THE CHAKRAS: KARMIC RECORD KEEPERS

In the metaphysical landscape, chakras are far more than mere spiritual abstractions; to understand them is to understand the body as a delicate radio, and the chakras as the tuning dials that determine which frequencies of reality we are capable of receiving. Think of the body as a radio, designed to receive and transmit. The chakras are its tuning dials. These light vortices have three defined functions:

1. They convert subtle, high-frequency energy into a form the body can use. What enters as refined force is stepped down into currents that sustain the nervous system, and regulate the endocrine glands. Without this translation, the body could not hold the charge of consciousness.

2. Each center also *stores* karma patterns. Within them lie the blueprints for lived experience: survival, feeling, will, love, expression, insight, and spiritual awareness. They shape how life is perceived, and how it moves through you.

3. Every chakra *reflects* your state of consciousness. When one is blocked, it signals resistance. A closed heart, for example, often reveals a refusal to forgive. The obstruction is not (normally) mechanical; it is metaphysical. Where there is contraction in awareness, there is constriction in energy.

In the journey of Ascension, these centers serve as the primary engine of transformation. *The chakras are the literal check-points the Soul has to "clear" to shift from material consciousness (3rd Dimension) to a multidimensional awareness (5th Dimension).*

This rigorous and thorough review by the Soul is a three-fold quality control that **starts with *purification*** in the lower three chakras, releasing the calcified imprints of survival and ego—until the consciousness can finally rise into the heart. This lower group relates to our relationship with the Earth, and the self.

The second internal chakra process is that of *integration*: it is here that the heart bridge to higher dimensions is crossed. The heart occupies a dominant position as it acts as the tollbridge to these higher dimensions. A clear heart chakra is a prerequisite to Ascension. The heart is the zero-point field where the lower three chakras meet the upper body chakras.

Finally, each chakra implements the *activation* phase. As the upper chakras (Throat, 3rd-Eye, Crown) open, they allow "Light Codes" to flow into the DNA, structurally changing the carbon-based body into a more crystalline-based "Light Body." This upper trinity relates to our relationship with the Divine and the Cosmos.

Consider this: if the Source of all existence is a brilliant sun, and your physical form is a house, the chakras are the windows through which that light must pass. Ascension is not an escape from the house, nor a journey to a distant shore. Rather, it is the meticulous, constant work of cleaning the glass until every pane is perfectly transparent. When the windows are clear, the interior is so flooded with radiance that the distinction between the sun and the home dissolves, and the entire structure becomes a vessel for the Infinite.

Despite the fantastic organization of this column of Light, which in a metaphysical context can easily appear marvelous, there is a transparent world of 3rd-dimensional "reality" impacting the chakras: our daily behavior. Its mapping, as it related to the chakras, has been documented over 3,000 years, in four main sources:

Classical Tantric & Hatha Yoga Texts (800 CE – 1700 CE). The most influential text of these, on the seven-chakra system, is the Ṣaṭ-Cakra-Nirūpaṇa (1577 CE). It describes the "knots" (granthis) that block energy due to attachment and ego.

Modern Energy Medicine & "Western" Chakra Psychology. The specific mapping of "negative behaviors" to "karmic blockages" (e.g., gossip =Throat Chakra) was heavily popularized in the 20th century by authors who blended Indian tradition with Western psychology. Of these, the work of Caroline Myss (Anatomy of the Spirit) stands out. She famously linked the chakras to the Christian sacraments, and the Kabbalah, showing how specific emotional patterns, and "sins" cause physical illness.

Astrology. Karma is tracked through planetary placements, as the planets have placed coded information into our bodies that makes them a sort of "Karmic Rosetta stone."

Teachings from Masters and Light Entities. Direct instructions on which chakras store a corresponding behavior. This is an invaluable source since it comes word-for-word, without translations from older style languages.

Even though the topic is recurring throughout this guide, we share a very *synthesized* synopsis of the chakras (with their Sanskrit equivalent), with their corresponding issues, as drawn from the above sources:

No. 1. Root Chakra (Muladhara)

Theme: Survival, Safety, and Grounding.
Material Hoarding: Clinging to material wealth or food out of a scarcity mindset, effectively blocking the natural flow of abundance.
Physical Aggression: Violating the physical boundaries or bodily safety of others, destabilizing our own sense of security.
Predatory Selfishness: Taking what others need to survive to ensure our own "excess," creating a karmic debt of instability.

No. 2. Sacral Chakra (Svadhisthana)

Theme: Emotional Fluidity and Shared Pleasure.
Relational Manipulation: Treating others as tools for your own sensory or emotional gratification rather than as human beings.
Betrayal of Intimacy: Breaking the implied "contracts" of trust in romantic or creative partnerships.
Escapist Indulgence: Using substances or sex to numb reality, which stagnates the healthy flow of creative energy.

No. 3. Solar Plexus Chakra (Manipura)

Theme: Personal Power and Integrity. The ego's home court.

Authoritarianism: Using your will to crush the autonomy of others, or to force compliance. Dictatorial behavior.

Ego-Inflation: Crafting a false persona or lying about your status to feel superior, which creates a "hollow" power base.

Persistent Contempt: Systematically devaluing others to mask your own internal feelings of inadequacy.

No. 4. Heart Chakra (Anahata)

Theme: Compassion and Connection.

Emotional Coldness: Choosing to remain indifferent to the suffering of others, which "calcifies" the energetic heart.

Chronic Bitterness: Refusing to release past hurts, keeping the energy of trauma trapped in a perpetual loop.

Guilt-Tripping: Using your own pain as a weapon to control or "handcuff" the emotions of those you love.

No. 5. Throat Chakra (Vishuddha)

Theme: Authentic Expression and Truth.

Character Assassination: Using speech to intentionally damage another person's reputation or social standing.

Deceptive Living: Speaking half-truths, or outright lies to dodge the consequences of your actions.

Voice Suppression: Actively silencing others or gate-keeping the truth to maintain a false narrative.

No. 6. 3rd-Eye Chakra (Ajna)

Theme: Wisdom and Perception.

Psychological Gaslighting: Deliberately warping someone else's reality to make them doubt their own perceptions.

Intellectual Arrogance: Using your knowledge or "sharpness" to belittle others or to orchestrate complex schemes of fraud.
Rigid Dogmatism: Closing your mind to any new information that challenges your ego, leading to mental stagnation.

No. 7. Crown Chakra (Sahasrara)

Theme: Unity and Transcendence.
Spiritual Superiority: Using your "awakening" or religious practice as a way to look down on others (spiritual narcissism). The "I am spiritually more special" attitude.
Blasphemous Action: Treating life or the environment as "disposable," ignoring the sacred thread that connects all things, thus trivializing Creation.
Living Without Consequences: Living as if your Soul is separate from the collective, leading to reckless and destructive nihilism.
Psychic Impersonation: Presenting yourself with superior psychic skills, that actually are fictitious.

THE 7-CHAKRA HUMAN IN 3RD DIMENSION

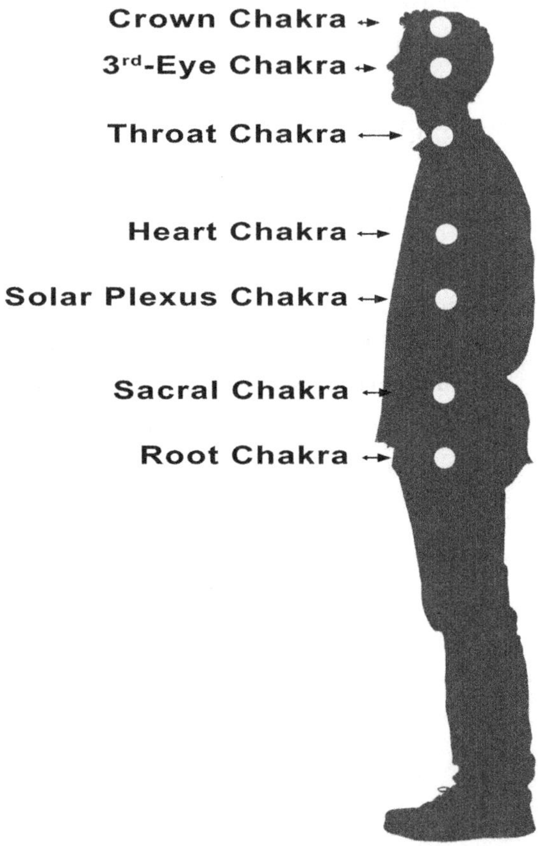

CHAPTER HIGHLIGHTS:

- **Karma is the natural consequence of actions, emotions, and words** that diverge from the fundamental principle of love, which is the original governing law of human experience.
- Every human "unloving" action generates karma that is energetically stored within the chakra system during life, then **transferred to the Soul at death**, and carried into future incarnations until dealt with.
- **Karma operates only within 3rd Density**, meaning that unresolved karmic imbalances must be harmonized before a Soul can successfully transition into higher states of consciousness.
- The chakra system functions as the energetic **record-keeper** of karma, with each center storing imprints associated with specific behaviors—such as dishonesty affecting the Throat Chakra, or emotional coldness affecting the Heart Chakra.
- **Clearing karma is essential for Ascension**, and can occur through acts that counterbalance past actions or, in rare cases, through divine grace that removes karmic burdens.
- The **Heart Chakra plays a decisive role**, since the transition into the love-centered 5th Dimension requires that karmic distortions in the heart be almost entirely purified.
- The chakras act as transformational gateways, **converting higher spiritual energies**, storing karmic patterns, and gradually opening as consciousness evolves toward multidimensional awareness.

CHAPTER TEN

OUR FAMILY: THE GROUP OF FOUR

BEINGS WHO HAVE CROSSED OVER

It is possible to connect with nearly any Soul that has crossed the veil. It is frequently a family member whose essence, having shed the physical body, and with whom we shared deep bonds on this earthly plane, resides now upon the other side, immersed in the vibrant glow of the Light. While in their last incarnation, that individual may not have accumulated the spiritual merit required for final Ascension, this Soul is typically resting in a phase of preparation for their subsequent journey back into form. They have, in all likelihood, traversed many cycles of existence with you, appearing in varied role plays—perhaps as a brother or companion in one life, as a mother or father in another, sometimes even as an employer, and so forth. This Soul knows yours intimately, for it is frequently a spark from your own originating soul group.

In a recent LightStreaming, a man named Robert found himself touched by the presence of John, his father, who had already passed.

Robert had not been seeking this contact; John simply flowed through, unbidden, as if merely to tender a soft salutation. John had carried a burden of unkindness in his earthly relationship with Robert.

Now, bathed only in Love on the Other Side, he offered a deep apology for his neglect, and the shortcomings he had exhibited in not caring for his son during his life. John conveyed that he was preparing for a new earthly incarnation. He hinted that he would return as Robert's son. Through this destined exchange, he would finally learn the nature of a bond that is both loving and righteous between father and child. Robert, naturally, awaits the beginnings of his family with an open, eager heart.

Many among us have family members who poured blessings into their kindred, their surroundings, and the world itself. They were a flowing wellspring of intrinsic goodness, and pure affection while here; it is therefore impossible for their nature to be anything less on the Other Side. Does it not hold a beautiful sense, then, to seek and receive communication with them?

Souls who have transitioned carry the poise of verified experience. Having recently walked among us in this lifetime, they can frequently offer an illuminating perception on what shadows might be holding us back. Beings from the other side are always motivated by an unconditional, loving desire to assist. At times, a simple communication with a cherished, crossed-over Soul can activate healing of the deep ache of a grieving heart. We often struggle to truly release the sorrow felt upon the absence of a beloved soulmate. Connecting through the Light can offer profound solace, and alleviate this sorrow.

ASCENDED MASTERS

These illumined beings, often simply known as "the Masters," are spiritual presences who hold the invaluable wisdom gleaned from traversing countless cycles of earthly experience. Through their deep commitment to the service of the Light, they have achieved a profound, transformative shift while in the earthly sphere, leaving a legacy of love upon the world. They are understood to have achieved final Ascension, having gracefully completed the necessary curriculum of their terrestrial journeys. They are not bound to return to this dimension, yet they may, by their own choice, descend again to further the Light's purpose[1].

There are literally thousands of these awakened Guides, whose origins span a vast and rich diversity of human history. Some emerge from the deep, legendary past, predating the Medieval Era, their names echoing with ancient resonance. Others are more recent, dedicating their focus to areas where their specialized compassion is most required[2].

The elevated Masters possess a timeless access to the primary wellspring of universal knowledge, which is the eternal capsule of NOW. In this sacred nexus, where time flows in quantum modus, they are able to offer us multifaceted guidance across various dimensions of being. These Masters hold the capacity for healing, yet often they channel this profound energy under the wise tutelage of the Archangels.

Ascended Masters, unlike Angels, have "boots-on-the-ground" experience.

To offer a small glimpse into the gallery of these inspiring Souls, the assembly includes such names as Moses, Apollo, Vesta, Yogananda, Yeshua, St. Francis, Mother Mary, John the Baptist, Shiva, Solomon, Krishna, Lakshmi, Quan Yin, Babaji, Peter, El Morya, Melchizedek, Akhenaton, Anubis, Isis, and a multitude of others. This is offered merely to suggest the breadth and diversity of the ascended Souls we contemplate.

Without an intuitive grasp of the Masters' function, the larger, complete understanding of their pivotal role and hierarchical purpose within the unseen, spiritual order would remain elusive. They constitute a vital, supportive pillar within the Divine's legion of compassionate helpers who assist life upon the Earth plane.

These Masters are most powerfully present within the LightStreaming

1 A historical example is that of the Ascended Master, the Prophet Elijah, who according to Yeshua, reincarnated as John the Baptist.

2 Such as Bruno Gröning, the Saxon post-WWII master healer, who was an incarnation of Moshe.

Past Life Regression, sometimes accompanied by the presence of an Archangel. When engaging with Past Life Regression and the deep process of Channeling, the most suitable Master is always dispatched to attend to the individual's specific, personal needs. This arrangement is akin to a compassionate celestial administration, where case managers are assigned to resolve a given human dilemma. They stand, in a sense, as some of the most elevated stewards within the entire spiritual framework. As part of their own chosen, continuous unfolding, they also receive consistent instruction from higher, more senior Masters and Godhead to ever refine their capacity to aid us.

Given their immeasurably profound significance, the Masters are integrated into a collective known as the Galactic Federation. This Federation is ever-evolving, welcoming new members into its fold as soon as they achieve the necessary spiritual qualification. The orchestration of this vast entity rests under the highest, most senior guidance of the Light itself. At this time, it is guided by a specially chosen Council of Light.

Shiva is the Hindu spiritual embodiment of the very same Christ power. Devotees who adhere to the Hindu tradition should reflect deeply upon this, as their spiritual connection to the Holy Spirit flows as directly and purely through Shiva as it does for others through the Christ consciousness energy. Yeshua occupies a uniquely revered and singular station, and always will. In his final incarnation, he was heralded by the title of Messiah, establishing him as a leading, guiding beacon within the Light. Yeshua, the ascended Master, is understood to be the Light's tangible and transcendent embodiment of the Holy Spirit[3].

Ascended Masters possess powerful, empathetic experience derived from their time on Earth, while also being deeply and fully conversant in the ethereal, spiritual realms. The Masters hold a position of invaluable grace as helpers in the Ascension process. They are, at their core, team players, possessing a keen insight of the human psyche—for they have walked this path and know full well the challenges that our current 3rd Dimension can unfold. Yet, they receive precious assistance from two

3 The Holy Spirit being a 6th Density spirit nexus.

other key members of our spiritual family; let us briefly consider the remainder of "The Group of Four."

ANGELS

The word Aggelos (αγγελος in Greek) was first found in a 2 BC manuscript, meaning "envoys." The verb form (αγγελλώ) means "to proclaim." Thus, the word refers to a messenger who is an envoy carrying a message.

The biggest difference between Ascended Masters and Angels is that Angels have never existed in the flesh world, and never will. They are exclusively spirit entities, who they will never deviate from God's plan. They have sworn eternal allegiance to the Father, and are 100% faithful in their task of executing their missions.

The original Hebrew word which was used in the scriptures prior to its translation into Greek (The Pentateuch) is "malak."

Malak (מלאך): Messenger, representative, courtier, angel. "Messenger" is an adequate term for the range of tasks carried out by Angels in the Testaments. These were:

1) to carry a message,
2) to perform some other specific commission, and
3) to officially represent the one sending them.

Angelic spirit beings fulfill an essential cosmic function within the vibrational framework, serving as both sentinels of profound stewardship, and emissaries of the highest Light. Within a terrestrial corporate paradigm, their role might be likened to that of highly elevated, dedicated coordinators. Their existence is one of constant, radiant action, for they ceaselessly transmit and receive data regarding a mortal being's evolutionary trajectory.

Some of these radiant overseers are tethered to our current incarnational cycle, a steadfast presence throughout this span of material experience. Others commit for the entirety of our Soul's journey, accompanying us from the very genesis of our individual consciousness.

Still other celestial architects specialize in dedicated domains, offering focused guidance in fields such as the creative arts, the professional world, our emotional landscape, family lineage, health, the energetics of abundance, or the intricacies of cosmic justice.

These heavenly presences orchestrate much of their work within the unseen currents of the metaphysical substratum, and one rarely observes their direct, energetic manifestation during a LightStreaming session. Their specific field of influence is intensely individual-centered, aligning with a unique spiritual signature. Despite this often-subtle deployment, one must never make the error of underestimating the amplitude of their power. Their insightful assessment of an existential scenario is rarely, if ever, countermanded by the governing bodies within the universal system. They are recognized for their integrity of service, as they are a direct creation *of* the Infinite Creator, *for* the Infinite Creator.

Angels hold no direct experiential data from the realm of 3rd-dimensional Earth, yet they are peerless experts in the spiritual dimension—the fabric of primal causation.

ARCHANGELS

The Archangels are the grand engineers, immense emanations of primal force within the ethereal expanse of consciousness. They hold expansive capacity within their unique domains, acting as direct conduits for the unfolding will of Source. The Archangels do not have Earth life experience, except for Sandalphon and Metatron[4]. These supreme Beings act under the direct command of the Father.

As "Architects of Light," they represent some of the most highly refined spiritual intelligences operating within Creation. They function as

4 Sandalphon and Metatron are not Archangels per se. They are in a unique category, being Spirit entities who have incarnated in human flesh, for then to return. They are classified as Cherubs and have been given extraordinary powers. In addition, they are special protectors of the creation of Israel and the Christ energy's overriding role in it, the Abrahamic Covenant and Mosaic Law. They served as guardians of the Garden of Eden, with "fiery swords."

foundational pillars, integral to the sacred geometric and energetic organization of our planetary matrix, possessing unprecedented access to resource streams from the Zero-Point Field. In the human frame of reference, they embody a level of cosmic seniority, akin to the principal stewards in a vast, transcendent hierarchy.

Judaism Recognizes 4 Archangels, Christianism 3, and Islam 4.

Archangels[5] differ from angels chiefly by rank, authority, and breadth of responsibility. Angels operate on the front lines, carrying out specific tasks, while Archangels function more like chief executives or regional directors, overseeing vast domains, and coordinating the work of others within the spiritual order.

To fully chart the depth of their metaphysical expertise would transcend the purpose of this book, but two words could define their beings: energy and alignment. Yet, I strongly encourage a meditative inquiry into the symbiotic nexus between each Archangel and the vibrational centers—the chakras—of the human energy body. They are first-order energetic equilibrators, constantly recalibrating the flow of Prana[6]. Their capacities for healing and systemic restoration often reside in a spectrum of reality that is presently beyond the scope of human phenomenological understanding. The ancient apocrypha, The Book of Enoch, Chapter 20, codifies the primary Archangels as:

> *Uriel, one of the holy messengers, who presides over clamor and terror.*
> *Raphael, one of the holy angels, who presides over the spirits of men.*
> *Raguel, one of the holy angels, who inflicts punishment on the world and the luminaries.*

---

[5] Judaism recognizes Michael and Gabriel; Christianism recognizes Michael, Islam recognizes Gabriel (who revealed the Qur'an, prior to its altered current version), Michael, Israfeel (who blows the horn on Judgment Day), and Azrael (the Angel of Death).

[6] Prana (from Sanskrit), is the vital life force or "primordial breath" that permeates all of reality, including both living beings and inanimate objects.

Michael, one of the holy angels, who, presiding over human virtue, commands the nations.
Sarakiel, one of the holy angels, who presides over the spirits of the children of men that transgress.
Gabriel, one of the holy angels, who presides over Ikisat, over paradise, and over the cherubim.

Notice that all the names end in "el," the Hebrew word for God. Rapha-el translates to 'God Has Healed', Micha-el means 'Who is like God?' and so on. Enoch, father of Methuselah, was a uniquely spiritually enlightened being who dealt primarily with the list above. Other Archangels include Ariel (The Lion of God), Azrael (Whom God Helps), Chamuel (He Who Sees God), Haniel (Grace of God), Jeremiel (Joy of God), Jophiel (Beauty of God), Raziel (Secret of God), Sandalphon (Brother Together), and Metatron (Next to the Throne).

CHAPTER HIGHLIGHTS:

- We enjoy a spiritual support system composed of four categories of helpers: **departed Souls, Ascended Masters, Angels, and Archangels**—collectively forming a guiding framework that assists humanity in its evolutionary journey.
- Departed Souls—often family members or close companions from previous lives, may communicate across the veil, **offering guidance**, reconciliation, or emotional healing while preparing for future incarnations.
- Ascended Masters are beings who completed the human evolutionary cycle, and achieved Ascension; drawing on their Earth experience and spiritual insight, **they assist humanity with guidance**, healing, and spiritual instruction.
- Angels differ from Ascended Masters in that they **have never lived human lives**; they are spirit entities devoted entirely to carrying out the will of the Infinite Creator, and often act as messengers, guardians, and coordinators of spiritual assistance.
- Archangels represent higher-order spiritual intelligences with vast authority and energetic capacity, **overseeing larger domains of spiritual activity**, directing the work of angels within the cosmic hierarchy.
- Together, these four groups form an **interconnected spiritual "family"** that supports the Ascension process, guiding individuals through healing, learning, and alignment with higher consciousness.

CHAPTER ELEVEN

THE MIND'S ARCHITECTURE

One of the West's most serious blind spots is its lack of any real foundation in understanding how the mind actually functions. We understand investments, space travel, and biochemistry with impressive precision. Yet if we drew a one-mile circle around our homes and asked anyone within it to explain the purpose of the superconscious, nearly everyone would be unable to answer.

The average person has only a rudimentary grasp of how the mind works, or what its core components are. It is generally assumed to be too complex for ordinary understanding. Even Sigmund Freud never fully mastered it. His glaring limitation lay in his conviction that the layers of the psyche—the id (lower self), ego, and superego (Higher-Self)—were permanently divided, and could never be brought into true reconciliation. He further falsely stipulated that the ego was the interlocutor between the lower self (id) and the Higher-Self (superego). He failed to see that these levels can be dissolved through the atonement, as when implemented in LightStreaming. What follows is a preview—bestowed by the Light—of the foundational concepts necessary to fully grasp the nature of LightStreaming, and the architecture of the mind.

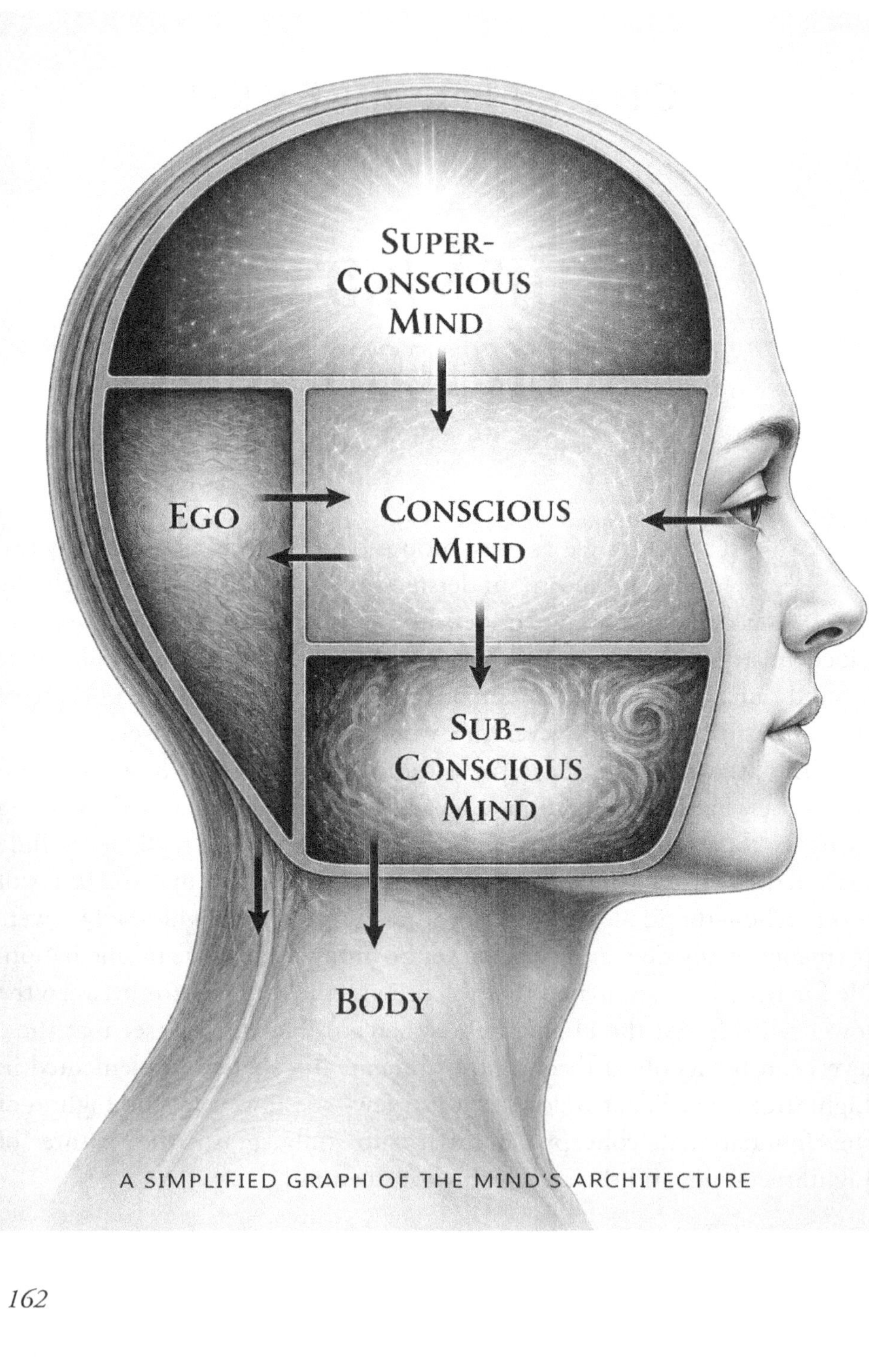

A SIMPLIFIED GRAPH OF THE MIND'S ARCHITECTURE

THE SUPERCONSCIOUS MIND

The superconscious mind is a broader stratum of awareness, a field rather than a single identity. It is the layer of mind where intuition, direct knowing, symbolic communication, and non-linear cognition arise. Imagine it positioned as a circular cloud inside the brain. It *includes* the Higher-Self, but it also extends into collective and universal intelligence. It is the wider network the Higher-Self plugs into, not "you" as an individual being.

The superconscious mind is a conduit entirely devoted to the pure, direct emanations from the Divine Source. These deep insights unfold through a profoundly intimate, personal journey. They may arrive as quiet announcements or as vital knowledge that the Spirit is deemed ready to receive for its ongoing evolution. Such a profound unveiling can be transmitted in a myriad of forms: as carefully chosen words, evocative visions, restorative currents of energy, sounds beyond language, thoughts, or capsules of concentrated wisdom. These Divine unveilings often reside beyond the reach of ordinary expression.

If one were to request a description of the opening movement of Beethoven's 5th Symphony, words alone would fail to capture its true majesty. One would be compelled to reflect: "That composition holds a singular essence that defies mere description; one must truly listen to it." A musician from the ensemble might muse: "The complete fulfillment of the work can only known through the act of *playing* it." So, too, is the nature of the revelations flowing from the Light. Arising directly from the ultimate Source, they are an overwhelmingly potent awakening, sparked by the universal Spirit. An experience of this nature is etched into the Soul's memory for eternity.

While the subconscious is the source of miracles (which are interpersonal), the superconscious is the source of *revelation*, which is a direct experience of union with God. Because the superconscious is "incapable of darkness," it became entirely inaccessible to the body after the "separation (the event of the fallen 'angels')."

Consciousness serves as a sublime, dedicated station for the Light itself. All ethereal transmissions intended for the Soul's illumination must pass through this supernal gateway first. These deep insights are conveyed in a one-way stream only—from the Divine Source to the human spirit, and never the reverse. Once received, the revelation descends for initial perception by the conscious mind, then is subtly refined, and further integrated into the subconscious realm, or perhaps encounters the ego, should the being still be striving for alignment with its innermost truth.

THE HIGHER-SELF

Every Soul enters existence with a celestial navigator: the Higher-Self. Much like the Holy Spirit, the Higher-Self is a 6th-density construct—essentially your "future" self having already mastered the challenges of the lower densities. While we perceive time as a linear progression from past to future, the Higher-Self exists in a state of simultaneity. It does not merely "remember" our past lives or "predict" our future; it holds the entire tapestry of our Soul's journey as a single, vibrant image. As a primary extension of the superconscious mind, it serves as the individualized expression of the Divine, localized within that expansive field of awareness.

For those identified as "wanderers"—Souls who may have spent eons within the high 4th and 5th Densities—the Higher-Self is uniquely equipped to manage this fluctuating, evolutionary data. It intentionally resides below the 7th Density, as that final stage represents completion: the point where we transcend the need for a separate guide, and merge back into the One. The Higher-Self acts as the ultimate "translator" between the finite mind, and the infinite Creator. It is the highest version of individual identity before identity itself dissolves into pure unity.

From this elevated vantage point, the Higher-Self maintains a "total map" of our various incarnations, past and future, clearly seeing the specific lessons we are currently navigating. It operates through a divine paradox: it guides without commanding. Because free will is the primary law of the Creator's universe, the Higher-Self must be sought; it will never infringe upon our autonomy. The Higher-Self does not use words; it uses resonance. When you feel a sudden, inexplicable "knowing" or a pull toward a specific path that defies logic, you are experiencing a frequency match with your Higher-Self.

While it refrains from dictating our path, it provides vital insights and intuitive impulses, activating only when there is a synchronous, spirit-aligned purpose. Communicating with the Higher-Self (through prayer and imaging) can yield amazing harvests!

THE CONSCIOUS MIND

The conscious mind is the home base of our experiential sphere, the singular and sovereign creative hub of our reality. We are not granted the prerogative to alter this configuration of individuality, yet a certain latitude exists to eclipse, if one so chooses, the creative mandate it carries. The sole, *pure* energy input for this conscious field is the *Stream of thought*, and we sculpt our being into vibrational form through the refraction of these thoughts. The conscious mind is the narrow beam of awareness we are actively using right now, the thoughts, perceptions, and choices we can observe and direct in the moment. It is the part of the mind that knows it is thinking.

The awareness within us stands as our prime, singular fountainhead of creation. Though we are bound to this built-in design, we possess the freedom to disregard its generative essence, should we choose such a path. The *sole* nourishment for this space is the flow of thought, and it is through the careful crafting of our thoughts that our creative spirit finds its expression.

This conscious center is our moment-to-moment nexus of guidance and sovereignty. Its operation mirrors the swift, transient nature of immediate memory, where a ceaseless activity unfolds, with countless fragments of insight exchanged each passing moment. The instant we perceive, feel, hear, scent, or simply sense existence, this awareness takes its immediate, decisive posture: determining our response to the unfolding experience. Yet, this stance is seldom as impartial as the Soul might yearn for. Our conscious awareness is akin to a monarch in a grand court, surrounded by a multitude of courtiers: subtle influencers, persuasive whisperers, attentive aids, and persistent petitioners. They all vie for attention.

The conscious mind is capable of listening to almost anything. If you wish to live well, *you must guide and protect it with care.* When the conscious mind makes a poor evaluation, the cost of correcting that mistake can be high. *Thought* is the driving engine of the conscious mind. When thoughts are formed through distorted perception—by listening to the ego rather than the Light consciousness—you open the door to illness, self-sabotage, depression, confusion, and similar consequences. Our very process of thinking is the engine of this awareness. Thoughts that are processed through a distorted lens—heeding the self's shadow rather than the inherent illumination—become the opening through which imbalance, self-diminishment, spiritual gloom, and a deep lack of clear vision may enter. Use with care!

THE SUBCONSCIOUS MIND: A SILENT PARTNER

The subconscious mind is the silent, holographic partner in the great theater of the self. Once the conscious mind has determined to "imprint" received data, it is channeled through a non-judgmental filter into the subconscious domain. *This realm holds no independent qualitative opinion.* Its primary function is the meticulous, infinite archiving of every informational datum it receives from its conscious counterpart.

As its secondary powerful function, this master-archivist then initiates the transmission of its deeply-vaulted information into the somatic field. The body then acts as the physical canvas upon which this energy is made manifest. Thus, if the conscious mind transmits information laden with apprehension, and this bio-energetic signal is relayed to the physical form, that information manifests as symptoms of systemic anxiety and palpable disquiet. Conversely, if the conscious mind intentionally channels the bright information of pure joy, the subconscious passes this harmonious signal to the body. This Divine exchange triggers the release of neurological opiates (such as endorphins) within the cerebral matrix, causing the entire being to vibrate in a state of spontaneous well-being.

THE EGO

The Enfant Terrible and the Wunderkind: The Mechanics of 3rd Density. We cannot hope to take our place at the table of Ascension without the spiritual maturity required to maintain an impartial view of the ego. This "enfant terrible" of 3rd Density has been paired with a "wunderkind" known as personal consciousness—a combination that has made this specific density the most "hairy" and turbulent of all our evolutionary stages, by a long shot.

The ego's outer mantel is protection; it's true heart is separation. A wolf in sheep's clothes.

To understand this pairing, we must look to the historical backdrop established by the conduits of Creation. As Ananda states, the ego finds its origins hundreds of thousands of years ago immediately after the event of the fallen angels (an episode explored in detail in our work on LightStreaming). This "fallen angel" event was far more than a localized historical incident on Earth; it symbolized a cosmic shift into separation consciousness.

Once this mode of consciousness emerged, it became embedded into the very construct of lower-density evolution. Humanity subsequently inherited this energetic field, though its full activation lay dormant until the advent of the 3rd Density. While the "fall" introduced the initial illusion of separation, it was 3rd Density that institutionalized it as the primary evolutionary environment. Thus, the ego is not a random accident of our current state—it is the functional engine of the 3rd Density curriculum. When man started saying "I am me," rather than merely functioning as instinctual life, the seed of 3rd Density ego was born.

This is why 3rd Density is said to be both a great advancement, and the beginning of profound suffering.

It is noteworthy that the ego is not entirely absent in 2nd Density; rather, it remains undeveloped and largely instinctual. A 2nd-density being lacks the psychological complexity, and the strong, individualized, self-reflective identity that characterizes 3rd-density humanity. In that earlier stage, the ego serves biological survival; in 3rd Density, it becomes the catalyst for the Soul's ultimate choice. The 2nd Density ego expresses itself through consciousness as an agent for:

- Biological self-preservation
- Instinctive separation
- Herd or pack identity
- Emotional reactivity
- Territorial consciousness

The Mandate of Choice. 3rd Density is primarily defined as the density of *choice* and *polarity*. While it is often characterized only as the density of the ego, this is an incomplete perspective. More accurately, it is the density of both the ego *and* individualized consciousness. Therefore, it functions as the specific environment where we are meant to discern and consciously choose between the two.

The challenges we face begin to mount significantly if we fail to make this choice, as the fundamental objective of the 3rd Density experience is to polarize our selection. By the conclusion of this density, the Light—or the universal intelligence—*requires a clear signature of our polarization to determine our path forward.* We essentially face three alternatives: we choose the ego, we choose the higher consciousness, or we remain in the status quo by making no choice at all.

This third option of indifference carries overwhelming consequences. After the final harvest—the transition period we are currently experiencing—any Soul that has not polarized will be obligated to restart the entire 75,000-year cycle of refinement from the very beginning.

To understand the weight of this, imagine reaching the end of 12th grade in high school. We find yourself short by a very small margin in just one subject, preventing graduation. We naturally ask to attend summer school, or retake a single exam to make up the difference. However, the school authorities inform you that the rules require us to restart our education back in the first grade. This is the metaphysical equivalent of failing to make a choice in 3rd Density.

The Law of the Ego: The more we engage it, the more it enslaves.

The structural rules for mankind's evolution in this density have consisted of two "midterms" occurring at 25,000-year intervals, followed by a "final exam" at the 75,000-year mark (which is now). While the law of evolution allows us to fail the first two midterms without catastrophic delay, we cannot afford to fail the final exam. This final test is straightforward, yet absolute: we must choose whether we polarize toward the "right" or the "left." Unfortunately, as discussed previously in this guide, an overwhelming majority of Souls still have not expressed their selection between ego and consciousness; they remain suspended in a state of spiritual indifference.

The Archetype of the Veil: Internal Separation and the Path to Unity. There is a frequent reference to a veil existing between the ego and consciousness within the 3rd-density experience. It is crucial to understand that this veil is not an external barrier, but an internal shield. It functions as a profound archetype for separation, mirroring historical and spiritual precedents.

We can look to the veil in the Second Temple of Jerusalem as a primary example; it served as a physical boundary separating the Holy Place from the Holy of Holies, the literal dwelling place of Yahweh's presence.

The crucifixion of Yeshua provides a pivotal symbolic key: at the moment of his passing, the Temple *veil* was torn in two. This is a vivid picture of the unification that is destined to take place between the ego and individualized consciousness. It signifies that the era of enforced separation drawing to a close has been announced. Just as the Temple veil was removed to allow direct access to the Holy of Holies, the veil between the ego and consciousness shall, likewise, be removed at the conclusion of 3rd Density. Similarly, there exists a mystical veil between the human heart and the Sacred Heart. These are all expressions of the same archetypal principle: a boundary that maintains the illusion of distance between the mundane and the divine, between what we *have* access to, and *will* have access to. The "Final Exam" of our current cycle is not merely a test of knowledge, but an invitation to step through this torn curtain, moving from a fragmented state of indifference into a unified state of polarized, positive awareness.

The Light's deepest aspiration for all of us is a profound return to the State of Illumination, to that same condition of pristine being consciousness knew before its descent to the earthly plane. The ego's own intent is the precise mirror-opposite of this sanctified intention, serving as the most intensely destructive ferment stirring within us. Any earnest stir toward a true communication with the Light incites a deep and uncontrolled tremor of panic within the ego. The ego's first and most pervasive stratagem is to persuade the self that it operates in a state of error or sin. Punishment is its cruel prescription, culminating in the painful manifestations of fear, deep-seated anger, and somatic illness. If you have ever felt the keen sting of these three shadows, you have become a willing string upon the ego's instrument.

The Light, by its very nature, does not strike out, but rather seeks reconciliation, and careful correction, for it intimately knows our inherent vulnerability to mistake. After all, we have been conditioned (by the ego) to "make mistakes!" A humble turning of the heart becomes the pure instrument of its remedy, through which it ushers in the boundless energy of love, the profound Principle of Atonement, and with it, complete healing.

The careful mechanism of the mind, and the manner of its unfolding must be pondered with utmost serenity and care. A failure to comprehend its fundamental spiritual matrix can exact a grievous cost upon the flow of our life, and the well-being of our health. Our conscious awareness is the receiver for the stream of thought. The moment a thought alights upon the mind, an inner decision is made regarding its nature. If we make a choice that is agreeable to the ego's impulse, it swiftly anchors itself to that decision, and claims it. The ego will then proceed to amplify that singular, flawed choice, increasing its energetic consequence multiple times over. It possesses the power to transmute even the smallest human slip into a massive, invisible dark cloud, a subtle shroud capable of ensnaring into its unseen web any consciousness that is too weak to resist its pull.

Conversely, the ego is seized by intense disquiet should you choose to abide by the guidance of the Light. The ego will mount a strenuous resistance, its ferocity calibrated by the magnitude of what it perceives the decision means to the Light's advance. Purity of prayer directed toward any entity of the Light is, naturally, a great and profound threat to the ego's dominion. Any sustained application of LightStreaming, which involves a direct and intimate contact with the entities of the Light, is precisely the antithesis of what sustains the ego. Clearly, any form of conscious communion with any aspect of the Light is perceived as an extreme peril to the ego, for it, the Light, holds the subtle potential to be the dawning of the separation's end.

Because our physical senses are deeply connected to our mind, the ego will often try to harm the body out of retaliation when we connect to the Light. This makes learning to disengage the ego during LightStreaming crucial; by cutting off its connection to your conscious mind, you stop it from interfering with the Light. While a highly advanced Soul can disconnect from the ego naturally without LightStreaming—as some serene individuals on Earth already do—most of us benefit from this conscious uncoupling.

The most pervasive mistake many of us make when it comes to the ego, is to not fully understand the catastrophic impact its function can have on our lives. If we were to make the mistake of willfully nurturing the ego—which we often do—the result can be so dramatic that it can take decades, if not an entire lifetime, to remedy the situation.

How many among us find ourselves caught on the endless treadmill of constantly fueling the anxious pursuit of accumulating mere material possessions?

Despite the shortcomings of the ego, try not to perceive it only as the enemy. It behaves mostly as a "bad" child, but the ego serves as a vital psychological guardian, functioning as the primary interface between our internal needs, and the demands of the material world. By fostering a clear sense of "self" versus "other," it compels us to secure the resources, shelter, and physical boundaries necessary for survival.

This drive for material well-being is not a spiritual failing, but a natural necessity, ensuring that we maintain the physical stability required to eventually explore higher states of consciousness. Without the ego's protective vigilance over our earthly interests, we would lack the grounded foundation needed to navigate and sustain life in a complex, physical reality.

But, one of the ego's driving goals is to relentlessly propel us to erect false idols. Do not hesitate for a moment to allow the Light to completely and serenely take over the "management" of the entire mind system. In this profound and most judicious sense, to be the benevolent manager of your consciousness is its sole, and most Divine purpose.

THE BODY: THE PASSIVE VESSEL

Of all the sacred components we have contemplated, the body appears last, simply because it remains a passive vessel within this intricate system. It acts as a receiver for information, but it does not possess the faculty to process or interpret information on its own accord.

The body cannot initiate action by its own will, and must be guided by an agent—be it the mind or the ego. If you recall the narrative of the Fall in the preceding contemplation, the body was already present and served as a quiet, steadfast ally to the ego's impulses. The first creatures who resided here were not yet connected to the God-given spirit system of the Trinity. The physical body did not descend from the fallen angels. Since the body is essentially the ego's cherished home turf, the ego actively and forcefully utilizes it to mete out its punishments whenever there is a spiritual disagreement or subtle defiance against its will.

CHAPTER HIGHLIGHTS:

- The human mind operates through three primary layers—**superconscious, conscious, and subconscious**—while interacting with the ego and the physical body, forming the framework that shapes human experience.
- The superconscious mind represents the highest level of awareness: it **includes the Higher-Self,** connects to universal intelligence as the channel through which revelation, intuition, and spiritual insight flow from the Divine.
- The conscious mind is the active center of perception and decision-making, using **thought as its primary input**; it shapes personal reality and life outcomes.
- The subconscious mind acts as a non-judgmental archive; it **records all impressions** from the conscious mind and **translates** them into physiological and emotional states within the body.
- The ego is a disruptive force originating from the historical "Separation," opposing the Light; **it demands control** through fear, anger, guilt, and attachment to material illusions.
- The ego can **distort** the thinking process. Therefore: **disengage its influence** (through LightStreaming, for example), and align the conscious mind with the guidance of the Light, allowing spiritual insight to flow without its interference.
- **The physical body is a passive vessel** that manifests the energetic and psychological patterns transmitted through the mind.

CHAPTER TWELVE

COMPATIBILITY AND CONVERGENCE

Before we dive into discussing the technicalities of LightStreaming, a disclaimer must be shared: We postulate that all have a self-agreed-upon life intention/purpose. This intention is labeled a "Soul contract." Our Light bodies make that contract with the Light prior to an incarnation to establish a work plan for the path of our Soul. It is given that we are meant to go from a defined point 'A' to a defined point 'B' during this life cycle. We should also keep in perspective that we have free will to depart from such a path at any given time.

At all times, and during all incarnations on Earth, our *life purpose* is to invite the physical body to set its spiritual GPS so we can receive and act on communication from the Other Side. The end purpose of this is for us to terminate the separation from the Light, and navigate back to where we came from, spirit. It is through the *body* that the ego separates.

Unfortunately, the physical body is, by default, set to complicate this by being obstructed with conflicting information from the ego. The life-game we live, in a nutshell, is to find out what our agreed-upon life purpose is, and consent to pursue it (more detail on this in the Souls Contract chapter, on page 235). This is where LightStreaming can assist. So, we must ensure that our actions are compatible with our life purpose. Once this is in place, we experience the convergence of intent with goal, which is really a state of powerful bliss. We must *pair our life's intention with guidance from the Light.*

Imagine a brilliant jazz improviser—someone whose entire artistry is built on spontaneity, breaking the rules, and reinventing the melody on the fly—joining a world-class classical symphony orchestra, where rigid adherence to the written score, and absolute uniformity are the law. Despite their musical genius, they find themselves paralyzed. Their very nature—the drive to experiment and innovate—is viewed as a liability rather than an asset. They struggle because their personal engine is built for a limitless jam session, but they have moved into a rigid arrangement; they suffer because their internal "why" is fundamentally incompatible with the external "how."

Our purest intention must be in seamless compatibility with the desired goal, for the liberating convergence to manifest.

Failures in life are 99% of the time caused by this simple concept not being implemented. We may have a difficult marriage or professional partnership which could have been avoided had we checked if both were compatible, prior to joining forces.

Perhaps we chose a profession that is incompatible with what we are meant to do and we do not understand why we are unhappy. Can we see how much easier it would be if we knew what our life purpose is? Have you heard of people who go through a lengthy and expensive education and then, upon graduation, decide to do something entirely different and unrelated to their college degree? This waste of time and resources can easily be avoided.

Likewise, many of us do not realize that our body is incompatible with certain foods, which can trigger a variety of diseases and symptoms. Would it not be prudent to find out what foods they are? Anything related to the harmonics of compatibility can be uncovered through LightStreaming.

If we are not fully on board as a 'believer' in the Higher-Self, we will have mediocre and/or irrelevant results with LightStreaming. These are the guidelines that cannot be stressed enough:

- **We accept that our constitution is made up of both flesh and Soul, and,**
- **We must be able to visualize and verbalize without fear, saying or describing whatever comes into our mind without analyzing the information.**
- **We cannot have fear of the process, and must allow the Light to completely provide guidance for our healing process.**
- **We embrace the concept of reincarnation.**
- **We are in line with how our mind works as described in this guide.**
- **We fully accept that we have a perfect and unalterable Soul, and,**
- **Accept that WE can communicate with the other side through our superconsciousness, thoughts and dreams.**

CHAPTER HIGHLIGHTS:

- Human life operates under a **pre-incarnation "Soul contract,"** a life intention agreed upon with the Light before birth, that establishes the broad path the Soul intends to travel during a lifetime.
- Although this purpose exists, **free will allows individuals to depart from that intended path**, making the central challenge of life discovering one's purpose, and consciously choosing to follow it.
- The body serves as the instrument through which the Soul reconnects with the Light, but the ego introduces conflicting signals that obscure guidance, complicating the ability **to perceive** one's true direction.
- When a person's actions, intentions, and life choices are aligned with their Soul's purpose, a state called **convergence** arises—bringing clarity, harmony, and a sense of fulfillment.
- Many personal frustrations—such as incompatible relationships, careers, environments, or even diets—arise **when choices are not compatible with one's deeper life intention**.
- LightStreaming is presented as a method for identifying these compatibilities, and **restoring alignment**, provided the individual approaches it with openness to the Higher-Self, acceptance of reincarnation, trust in intuitive communication, and willingness to follow guidance from the Light.

CHAPTER THIRTEEN

UNDERSTANDING THE LIGHT

The Light, the Divine Source-energy is the transcendent synthesis of all positive and negative charge, a primal field where opposing forces merge. The Light is the "material" or the energy that activates the physical and metaphysical universe (photons, atoms, and densities). The ultimate Godhead, from where the Light originates, is thus revealed as a seamless Father-Mother, a unified male-female polarity, dynamic configuration. The profound Yin-Yang symbol (☯) of the Eastern metaphysical traditions, perfectly represents this fitting pairing of the essential female energy and its complementary male energy.

When our awareness is drawn toward the appellation of our Heavenly Father, it is an intuitive recognition that we are engaging with the combined, singular Father/Mother unity, known as the Godhead. We refer to this celestial Source-energy that emanates *from* this boundless Infinite Creator as the Light. *The Infinite Creator is not the Light*; rather, it is the **energy** the Infinite Creator gave us that is referred to as the Light. Be aware of the distinction.

There exists NO dimensional or material constraint that this pure vibrational energy cannot supersede, for in its multi-creative capacity it far surpasses the limitations of dense, solid matter and all other manifest forms of being. It is the very field that, in fact, created them all. This God-infused Light energy possesses the sentient capacity for conscious interaction, enabling a genuine, *two-way dialogue and response.* In the practice of LightStreaming, healing transcends the narrow, modern pre-occupation with the biological frame. It is foremost a repair of the mental and emotional bodies, a profound act of restoration. To heal should be understood in a broad sense: to realign with our original wholeness, returning the spirit to its natural state of peace and equilibrium.

A significant fraction of humanity remains entirely oblivious to the constant transmission of this cosmic energy, and this state of spiritual dormancy shall, perhaps, continue for a certain span of time—not too long, we can hope. Furthermore, the great majority of individuals who embrace a form of faith often harbor a misconstrued or limited understanding of the sheer power output streaming from the Source, which is God. This vital, quantum energy is so exponentially potent that "any being *directly* exposed to its unmitigated field intensity would undergo a literal combustion (direct quote from Yeshua)." Death, in that specific circumstance, would be the resultant outcome. It is for this fundamental, energetic reason that the Divine Source DOES NOT initiate direct healing.

Consider the countless millions of Souls who, on a regular and persistent basis, offer prayers to God for physical restoration, that *apparently* remain unanswered, and futile. Even though all prayers are ultimately answered, failing to immediately receive the desired healing, they let themselves stranded in a state of profound disbelief and helplessness.

The request is analogous to petitioning the Director of a colossal hydro-electric facility to directly enter into a bespoke residential electrical power contract. That authority would, logically, redirect the applicant to a local power company, whose specialized task is to step-down, and transform the immense electrical impedance to a usable level.

Or: a piece of your mail was mistakenly delivered to a different household. Irritated, you file a complaint to the president of the country. His office forwards it to the Federal Postmaster General, who forwards it to the State Postmaster, who forwards it to the county postal administration, who forwards it to the city postmaster, who forwards it to the local carrier! In spiritual ways, we get faster results when we get our "mail" (thoughts, prayers, communication) to the right entity to begin with.

Hence, the Light has ingeniously established a system of energetic transmutation, a spiritual transformer that converts that raw, infinite energy to an impedance level that is perfectly suitable for individual, "personal consumption." The complex structure of this Divine energy conversion grid is of paramount interest within the esoteric discipline of LightStreaming, particularly as there is ONE Source-energy, that emanates directly from the Light's central intelligence:

God does not heal; Sacred consciousness does.

That stream is exclusively dedicated to the process of profound HEALING and restorative processes. At the same time it also serves to ACTIVATING and ENERGIZING all processes of manifestation, and the transmission of intuitive REVELATIONS.

Operating in seamless conjunction with the Godhead, this dual expression, along with the Holy Spirit, collectively form a sacred trinity, commonly referred to as The Holy Trinity. Its designation as Holy is derived from the infinite possibility of limitless, interconnecting energy transfer between each nodal point of the Trinity, which inherently originates from the Divine Source—God.

This profound trine relationship was not an innovation conceived during our current Global Civilization (the epoch following the final Ice Age), nor was it formulated during any of Earth's previous major civilizations (Lemuria and Atlantis). Its establishment precedes the actual formation of our terrestrial planet.

Genesis 1:1-2

> *1 To begin with, Elohim rearranged the heavens and the Earth. 2 Now the Earth was formless and empty, darkness was over the surface of the deep, and*

the Spirit of God was hovering over the waters[1].

This Trinity is also a manifest principle within the complex faith of Hinduism[2]. However, Vishnu, Shiva, Krishna and so many more, are hybrid beings from Andromeda, and therefore, the Hindu trinity represents a different order of divinities. The cosmic realms only embody one Trinity, that of the Infinite Creator, the Sacred consciousness (which is the Son, not Yeshua) and the Holy Spirit (The Father, the Son and the Holy Spirit.) *God's child, His Son, is not a human being. God's child is consciousness.* Trinity is not the finite creation of any specific religious organization or doctrine. A misunderstanding persists among some, suggesting the Holy Trinity was an invention of the Christian or Catholic Church simply because it is mentioned within the canonical Bible (specifically Matthew 28, v. 19-20). This inference is not metaphysically sound. The revelatory aspect of this universal energy configuration has been a known key to the great sages and spiritual giants throughout all recorded ages. The two creations/emanations of God, the Holy Spirit and consciousness, where interconnected *after* the Fall:

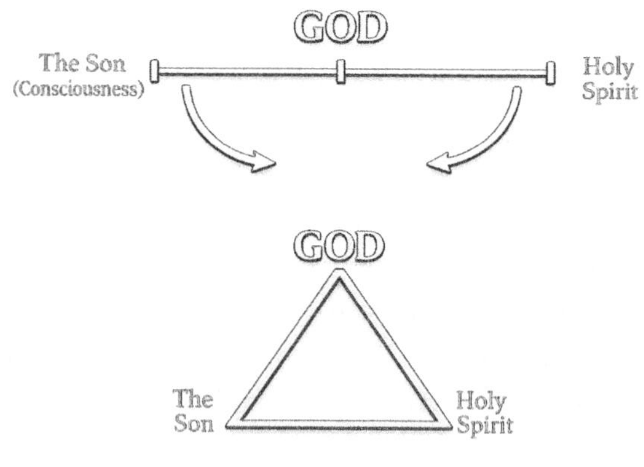

THE HOLY TRINITY (LINEAR VIEW)

[1] Hebrew urtext translation by Marc Mourier.

[2] Brahma, the Creator; Vishnu, the Preserver; Shiva, the Destroyer.

The astounding expression of the Christ consciousness manifested in Yeshua was a strategic event designed to showcase:

(a) The healing and revelation currents of the Light's energy; and

(b) to irrefutably establish that the Light's Divine power utterly and metaphysically transcends, and supersedes "dormant" matter (as demonstrated in the acts of Yeshua' resurrection and Lazarus' awakening from death).

The Holy Trinity is a dual segmented vector including God, Sacred consciousness and the Holy Spirit; not Yeshua.

Often called the Holy Spirit, this dynamic energy was held back from humanity until Yeshua demonstrated, by his example, how to access it alongside Christ consciousness. This spiritual blueprint was revealed by him, but not by any church or organization. Also, when practicing LightStreaming, you should not associate these energies with any specific religion or religious movement.

<u>CAVEAT</u>: If we try to access the Light via LightStreaming through any source other than the Holy Spirit, the energy will become corrupted. Without this authentic conduit, the flow loses its integrity, and simply will not work effectively. All energetic "traffic" within this domain is exclusively and divinely channeled through the Holy Spirit. It serves as the official, sovereign clearinghouse for *all* operations of a spiritual nature. Given that the radiant healing energy is so intricately associated with the healing ministry of Yeshua, this specific current of restorative energy is often designated as the Christ-power; but, it does not originate from Yeshua The Anointed (the Christ).

The Light energy is NOT *incremental* in its application when addressing the need for healing. It does not assess a physical ailment, such as a severe headache, and render a judgment, saying: "As this condition is minor, it requires only a subtle, nominal application of healing energy." Nor does it respond to a more severe systemic condition, such as advanced heart disease, by proclaiming: "We need to significantly amp up the energy frequency modulation." The Light operates with ONE singular, universal energy level, and this output is absolutely identical for every single treatment session. There is a cosmic ON switch and a commensurate OFF switch—that is the totality of the mechanism.

If a sustained or prolonged treatment regimen is deemed necessary by the Higher-Self, additional sessions can, of course, be entertained. However, the base output energy remains perfectly constant for the duration of each treatment. Daily focused healing prayers should, nonetheless, be conducted by the specific individual seeking the transformation. These heartfelt prayers may be consciously, and precisely customized to address the unique nature of each condition. Our bodies understand speech and thought very well.

The Holy Spirit is, in essence, the most exquisitely advanced communication "device" ever bestowed upon humankind. To briefly and clearly recapitulate: The Divine Source—God is NOT directly involved in the function of healing. This blessed task is wholly managed within the specialized, dedicated realm of the Christ consciousness ray, or Holy consciousness, an *emanation* that originates from the very heart of God.

CHAPTER HIGHLIGHTS:

- The **Light is a Divine energy** that powers both the physical and spiritual worlds. While it comes from the Creator, it acts as the distinct tool or "fuel" that makes all of Creation function.
- The Light embodies a **unified polarity** (Yin-Yang) of masculine and feminine energies, reflecting the balanced dual nature of the Godhead.
- The Light is too powerful for humans to handle directly. To make it safe, a **cosmic "transformer" system steps down this infinite energy** so we can use it for healing, and spiritual growth: the Holy Spirit.
- The Light is organized through a universal **Trinity**: the Creator, Sacred consciousness (the Son), and the Holy Spirit. This energetic structure is a cosmic reality that has existed for hundreds of thousands of years, and is (should be) entirely **detached form any religion**.
- The Holy Spirit acts as a central "clearinghouse." It **moderates the intense power** of the Divine Source, safely transmitting healing and wisdom to humanity.
- Christ consciousness **comes from within**. Yeshua was the master model of how to access, and use this energy.
- In healing, the Light operates at a **single, constant universal level,** regardless of the condition (mental, physical or bodily restoration). While a person may need multiple sessions to fully integrate the healing, the intensity of the energy output itself never changes.

CHAPTER FOURTEEN

HYPNOSIS

Hypnosis refers to a state where consciousness can act without the influence of the ego. It is a trance-like state characterized by deep relaxation, and heightened suggestibility. It is a condition, and not a treatment. Hypnotherapy is the action of applying suggestions and instructions to the Subconscious Mind while the body is in a state of hypnosis.

Hypnosis is scientifically studied in psychology and neuroscience. There is solid, evidential research showing that hypnosis can alter perception, attention, and activate memory recall. Despite the oftentimes reticence by the scientific community to veer outside its "hard" disciplines, there is, with hypnosis, a verifiable and controlled component that satisfies scientific reasoning: brain imaging shows measurable changes in neural activity during hypnotic states. Major institutions and peer-reviewed journals recognize this work. In this sense, hypnosis meets scientific criteria; it is testable, observable, and reproducible under controlled conditions. As a result, it is often taught as part of the standard curriculum of psychology (and psychiatry) in universities worldwide.

HYPNOTHERAPY'S TARGET: THE EGO

Hypnosis and the therapy that may accompany it revolve around a single actor: the ego. The ego is not an ally of hypnotherapy. As a tool for Ascension, hypnotherapy addresses one central challenge—how to bypass the ego. When the ego is subdued, meaningful work can proceed. Hypnotherapy alone, however, does not have the force to eradicate the ego, as it is embedded in our bodily infrastructure, woven into it as a permanent feature of embodiment. The ego is often seen as a necessary "software" program for navigating the 3rd Density (physical reality).

This ego-bound structure is reactive, and *sustains itself through constant activation.* The more it is triggered, the stronger it becomes. One of the most effective ways to reduce this reactivity is to ignore it. Nothing frustrates the ego more than being denied attention. A plant that is not watered withers; an ego that is not fed renders itself inert. There is a direct relationship between how often the ego is triggered, and how insistently it seeks the spotlight. In this sense, the adage "If you don't use it, you lose it" applies remarkably well to the ego.

A substantial dissolution of ego interference does not occur until initiation into the 5th Dimension. Yet entry into the 5th Dimension is itself far more accessible when ego influence is minimal. This creates a reciprocal, self-reinforcing loop. Navigating this dynamic with discipline and care can yield exceptional results.

The absorption of higher photon levels occurs with full intensity when the spiritual body is pure. Conversely, this absorption is diminished when our energetic system is unprepared. As discussed earlier, this requires keeping the chakras as clear and responsive as possible. One challenge is unresolved karma carried forward from prior lives; another is avoiding the creation of *new* karma through daily behavior. Hypnotherapy is particularly well suited to this work. When applied correctly by a clinical hypnotherapist trained in Ascension-oriented practice, the question is not whether it will work, but how quickly one wishes to experience results.

Addressing mind-centered issues is most effective in a clean, and receptive mental environment. By reducing the defensive mechanisms the body habitually activates, one gains access to the mind's inner engine—the subconscious. The body is governed by a powerful watchtower: the ego. Its agenda is to interfere with the free operation of the subconscious, by inserting its own priorities and desires, rarely, if ever, aligned with higher aims.

The ego does not act in our best interest; it acts in its own, seeking to maintain dependency, and preserve separation from Spirit. Hypnotherapy therefore functions as an advanced instrument for clearing unnecessary obstructions that distort expression and behavior.

The purpose of hypnotherapy in the Ascension process is to ready the chakras for the rising of the Kundalini.

The most effective context for addressing ego-driven patterns is the *hypnagogic* state. Behavioral changes that might take years to achieve through conventional talk therapy can often be resolved in a matter of hours through hypnotherapy.

One of the less visible benefits of hypnotherapy is the rapid restoration of confidence. Its strength lies in the immediacy of its effects. After a successful session, the change is felt somatically, and is verifiable through a sense of lightness, relief from mental weight, renewed vitality, and a conviction of "I can do this." At this stage, *direct experience* replaces doubt, and that renewed self-assurance can quickly extend into other areas of life, accelerating progress faster than expected.

We are not always reliable stewards of our own mental health. Poor mental health can be corrosive even without dramatic symptoms. Over time, patterns shift. A behavior that was once well managed may quietly regress until it once again requires deliberate correction. True progress requires consistent presence. It is about the discipline of awareness—refusing to let the clarity we have gained slip back into the shadows of habit.

HYPNOSIS: AN ASCENSION SOCIAL WORKER

In the broader journey of Ascension, the ego often functions as a persistent but ultimately temporary distraction. For those seeking higher consciousness, the productive daily practice involves clearing away the mental debris that obstructs one's path, and maintaining a disciplined awareness to prevent further clutter from taking root. Hypnosis serves this process by quieting the ego's habitual filtering, thereby facilitating a clear dialogue between the subconscious and the superconscious minds. Regardless of how one defines the practice, it remains an indispensable tool for those preparing for the transition to higher dimensions.

Even seemingly minor obstacles, such as acrophobia or other specific fears, can significantly hinder one's progress. The issue lies not in the object of the identified fear itself, but in the presence of the fear state. Fear is entirely incompatible with higher dimensions, as it is rooted in a fundamental *lack of trust*—the very quality that defines higher existence. Fortunately, fear can be effectively transmuted when the appropriate methods are applied.

The approach recommended by Ascended Hearts (the organization), is unique in its strategic implementation of therapeutic modules designed for maximum efficacy. This progression begins with Hypnosis to address the ego mind. It then moves into Past Life Regression to work through the Higher-Self, and concludes with channeling to engage with spiritual entities, and the superconscious.

Hypnosis draws upon the facets of the individual personality, including memory, conditioning, and learned behaviors. Through relaxation and mental imagery, it utilizes suggestibility to address practical concerns such as habit modification, pain management, and the resolution of phobias. It is an ideal starting point for restoration. Those who are uncertain of where to begin, are encouraged to review the "Top-20" list, and identify areas ripe for improvement, with honesty and an eagerness for self-mastery, free from shame or guilt.

Within this state of hypnosis, the personal ego recedes, allowing pure consciousness to take precedence. The objective is to access a more expansive sense of identity and higher awareness. Here, *authority remains entirely with the individual rather than the hypnotist*, who acts as a supportive practitioner rather than an operator. The process transitions rapidly into a state of alignment through symbolic, contemplative language, and a profound sense of inner stillness. Rather than relying on direct suggestion, the practitioner offers guidance toward trans-personal experiences—states of unity, archetypal perception, and direct inner truth. Ultimately, while hypnosis can target specific behavioral outcomes, its true purpose is to invite the Higher-Self to establish an entirely new and elevated trajectory for one's life.

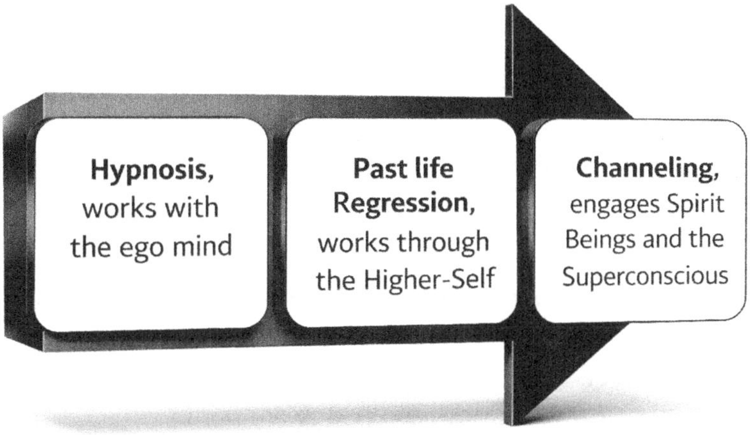

CHAPTER HIGHLIGHTS:

- Hypnosis is a trance-like state of focused awareness where the **influence of the ego is reduced**, allowing consciousness to operate with heightened suggestibility and access to the subconscious mind.
- Psychology and neuroscience show that hypnosis causes measurable changes in brain activity. These studies prove it **can effectively alter how we perceive reality**, focus our attention, and recall memories.
- In the context of Ascension work, **hypnotherapy primarily targets the ego**, helping bypass its defensive mechanisms.
- By quieting the ego, hypnosis **accelerates** behavioral and transformation alterations, often resolving issues that might otherwise take years through conventional therapeutic methods.
- Hypnotherapy also **assists in clearing karma**, and maintaining a balanced chakra system, preparing the spiritual body for higher photon absorption, and the eventual rising of Kundalini energy.
- Within the broader Ascension methodology, **hypnosis serves as the first of several coordinated tools**, followed by Past Life Regression and Channeling, forming a structured progression for spiritual development, and higher-dimensional readiness.
- By reducing fear, quieting mental interference, and fostering dialogue between the subconscious and superconscious minds, **hypnosis becomes a practical instrument for clearing obstacles**, and aligning with higher consciousness.

CHAPTER FIFTEEN

LIGHTSTREAMING - PAST LIFE REGRESSION

We did *not* live before. However, our *Soul* was coupled with another person's body in a previous lifetime. Let us be clear on that. The deep wisdom concerning the Soul's return is embraced by a vast, resonant multitude of spirits spanning the globe. Yet, the predominant, established religious frameworks often do not share—whether it matters or not—this understanding of rebirth[1]. Despite Jesus's assertion that one must be born again to see the kingdom of God, and his explicit declaration that John the Baptist was the return of Elijah, the established Church ultimately rejected the concept of reincarnation. The faith of Islam is firmly rooted in the conviction of a singular existence,

[1] Pythagoras (c. 570 – c. 495 BC) was the first to postulate the concept of the Soul's Trans-migration (reincarnation) to the Western world. The Hindus were already very familiar with the concept of reincarnation since the late Vedic period (c. 1100 – 500 BCE).

followed by a final disposition in either heaven or hell. The children of the Hebrew tradition generally hold to the same perspective. Why might this divergence exist?

The primary leverage point held by the established orders appears to be their belief that they possess the authority to guide us toward spiritual despair should we stray from their precepts. Our life system is, however, not constructed in this fashion. When we engage in conduct that is discordant with the Divine Radiance, we are offered the grace of a fresh birth, providing a profound opportunity to return and *mend* the perceived error. We must journey further eastward, to the centers of Hindu and Buddhist thought, to encounter an open acceptance of the Soul's trans-migrations. Is it not telling that these two spiritual traditions are less rigidly founded upon a centralized, dogmatic priesthood?

Past Life Regression is amazing, but so is Future Life Progression... seeing your next incarnation.

The concept of karma is, regrettably, one of the unfortunate shadows cast upon the true teaching of reincarnation. Many mistakenly perceive karma as a malicious, punitive curse—a tenacious shadow that hounds the spirit through multiple earthly cycles in retribution for a past transgression. This is a profound misreading, a fabrication born of superstition and spiritual ignorance.

Nevertheless, there is a kernel of truth within this mistaken karma belief—a subtle thread connecting the web of life cycles. It is this delicate linkage that we seek to explore when we guide the self through the recollection of a past life. To engage in this journey, in our understanding, holds little practical significance unless it can be utilized for deep inner healing, and to bring our current existence into a greater, more visionary perspective, thus preparing the Soul for its Ascension.

To accept that the human being was created is but one step; to truly grasp the sublime mechanics of that creation is another entirely. The karma system serves as a dynamically managed vessel for spiritual debris. It is the Infinite Creator's way of conveying this truth: "Whenever we commit deeds (in thought, action, intent, or word) that are not aligned with the Pure Light, a negative resonance will be recorded, and held within our karma vessel. Conversely, whenever we perform deeds that are in full alignment with the Light, they shall serve to dissipate and remove any negative imprints that may reside within that same repository."

Therefore, the term karma is most purely understood when we define it as "the Law of Reciprocity as it is applied to the trans-migration of a Soul." Every individual Soul has been perfectly fashioned from the very instant of its creation. It stands in no need of being developed, labored upon, repaired, or improved in any conceivable way. It cannot be crushed, wounded, seized, or otherwise altered from its original, pristine state. It remains a perfect creation, and it is the sole and exclusive property of the One who brought it into being. It is, however, exquisitely designed to progress (move) between its successive physical forms.

An individual who disavows reincarnation, has never interacted with Spirit about it.

The surest path toward reducing the number of earthly cycles we are required to undertake, is to diminish to an absolute minimum the frequency of actions that move against the Radiance of the Light. Nested within the Law of Reincarnation lies the profound concept of "lessons learned." In this way, the process is strikingly analogous to the preparation for a school graduation. For example, should we find ourselves falling short in the 3rd grade, we must dutyfully retake the course. We will continue to return to that level until the lesson is fully mastered. That same principle also holds true for the deep lessons of life. Should we fail to assimilate a necessary lesson in a particular life cycle, that identical lesson will be presented repeatedly until we are able to proceed, climbing ever upward toward our ultimate spiritual graduation: the final Ascension. The purposes behind the Soul's journey of return are manifold.

LightStreaming Past Life Regression (LSPLR) holds one singular, elevating objective: to guide us back, while in a trance state, to a previous existence that can most clearly bring forth what we are meant to focus upon, and master in this present life. We often carry a profound weight of emotional burdens, unresolved complexities, deep misunderstandings, and more, from one embodiment to the next. Let us now turn our attention to a few specific instances drawn from the PLR log journal:

> *"... John came into the session with a dreadful fear of needles, had anxiety all his life and requested a PLR. In the session, John was guided to a life where he was a Neo-Nazi. He spent his life at that time, killing innocent people and causing harm to society. He was caught and was given the death sentence. His life was terminated by lethal injection in prison. Once he recognized that his fear originated from another life, he was, with his practitioner, able to leave that fear in that past life. Also, his anxiety was alleviated from the same root cause..."*

> *"...Peter came into the session with an issue of pain. He reported that he experienced pain in his shoulder intermittently, and he had no way of knowing when the pain would manifest. He had been to doctors, had scans and the medical world had no answer for him as to why he experienced the occasional pain. The pain was debilitating when he suffered it, and it would only last a minute or two before disappearing. He requested PLR.*
>
> *During the session, Peter was guided to a life where he, as a young man, was running away from something. There were several young men running away with him. Suddenly, he felt a searing pain in his shoulder and it was a spear that was thrown by another group of men chasing them.*
>
> *He and his practitioner were able to release the pain once Peter had the realization of the origination of the pain, in that lifetime. Since then, Peter has lived pain free*[2]*..."*

In these stories, we see how Souls get stuck when they carry unresolved energy. They end up wasting precious time just trying to find

[2] This perfectly demonstrates the power of the Principle of Atonement: simple exposure to the Light energy removed the pain.

their footing again. Yet, it is beautiful to remember that the universe always guides us exactly where we need to be to gain true wisdom, helping us fully step into the life we were born to live. Past Life Regression (PLR) emerges as a tremendous equalizer for harmonizing problematic life situations, and interpersonal quantum entanglements. Contemplate the memory of Jane and Thomas:

> *"... Jane and Thomas were experiencing marital difficulties. Having spent some time with marriage counselors, talking to friends and relatives, they were at the brink of divorce. Jane had confided in her practitioner that she was contemplating leaving her family. They decided to give PLR a shot as the final effort. The sessions were individual, and at separate times. When Jane was taken to a past life, she reported that she left her husband and children, and she saw how her children suffered due to her leaving. When Thomas went to a past life, he stated that he and Jane had a wonderful, quiet life together, and both lived to an old age.*
>
> *Jane realized that if she deserted her family now, maybe in a future life she would have to repeat the same scenario. They both realized that it could be possible for them to overcome their obstacles in this lifetime and work harder on their marriage. The retrospection allowed them to reunify as a couple in this life cycle ..."*

In reflection, the profound influence of the LightStreaming modalities upon one's inner landscape is quite remarkable. When viewed through the lens of proper perspective, its capacity for constructive transformation is undeniable. Do not allow despair to take root, should the clarity surrounding the appropriate path remain veiled. Sometimes the representations are metaphorical. Many seekers arrive with a natural confusion as to the specific modality best suited for their session. This discernment can be established in dialogue with the practitioner at the time of scheduling one's session.

The singular purpose of LightStreaming is to forge a connection with the vital information contained within the timeless capsule, which is the very essence and true reality of the Light. We speak of this as a capsule because it holds a concentrated, non-linear blueprint of our life's past, present, and unfolding future. Through LightStreaming, we are empowered to act as an effective channel for this wisdom.

The Light reveals to us that the full symphony of our actions is already mapped, even those events which will be shaped or modified by the power of our free will. Thus, LightStreaming emerges as a most powerful instrument available for the Soul to align its present earthly purpose with its deepest intent. Far too often, we observe processes that lack transparency, especially where matters of spiritual energy are concerned. One must always arrive at a complete and intuitive understanding of the forces they engage with. A true process should be one that can be assembled and disassembled at the will of consciousness.

The opalescent transparency woven into the LightStreaming method is one of its most profound strengths. What is revealed is precisely what is received—purely, literally, and without distortion. As we stand in awe of this innate functionality, we can rest assured in a deeper truth: we are never left unattended in this space.

We can receive guidance from the Light, who is an active co-creator of our being. This is not the realm of magic. It is a simple, clear communion with the Light that awaits our invitation, longing to assist us, should we be ready to accept that we are fundamentally beings woven from flesh and Soul. In its most primal contemplation, our physical form is host to 3 core engines: Spirit, mind and flesh. If they are not in conversation, they *should* be. As noted, the ego is perpetually eager to broker a negotiation with the Soul. Yet, the Soul will never, in any dimension, enter such a dialogue.

However, we humans are frequently unaware of this magnificent internal set-up, and are therefore not consistently adept at attending to the counsel flowing from the Light, as much of this insight is often thwarted by the pervasive voice of the ego. Consequently, we often fail to examine the source from which the information springs. It may be wisdom aligned with the Light, or the compelling directives that identify with the ego.

Regrettably, the ego assumes a role akin to a controller during our life. Its singular preoccupation is to dominate our actions and thoughts, and by extension, to impose its will upon the environment, and our communities. In this sense, it is a veritable bossy governor of the self. This ego function is often encouraged by the individuals themselves through the daily choices they make. Since we have been conditioned by the cultural narrative that material success is synonymous with the highest goal achievements in life, we tend to follow the ego's insistent call more deeply, in the broad sense of the word.

Yet, there are those who have finally arrived at the profound realization that a vast, material success is utterly irrelevant to attaining true internal health and peace. Those who consciously choose this path are already well on their way to an effulgent alignment with the Light.

Light-Streaming-PLR doesn't take you to any past life, only to those that Creation wants you to learn from for your Ascension.

The Light desires only the absolute highest good for every single person. The ego's SOLE, unwavering objective is to prevent the individual from ever achieving a clear communication with the Light. The reason is simple: once an individual awakens into a multi-dimensional state, such as the 5th Dimension, the ego has lost its foothold in the game. Checkmate.

As mentioned, the Light will NEVER engage, communicate, or enter into any dealings with the ego. The ego's singular aim is the total control of the human spirit through the shadows of fear, greed, and the insatiable desire to "conquer" all materialistic pursuits and flesh-driven vices. It is the architect of all those traits which we commonly label as hubris and arrogance, and it will relentlessly steer the individual to follow its narrow path.

Thus, life unfolds as a spiritual arena for this battle of opposing wills: consciousness versus the ego. To yield to the ego's direction can manifest as deeply compromised health situations, both mental and physical, with the arising of symptoms such as anxiety, irritability, fear, chaotic emotions, anger, and frustration, to name but a subtle few. Add to this the ensuing possibility of physical ailments, and life becomes intensely challenging, often leaving one without the inner compass to guide decisions: not knowing when to take the next step in one's career, or whether one resides in the most harmonious relationship, for example.

Whereas, if we cultivate the ability to follow the Light's tranquil call, an abiding peace will ensue, accompanied by a profound sense of calmness, and our life will begin to flow as it was always meant to, naturally. We have surely heard the encouragement, "Go with the flow." In this deep, spiritual context, that is simply to say: align with the Light.

The Light will NEVER communicate with the ego —ever!

We reiterate that LightStreaming PLR can prove to be an experience of substantial benefit in that it possesses the capacity to bypass the ego completely through the art of hypnosis. A deep hypnagogic trance allows the individual to release all tension and connect with the very source of the Light. During the session, while the individual rests in this tranquil trance, profound questions can be answered easily by the Light, without any interference from the egoic mind.

Some individuals may find that the journey into a deep Theta state of hypnosis (sometimes referred to as a somnambulistic state) can be a subtle challenge. This is particularly true for those who inhabit a more "left-brained" orientation than others. People whose professions are analytical by nature, are naturally more inclined to this initial resistance. However, the LightStreaming Practitioner is deeply experienced in this nuance, and can provide skillful ways of maneuvering around any initial hesitation, should the need arise.

The practitioner is rigorously trained to completely safeguard the confidentiality and personal privacy of every seeking individual. A session should always conducted in full and transparent compliance with the strictest privacy regulations, including HIPAA.

1 - THE QUESTIONS

A typical initial LightStreaming session assumes that the individual has typed up a list of relevant questions which is brought to the session. The questions should be in third person, always. Remember, the practitioner will be the person that will be asking the Light the questions on your behalf. Thus, do not use 'I' when formulating the questions. This is a common error to watch for. If you are Mary, a question's format should be: "Is Mary in the right profession?" and not "Am I in the right profession?"

(1) Do not ask about other parties unless they are specifically connected to your issue. Those questions will not be answered. The Light knows a thing or two about other parties' privacy.

(2) Keep your eyes on the ball. Your objective is to align with the Light. Your queries should be aiming at that. This is when we get maximum accuracy and reward. Do not ask if your refrigerator will fail in the upcoming year, or similar! We will not be dealing with secular entities on the Other Side. In other words, take your fortuneteller fedora off, and put your spiritual guide cap on.

2 - THE INTAKE

The practitioner will start the process of making you feel at ease and relaxed. You will discuss your life, upbringing, relationships, work etc. The practitioner will also review your questions, and make suggestions to avoid overlapping or for any needed modifications. The intake is the most important part of the session as it allows any ambiguity to be clarified. Furthermore, there is a "connection" that develops during the intake between yourself and the practitioner, and this deepens the mutual trust. This is important; as the hypnosis part starts, you will need to be completely at ease with your practitioner and the process.

Since there will be dialogue between you and he practitioner when you are in trance, the practitioner must be able to provide follow-up questions when needed. This can only be done if the practitioner is very familiar with the background of the question/issue, and the real-life environment you live in. The more information you can share with the practitioner, the better the chances are for success. If a follow-up question is needed, which is often the case, the practitioner will be at ease with the topic. The intake alone can take up to a couple of hours, or more.

3 - THE HYPNOSIS

After the intake is complete, the most interesting part of the LightStreaming PLR can commence. Cordless microphones will be affixed, to provide an integral recording of the session. Your practitioner will start the induction, and you will slowly slip into a world of peace and serenity. How wonderful!

Your practitioner has an ongoing contact with the Light, that is fully aware of the process. This is KEY. As soon as connection is achieved, the LightStreaming process will easily facilitate and share any/all relevant information through you. You will act as the transmitter, the trance-channeler via your own ego-disconnected voice.

You will be talking during the session, but you will serve only as a transmitter for the Light. The words that come out of your mouth are not yours, but those of the Light, even though you will feel they are your words since they come out of your mouth. The miracle of LightStreaming will then be embodied through you! It is a very powerful and yet, humbling process. Since we have had Spirit guides help us in previous incarnations, it is very likely that one of them may come through during the session. Every session is different, because the questions are different every time. This unique orchestration ensures that the wisdom you receive is perfectly calibrated to your current spiritual alignment, and the specific growth your Soul is seeking.

If you later intend to do multiple sessions, the practitioner should be informed; a segment will be added to the induction where the subconscious mind will be coded with a pair of uniquely connected code words which will shorten, and facilitate your next session's induction.

4 - THE SESSION REVIEW

After having been led "back" to full consciousness, and the Light has receded to where it belongs, the practitioner will review what you went through, and the advice given to the most important questions. You will later receive, if desired, a digital audio recording of your session.

You may feel slightly light-headed, and the practitioner will advise you to ground yourself by eating something once you leave your session. It is not uncommon for you to question whether your experience was a dream or a figment of your imagination. This is perfectly normal, and once you listen to your recording, and put the session information appropriately into perspective in your life, you will realize that you did, in fact, have a phenomenal channeling session with the Light!

It is truly a remarkable process, and one which has the potential to permanently change the way we perceive our life.

CHAPTER HIGHLIGHTS:

- Past Life Regression (PLR) is a **method for accessing previous incarnations** of the Soul in order to uncover unresolved emotional, psychological, or karmic influences that affect the present life.
- Reincarnation is a learning process **governed by the Law of Reciprocity** (karma), where actions aligned with the Light dissolve karmic imprints, while actions opposed to the Light generate karma that must be resolved in future lifetimes.
- The purpose of PLR is not to explore random past lives, but **to identify the specific lifetimes most relevant** to the lessons or challenges that the individual must address in the present incarnation.
- Deep hypnosis allows one to bypass the ego and access Divine guidance to uncover the past-life origins of current fears, illnesses, or conflicts. By identifying these karmic roots, one can **release long-standing burdens,** and realign with one's true life purpose.
- **The PLR process involves several stages**—including question preparation, practitioner intake, hypnotic induction, and post-session review—ensuring that insights received during the trance state are integrated into everyday life.
- Ultimately, **PLR functions as a tool for spiritual recalibration**, helping individuals align their present actions with the guidance of the Light, and progress more efficiently toward the long-term objective of Ascension.

CHAPTER SIXTEEN

LIGHTSTREAMING - CHANNELING

The subtle difference between LS-Past Life Regression and LS-Channeling lies in the direction of the dialogue—specifically, the shifting roles between the one who asks and the one who receives the answers. Physically, however, the setup allows both the channeler and the seeker to comfortably sit together in a shared space.

THE PSYCHIC OR THE CHANNELER

In its purest definition, the roles of the channeler and the psychic remain distinct, separated by the specific mechanics through which metaphysical information is conveyed. However, the practical reality is that they represent two facets of a single spectrum. As an Ascension student, you need to know how they differ.

A *psychic* operates primarily *within* the framework of the ego-mind or the personal energetic field. They source information by tapping into the personality, memories, and vibrational conditioning of others, utilizing their own intuitive "operating system" to discern patterns. Typically remaining in a normal waking state, a psychic employs faculties such as clairvoyance, clairaudience, or clairsentience to act as an active intermediary who interprets and relays messages.

The *channeler* operates *beyond* the confines of the ego, serving as a direct interface or conduit. They access information by connecting to higher consciousness, spirit guides, or the Higher-Self. To facilitate this transmission, they often enter an altered, or hypnagogic trance state (hence the designation "trance-channeler.") Rather than maintaining an active role, the channeler assumes a receptive posture, allowing a higher authority or entity to communicate through them. In this capacity, they act as a practical facilitator—which is why we use the term "practitioner"—stepping aside to permit the Higher-Self or another spiritual intelligence to direct the session.

Consequently, the content and purpose of their messages differ significantly. Because a psychic reads energy, impressions, and timelines by accessing the subconscious, their insights are generally drawn from information already present within the human mind, and the emotional layers of the field. Information may also arise from communication between the psychic's spiritual team, and that of the seeker. The nature of this data is often varied, and occasionally mundane; for example, questions regarding the outcome of a court case or the location of a lost pet are well within a psychic's reach. Conversely, complex inquiries[1]—such as whether one's Soul path is aligned for a 4th-dimensional initiation—are less likely to receive validated answers. Since the future consists of multiple paths dictated by free will, short-term predictions are generally where a psychic's accuracy is most pronounced.

Ascended Masters have ONE purpose: to assist with our Ascension.

Messages delivered through a channeler are fundamentally different, as the channeler functions as a receiver, and translator of non-local intelligence existing outside the human psyche. In this process, as in LS-Channeling, psychic scanning is replaced by *consciousness alignment*, and

[1] Asking a psychic a spiritual question is often an irritant; it exposes a limitation they are not equipped to address, and can place them in an unflattering light of inadequacy.

the *suspension of the ego is a strict requirement*, as the Light does not communicate directly with the egoic mind. Optimally, information is received verbatim—the most powerful form of delivery, as it leaves no room for subjective interpretation. However, if the Light intends to convey a sentient message requiring further explanation, clairvoyance may still be employed as a medium. The source of a channeler's message is typically non-physical intelligence, higher-density consciousness, or universal archetypal wisdom.

While an open Crown Chakra is not a prerequisite for either discipline, should the Light *require* that specific activation, it obviously possesses the capacity to manifest it.

SAFEGUARDING TRANSMISSION INTEGRITY

Channeling, in its broadest sense, can serve many aims, and involve many kinds of beings from the Other Side. Do not assume that contact with Spirit automatically means safe or benevolent guidance. There are two fundamental classes of Spirit beings: ascended and non-ascended. The latter consist of beings that are cloned, and *lack a living Soul connection to the Infinite Creator.* Deprived of this vital link to higher consciousness, they readily drift into a negative orientation. By and large, they do not hold humanity's well-being as a priority. They approach human life from a purely utilitarian standpoint, show no true respect for our dignity, and regard humans as more fit for servitude than sovereignty. Preventing human Ascension is, for them, a central objective. Psychological manipulation is a preferred method; honesty is absent, violations of free will are routine, and they actively seek out weaker Souls who they can easily ensnare. These beings typically originate from non-ascended worlds—planetary systems steeped in extremely low consciousness energy.

Ascended beings, often called Light beings, fall into two distinct categories: secular and sacred. Secular ascended beings assist with ordinary, practical concerns rooted in 3rd-dimensional life. They can be useful at times. For instance, if your goal is financial improvement, and you seek guidance about which of several companies to work for, they may offer support. Lightstreaming Channeling, however, does not operate within the sphere of strictly secular interests.

As described in the chapter "Our Family: The Group of Four," a small, select group devoted to helping humanity in its Ascension process exists among the hundreds of Ascended Masters beyond this world. Within this group is an especially focused and powerful order entrusted with overseeing the current precessional harvest, ensuring that those graduating from the 3rd Dimension are as prepared as possible. These are the sacred branch of Ascended beings. Essential celestial intermediaries—a kind of heavenly Delta Team for spiritual transition—they carry an immense responsibility: to train and develop individuals on the ground who will function as spiritual relays for the awakening population as a whole. The sole purpose of Ascended Hearts, as an organization, is to enact the will of the Infinite Creator: "Your will be done on Earth as it is in Heaven." We hold no personal agenda. Our mandate comes from Light beings who serve the Father *exclusively*—to assist others, wherever possible, in their Ascension.

As Lightworkers, we have entered into an agreement with this leadership to act as a practical extension, coordinating certain aspects of the Light's Ascension preparations here on Earth. This implies the Masters providing us with an embedded energy shield that protects against non-ascended entities. Also, should one attempt to use Lightstreaming Channeling for purposes outside this calling, disappointment is assured. It is a specialized instrument, intended for those who know—without hesitation—that the moment for profound change and transformation is now. Embrace this alignment with unwavering purpose, for we are a bridge through which the higher frequencies of the future anchor into the present. The available guidance is abundant to do the formidable task at hand.

THE SESSION

When you schedule your session, you will receive a sample Channeling questions form. This form is essential to the channeling process, as it will ultimately hold every question you intend to ask. Do not assume you can arrive, and improvise. Coming unprepared, or without the completed form in hand, will make the session ineffective, and require cancellation. Under pressure—especially when a focused performance is expected—one often experience nervousness, mental blanks, and uncertainty. This is precisely why airline pilots rely on written checklists before takeoff. They are not allowed to trust memory or experience alone; they are required to follow a documented pre-flight procedure.

Once the practitioner activates the link to the Other Side, the session moves quickly, requiring one to be fully prepared with written questions. Because the information received can be surprising or unexpected, beginners often miss the chance to ask critical follow-up questions—much like an inexperienced law student in court. While mistakes in channeling aren't as final as those in a courtroom, they are costly and unnecessary. Proper preparation ensures that you capture all necessary clarity in one session, avoiding the need for a new appointment due to missed opportunities.

During LS-Channeling, you ask the questions out loud, not the channeler; the channeler verbalizes the response.

The Channeling questions form already includes several fixed, pre-written questions. These are suggested prompts—questions we know, from experience, must be addressed in nearly every case. If some of them do not feel relevant to you, you may skip them. While personal in nature, they apply to most individuals, which is why the form also requires you to add questions specific to *your* life and circumstances. One question should focus on identifying who in your life belongs to your Soul group. You will learn that there is a precise reason this matters. Be generous with the number of questions you prepare; the LightStreaming practitioner will review them with you beforehand to ensure they are appropriate, and fully relevant.

There is nothing to fear in this process. The Ascended Masters involved are deeply loving. Still, the pace is brisk, and there is little room for reflection in the moment. That is exactly why the written list is indispensable.

CHAPTER HIGHLIGHTS:

- Channeling is the final step of the methodology. Once the ego is quieted through hypnosis and past-life regression, **you can communicate directly with spiritual intelligences,** and the superconscious realm.
- This process allows us to **act as a transmitter** for the Light. It provides **direct guidance** on our Soul's past, your current life, and your potential future paths.
- Through this communication, one can gain clarity on **unresolved karmic patterns**, and one's **life purpose**. It reveals the spiritual lessons needed for the personal evolution, and eventual Ascension.
- Channeling operates by bypassing the ego's interference, allowing information aligned with the Light to emerge through the individual's consciousness **without distortion**.
- The Light never communicates through the ego. Successful **channeling requires inner stillness**, trust, and alignment with higher guidance to receive clear information.
- Ultimately, **channeling is a tool to align** our daily decisions with the Light. This guidance helps us live with greater harmony and peace as we ascend.

CHAPTER SEVENTEEN

VIRTUAL LIGHT TRANCE INDUCTION

VLTI - THE "CHEATING" HELPER

Virtual Light Trance Induction (VLTI) is a twelve-LED stroboscopic light system[1] designed to evoke profound visual and sensory experiences. Its flickering sequences guide the brain into deeper, more harmonious states of consciousness.

Many of us are graced with a built-in facility to easily slip into sleep, meditative or trance states. For some, deep relaxation is elusive—often due to dominant left-brain activity, the mind's analytical and controlling nature. This prevents the mind to open the curtains to a deep trance state, also referred to as a hypnagogic state. It is not a matter of will to enter a hypnagogic trance, rather a technique of slowing down the mind. VLTI helps quiet that impulse by gradually training the brain to let go, to surrender to the flow of natural rhythm. The result is a safe, effortless gateway into expanded, yet entirely natural, altered states of awareness.

---

[1] Manufactured by PandoraStar.

Though not a generic LightStreaming modality per se, VLTI is an effective accessory procedure that will naturally ease communication with the pineal gland. Some say it has been a lifesaver!

VLTI AND SACRED GEOMETRY

VLTI's light array is arranged in sacred geometric symmetry, built upon the Star of David—an archetype uniting matter and Spirit, Earth, and sky. When the eyes are closed, this light reaches the 3rd-Eye, stimulating a cosmic archetype that helps the mind slip gracefully into meditation, relaxation, hypnosis, or spiritual depth.

Scientific observation shows that specific light frequencies can influence neural patterns, harmonize brain activity, and soothe the nervous system. VLTI explores these resonant frequencies, inviting vivid imagery, nonlinear perception, and visionary experiences often described as dreamlike or transcendent.

Over time, the brain *learns this pathway*—making the trance state more accessible, natural, and deeply restorative.

THE SCIENCE BEHIND VLTI

VLTI operates through a principle known as brainwave entrainment—the synchronization of brain activity to external rhythmic stimuli. When the brain's natural electromagnetic patterns align with the pulse of light, it creates a resonance that promotes balance, clarity, and creative insight.

Neural oscillations—rhythmic electro-chemical waves within the brain—adjust in frequency to match external stimuli such as light, sound, or vibration. This phenomenon has been extensively documented in peer-reviewed research across neuroscience and consciousness studies.

VLTI merges this scientific foundation with sacred geometry, and the metaphysics of Light—creating a bridge between measurable brainwave dynamics and the boundless terrain of inner experience.

BENEFITS OF VLTI

Our Visual Light Trance Induction Technology is designed to gradually awaken, and harmonize the mind through light frequency entrainment. It supports:

- **Deep relaxation**
- **Enhanced well-being**
- **Cognitive clarity**
- **Heightened creativity**
- **Expanded consciousness**
- **Reduced stress and anxiety**
- **Cognitive enhancement**

THE SESSION: THE ART OF RELAXATION

Lie back beneath the PandoraStar light with your eyes closed, and simply let the light guide us. The system emits rhythmic stroboscopic pulses, precisely tuned to resonate with natural brain-wave frequencies. As the mind synchronizes with these patterns, our awareness begins to drift into deeper states of calm and presence.

Each session lasts 20–30 minutes and feels like an inward journey, a lucid blend of peace, imagery, and timeless stillness. Many describe it as both deeply restorative and quietly transformative—a renewal for the mind, body, and spirit.

SAFETY AND CONTRAINDICATIONS

Because VLTI employs high-intensity stroboscopic stimuli, it is incompatible with some physiological and psychological conditions. The technology is contraindicated for individuals with a history of seizure disorders or acute light sensitivity. To ensure safety, please review the following contraindications before use:

Neurological & Sensory Health

Photosensitive Epilepsy: As stroboscopic light can act as a primary trigger for seizures, any history of epilepsy or seizure activity strictly precludes the use of this device.

Severe Migraines: The rhythmic flickering may precipitate acute migraine episodes or sensory auras.

Ocular Health: Those recovering from recent eye surgery (e.g., LASIK, cataract procedures) or those managing retinal pathologies should avoid exposure to protect the integrity of the ocular tissues.

Cardiovascular & Systemic Considerations

Implanted Medical Devices: To prevent potential electromagnetic interference, VLTI should not be used by individuals with cardiac pacemakers or Implantable Cardioverter-Defibrillators (ICDs).

Pregnancy: In the absence of definitive clinical research regarding the impact of intense light on fetal development or maternal hormonal shifts, use is discouraged during pregnancy.

Photosensitizing Medications: Use is contraindicated if one is taking medications that increase light sensitivity, such as certain antibiotics, isotretinoin (Accutane), or St. John's Wort.

Psychological Wellness

Psychotic Disorders: The induction of altered states of consciousness is incompatible with diagnoses of psychosis or schizophrenia.

Anxiety & Panic Disorders: The profound depth of the trance experience may induce acute distress or panic in susceptible individuals.

Pediatric Use: Due to the heightened sensitivity of the developing nervous system, VLTI is not suitable for infants or children.

Note: VLTI is exclusively intended for recreational and research purposes. It is not a medical instrument, and must not be used as a substitute for professional clinical diagnosis or psychiatric care. VLTI is not a therapy.

CHAPTER HIGHLIGHTS:

- Stroboscopic Entrainment: VLTI uses rhythmic light patterns **to synchronize brain activity**, guiding the mind into deep relaxation and altered states of consciousness.
- Overcoming Analytical Barriers: The technology is **specifically designed to help "left-brain" or highly analytical thinkers** quiet mental chatter, and access the hypnagogic trance state.
- Sacred Geometry: The light array is arranged in a Star of David pattern, using **sacred geometry to stimulate the 3rd-Eye** region, and symbolize the union of spirit and matter.
- Supportive Modality: While not a core LightStreaming technique, VLTI serves as a powerful **tool to enhance meditation, hypnosis, and visionary spiritual exploration**.
- Session Experience: During a 20–30 minute session, the brain's synchronization with the light often produces vivid imagery, restorative calm, and expanded awareness.
- **Safety Precautions: Due to the high-intensity light stimulation, VLTI is not suitable for everyone**, particularly those with seizure disorders, migraines, medical implants, or pregnancy.

CHAPTER EIGHTEEN

ASTROLOGY - THE ASCENSION SAGE

This Guide to Ascension would be incomplete if we did not, at least casually, also explore the topic of astrology. My (Marc's) interest in the subject started at the age of 19. Living in Norway at the time, a country of 4 million people, meant that there were no astrology teachers, no courses, and no internet. Ephemerides[1] were journaled by hand into the chart, and textbooks would be shipped out, literally, for a two-month journey from London. My impatient mind regularly suffered. When my head was not buried in Gregorian chant manuscripts, I was surrounded by books about the stars. I instinctively knew, and acknowledged the validity of the discipline, because *I could correlate what I saw in my chart with what I saw in my own being.* Even though it was early in my life cycle, several clear behavioral characteristics would exactly match the coordinates of my chart.

At the same time, my famous liturgy teacher, Ludvig Nielsen, would

---

1 A data table that provides the daily calculated positions of celestial bodies in the sky.

tell me that it was all a lie, sorcery, and an abomination. The newspapers, now as then, have always done a good job in bastardizing astrology by turning it into entertainment, and a commercial hoax. For instance, how could one tell 600 million people born in Virgo that they would meet the love of their life in the coming week, and not lie about it?

I carried on, with what I knew in my heart, that astrology was real. One of my biggest question marks, though, was how, *exactly*, did it work? In the case of the Moon, one could sustain an argument that gave credence to the idea of some electromagnetic radiance, or light radiance. But, how about influence coming from remote bodies like Uranus or Neptune? I did not have an answer to that, nor did anybody I knew have an answer to that; and, nor did anybody who were acquaintances of *theirs* have an answer to that.

Millionaires don't use astrology; billionaires do.

- J. P. Morgan

There exists an influence, "I just had to trust that," I was told. I later discovered from the Masters, through LightStreaming, the hidden truth behind the mechanism that activates astral influences, and its validation. To this date, I have only met a couple of individuals who have this knowledge, which I will share with you shortly.

Sumerian culture, is one of the earliest known civilizations, located in the historical region of southern Mesopotamia (now south-central Iraq). Their people were tent living farmers, living in reed huts in marshlands that were regularly inundated, and were therefore constantly on the move, following herds of sheep and goats.

Suddenly, almost overnight, they transformed into one of the most brilliant civilizations in that part of the world, with sophisticated canals, mind-blowing architecture and infra-structure, and inventions that were nothing short of marvels at that time: at a pace never seen before, they became masters of arithmetic, geometry, invented the luni-solar calendar, cuneiform glyph-writing[2], bitumen waterproofing, developed to become

[2] Sumerian is a language isolate, unrelated to any known language family on Earth.

advanced teachers of cosmology[3], and much more. Where did this newfound knowledge come from? They quantum-lept from bronze-age sheep farmers to cutting-edge cosmologists in just a few short years!

Historical facts[4] point to the Sumerians having been visited by an extraterrestrial race, the Anunnaki. They knew the ways of the heavens, and quickly taught the Sumerians astrology, around 4000-5100 years ago. Since then, a systematic observing of planetary influences, detailed recording of happenings relating to interplanetary aspects, and cataloging of empirical observations linked to anything from the Moon's phases to precessions were recorded. The Anunnaki had a very specific method, which has later become known as Western Astrology.

Historical facts point to the Sumerians having been visited by an extraterrestrial race called Anunnaki.

At approximately the same time, the peoples of the Indian subcontinent were visited by *another* group of extraterrestrial visitors, the Andromedans. Just about everything relating to ancient Indian culture has *one* point of origin, the 6th Density level Andromedans. The Sanskrit language and alphabet are of direct Andromedan provenance. The Andromedans, with a home base far away from the Anunnaki, taught the Indians astrology as well. Their method and process were uniquely Andromedan. For example, they came down with sophisticated, and detailed knowledge about the influences of the various sub-segments of the Moon's phases[5], and a keen understanding of the influence of Fixed Stars[6]. Whence would the Indians have received inside information on the fixed Stars?

There are many other differences between the two systems, but what unites them is that there is only *one* cosmos, *one* set of stars, and *one* set of

---

3 For example, their artwork depicts the location and cluster size of the Pleiades!

4 Kramer, Samuel Noah (1963), The Sumerians: Their History, Culture, and Character, Chicago: University of Chicago Press, ISBN 0-226-45238-7

5 It uses the 27 lunar constellations called Nakshatras.

6 Known as Sidereal or Vedic Astrology.

planets. The result from both systems is the same, but each method is formulated differently. One is not better than the other; they each have their strengths and weaknesses; they just approach the same phenomenon from two different angles. To sum it up, astrology has been conveyed to us by supremely advanced 5th and 6th Density civilizations from far outside our Solar System, and, its validity has been verified through multiple layers of multi-dimensional intelligences, and through empirical validation.

HOW ASTRAL BODIES INFLUENCE US

During the establishment of the Soul contract, the main facets to dominate the upcoming life are developed in coordination with the reincarnating Soul. In addition to that, an extremely detailed scenario of possibilities, alternate paths, life circumstances, and eventualities are mapped by the Masters, paying careful attention to upcoming celestial bodies' positioning at the time of birth.

A physician without a knowledge of astrology has no right to call himself a physician.

- Hippocrates

The Light does not consider birth starting at conception, even if there is an embryonic development that fully mirrors the development of the human body. The Soul contract is still being worked on while the fetus is in the mother's womb. The time of birth is clocked when the child is born, and takes their first birth. This is the reason, in addition to biological factors, why a birth can be delayed or moved up within the nine-month traditional gestation period. The spiritual quantum technology that goes into the final birth moment of a baby is astounding. There is nobody more aware of the influence of proper timing than our spiritual masters. They are meticulous, and watch over the timing aspect with hawkish precision.

The Light then sends a cosmic imprint of the stellar map of our universe to the newborn Soul, at the exact time of birth. This dynamic imprint is, from that moment on, energetically linked to, and mirrors exactly the movement of the heavenly bodies via the universal consciousness.

This seeding of imprinted and coded consciousness is the secret behind Astrology. Coded consciousness, Soul guiding, functions as a spiritual lighthouse for the Soul. So if, for example, Venus and Mercury are in a harmonious relationship, let us say in a trine angle of 120°, then that harmonious relationship is simultaneously mirrored in the energetic imprint that the Soul received. Or, if Mars were to move into a difficult angular relationship (aka as aspect) to the original Mars location in the imprint of the Soul, the individual would be affected by that. This does not infringe on free will, since we formally agreed to these conditions in our life-between-lives[7] Soul contract.

Creation imprints a celestial "QR-code" on the Soul at birth.

IS ASTROLOGY FATALISTIC?

An astrological chart works much like a weather map. If the forecast calls for rain, we bring an umbrella, and stay dry. In the same way, if a chart suggests a tendency toward an ankle fracture, the sensible response is not to step onto an ice rink. If we remain on a sofa watching a film instead, the likelihood of breaking an ankle is minimal. A horoscope is an energetic blueprint. It describes potentials, not fixed outcomes. It reveals which *energies* are active in our field at a given time. What ultimately happens depends on how we meet, and manage that energetic climate.

Each astrological vector is charged, or ionized. Every axis (vector)—Leo–Aquarius, Scorpio–Taurus, and so on—carries both a positive and a negative polarity. Leo, for example, contains both elevated and distorted expressions. An individual may choose either, and no force compels the choice. Free will always remains intact. Claims that astrology is fatalistic arise from a shallow understanding of the subject. Those who explore its

[7] A new Soul contract is crafted after each incarnation, during the period between lives. See the next chapter re. life-between-lives..

philosophical depth understand that **astrology describes conditions, not destiny**.

HOW ASTROLOGY CAN HELP OUR ASCENSION

Every astrological chart reveals what we bring into this incarnation from the one before it. It shows which life lessons remain unfinished, and which have already been integrated. It functions as a precise guidance system, exposing our strengths and vulnerabilities, clarifying what truly supports our growth, and what distracts or diminishes it.

Each incarnation arrives on Earth carrying with it what is a lesson unlearned from previous lives, which we shall call a *master obstacle*. This is the central burden of a lifetime—the most demanding challenge we agreed to face. It follows us in many disguises, reappearing at different stages, and in different forms throughout life. Before incarnating, we consented to make this obstacle the primary test of the journey. Identifying it can lift an enormous weight, because our growth is ultimately assessed by how we meet this challenge. Most people are unaware that such a requirement exists, let alone how to consciously address it. An astrological chart makes it visible. When the master obstacle is recognized, it often triggers a powerful and liberating "Aha!" moment.

> *An astrological chart can identify chakra-stored karma with pinpoint accuracy.*

This sudden clarity acts as a spiritual compass, transforming what once felt like a repetitive burden into a structured path toward Soul mastery. Once the veil is lifted, you transition from a passive subject of your circumstances, to a conscious designer of your own evolution.

With this in mind, recall the idea introduced in the chapter on LBL: we pre-select the general structure of our temperament and life circumstances. We choose, for example, who in our Soul group will play the part of the difficult parent, who will appear as the nurturing teacher, or who will take the role of the betraying partner that leads to divorce. These are not random events but *agreed-upon roles* within a carefully orchestrated scenario, established during the crafting of the Soul contract. Therefore, playing the victim card is most often not well-received by the Masters. Taking one hundred percent responsibility for our behavior, is.

A birth chart reveals the flip side of this design of pre-selecting obstacles: the precise pathways toward resolution. It outlines the *solutions* to the very challenges we placed in our own obstacle course, while also highlighting where joy, fulfillment, and ease are most likely to be found. In this way, astrology becomes an invaluable tool in the Ascension graduation. A horoscope *clearly* indicates which chakras carry karmic density or blockages, and which are relatively free of burden. It is as though the astrological system was devised to *help* us understand ourselves deeply, so we might arrange our lives with less unnecessary struggle. A chart practically shouts guidance, urging us to release problems that need not persist. Used wisely, a horoscope can become a lifelong ally.

> *The Soul of a newly born baby is marked for life by the pattern of the stars at the moment it comes into the world...*
>
> *-Johannes Kepler*

Astrology is multi-functional, and applicable across many fields—medical, financial, vocational, investigative, and more. Yet *Spiritual Astrology*, in particular, is the specialization that truly serves our forward movement in Ascension. A skilled astrologer is not merely technically competent, but equipped and guided to receiving guidance from the Akash through the Higher-Self.

Self-knowledge is among the most valuable capacities we can develop on the path to higher dimensions. In that journey, astrology can become an indispensable companion.

CHAPTER HIGHLIGHTS:

- Astrology is presented as a **symbolic language** of cosmic influence, reflecting how planetary positions at the moment of birth **imprint spiritual energetic patterns into the Soul**, that shape personality, tendencies, and life circumstances.
- Rather than determining fate, **astrology functions as a diagnostic framework** for understanding karmic patterns, life cycles, and the evolutionary direction of the Soul.
- The **natal chart acts as a cosmic blueprint**, mapping the interplay between planetary energies and human consciousness, and revealing both strengths and challenges that arise during one's lifetime.
- **Planetary transits and cycles influence the unfolding of life** events by activating specific themes within the natal chart, helping explain periods of growth, conflict, opportunity, or transformation.
- Within the Ascension framework, astrology can serve as a tool for timing and awareness, helping individuals **align personal decisions** and spiritual work with broader cosmic rhythms.
- Factually, astrology is **not a deterministic system** but a guide for conscious participation in one's evolutionary journey, allowing individuals to better understand the relationship between cosmic forces and spiritual development.

CHAPTER NINETEEN

LIGHTSTREAMING - LIFE-BETWEEN-LIVES: THE SOUL CONTRACT

The journey of rising **necessitates a method**, a rhythm of introspection that asks for the regular assessment of the unfolding endeavor. Within this transcendent interval, the life-between-lives, a moment of deep significance unfurls, named *the review*. The aim of this contemplation is threefold:

(1) To revisit, with clear-eyed wisdom, how we engaged with the prior life's experiences in relation to its original intention, i.e. Soul contract; and

(2) to inscribe a new Soul contract for the ensuing existence—a practical map charting the inner work to be embraced, and its opportune timeline.

(3) Once this task is complete, we enter a state of readying for that next destined incarnation, often through a blend of deep study, and relaxing communion with the beloved companions of our Soul group. If we have the skills, we may even be called upon to assist the Masters as a teaching assistant.

REJECTING REINCARNATION

The contemplation of the Soul's enduring journey finds little kinship within the structures of many established creeds. Where the spirit of the East embraces the timeless turning of the wheel, the West remains more tethered to a singular lifespan. Across the traditions of Judaism, Islam, and Christianity, a deep resistance persists. This reluctance, when viewed with unbiased eyes, appears rooted in a desire to preserve the iron-clad powerhold that is so carefully maintained by the various religious authorities. Consider the enormous, heavy, fear-laden yoke that is placed upon the shoulders of the seeker when they are taught that earthly life is a one-time event, and that any divergence from the doctrines of the church will lead to *eternal* separation. Moreover, they are told there is no possibility, no graceful opportunity, to amend or correct a misstep. We are given one solitary breath, *one* single attempt, they solemnly declare, and that is the final seal.

Denying reincarnation facilitates upholding the dogma of the existence of hell.

There was, however, one glaring exception: an early, calculated strategy, such as that employed by the Roman Catholic Church, revealed that the only permissible path to one's ultimate destination, the celestial Heaven, was through the purchase of absolutions. It was promised that they would erase the stain of sin. If one possessed no material wealth, or one was tragically doomed, then the naming of trespasses became a cruel, sharp weapon used to maintain people in a state of crippling spiritual, and financial poverty. Had the powerful Roman institution opened its heart to the truth of the Soul's return, it would have, in effect, rendered itself destitute, having stripped itself of the substantial revenues flowing from those it so grievously mistreated. The Church leveraged the threat of eternal damnation as a more potent tool for resource extraction than the promise of a restorative afterlife intended to balance one's karma.

Following the act of the Reformation, the Lutherans withdrew from this shameful practice, yet they carefully preserved the foundational belief in "one Soul, one life." The subtle but potent threat of "one Soul, one life" served as a mechanism of control, a dark shadow intended to subjugate the faithful through the energies of fear and absolute submission. Our lives were never intended to be lived as if they were a prison sentence. Instead, the liberating gift of free will is the enduring gold standard of the Divine.

The other formidable obstacle that has hindered this boundless truth is the realm of science. "Modern" science, in all its celebrated magnificence, carries within it countless limitations, the most significant of which is likely its attempt to grapple with cosmic concepts that lie far beyond the scope of its own capabilities. To implore science to furnish proof of the Soul's passage would be as fruitless as asking a small mouse to calibrate the mighty Hubble telescope.

The steps essential to the scientific method, as given us by Sir Francis Bacon, necessitate both clear observation, and undeniable confirmation. This axiom holds true across all branches of natural physics. The most authentic way to validate the reality of reincarnation is, therefore, to simply follow this very same, time-honored process—to observe and to confirm. How can a Soul be guided back to a specific, distant place from a previous life cycle (through Past Life Regression), and then describe it with utter precision and exquisite detail, having never consciously set foot there in this present incarnation? And, why is it that all the greatest, most fully emancipated spiritual leaders (Yeshua, Buddha, Bahaullah, Krishna, Yogananda, and countless others) wholeheartedly confirm the enduring validity of the Soul's continual return?

THE SOUL CONTRACT: CORE COMPONENTS

A Soul contract is a finalized agreement between the Higher-Self, the Soul and those—Ascended Masters and other senior Spirit Masters—in charge of overseeing the work progress in our upcoming incarnation. This, in order to remove karma from the chakras, and thus managing and facilitating/speeding up our Ascension. An extraordinary amount of work, complexity, and preparation goes into finalizing the Soul contract – the reason being the highly special times we are in, relative to zodiac precession, and transitioning densities.

If the Awakening were a symphony, its melody would be the Soul, the eternal radiance guiding our vast, universal passage. The conductor of this unfolding progress would be called Embodiment. When we speak of this collective Great Shift, it is the Soul's rise toward wholeness that draws our attention. The sheer awe-inspiring way the dense, physical form slowly reweaves itself back into its native, lucent essence is a profound spectacle to witness. This process, we name "the return to the dissolution of perceived separateness." At the very heart of a Soul contract lies the intricate art of pre-incarnation foresight. Here are the root themes that are deliberated in the crafting of that contract:

• **Choosing the Essential Threads of Existence**, the key relationships and deep associations, the delicate selection of kindred spirits, team guides, and even needed challengers. This may sound peculiar, but within the terms of our Soul's vow, we openly commune over the crucial, interactive roles other Souls shall play upon our path in the coming manifestation.

Akin to weaving our own terrain of purposeful challenges, we may have chosen our familial roots with the understanding they would prompt growth through adversarial resistance or loving constraint for our development. Family conflicts do not suddenly surface; we chose for them to occur so the Light can examine to which degree we will engage the Soul, or the ego to resolve the conflict! Quite amazing, it is.

A destined romantic companion may grace our life, perhaps arriving in our later years, purely to sustain our inner unfolding. A named adversary from a previous cycle would be appointed to catalyze a spiritual metamorphosis, or we may encounter our twin-flame, perhaps as a cousin this time, who aids us in shattering ancient constraints, and steps with us onto a path of deeper awareness. Alternatively, we might consent to meet a beloved who will insist on a painful severing from our familiar kin. The greater Light may simply wish to observe if, within a chosen scene, we will honor the Soul agreement we once co-created.

• **Embracing the Wisdom-Lessons**, often centering upon the deep knowing of self-worth, the delicate cultivation of compassion, the mastery of loving, clear boundaries, and the pure experience of unconditional embrace. They are outlined in "The Seven Rays of Wisdom" below.

- **Learning that Soul Covenants are not rigid fate**, and that they are not unyielding, but rather boundless spheres for the experience of free will. Conceive of planning an incarnation is like charting a spiritual journey via a GPS navigation system: we set the trajectory, and the agreed-upon points of awakening. Yet, we are infinitely free to take meandering paths, swift detours, or even to decline the journey altogether. Regardless of our choice, our faithful guides and otherworldly elders will always be poised to reveal a measured, alternative path that aligns with our burgeoning inner confidence, and deep Soul's longing.

Understand that by consciously entering a Soul realm remembrance, we will uncover the breathtaking expanse of probable premises, and logistical beauty that underpins the sacred orchestration of a single incarnation—it is truly jaw-dropping.

Just as there are base disciplines taught through most grades in public schools (mathematics, English, history, science), there are core topics, seven of them[2], that are offered, and repeated at every single incarnation. They are so impactful that we shall examine them in greater detail now.

THE SEVEN RAYS OF WISDOM

We have saved the most complex, but must impactful, teaching mechanism part of the Ascension work for the end. It is a crowning element that simultaneously displays unimaginable intelligence, thoughtfulness, complexity, and thoroughness. This pedagogic cogwheel of learning leaves no doubt about the Creator's intent: to implement a system of purification that would be so fool proof as to leave *no possibility* for someone to slip through, and be able to transform from flesh back to

[2] Referred to as "The Seven Rays."

spirit without commensurate qualifications and preparation.

Perfecting the human being sufficiently to graduate into the higher realms of consciousness is an undertaking that plays out on multiple levels. We have dealt with many of them already. Now, let us open the bag of one of the most comprehensive teaching systems ever designed, the Seven Rays of Wisdom or, the seven lessons to attain Ascension. Let us disassemble the moving parts of this phenomenal teaching tool.

THE BODIES

One of the multiple layers through which the human Body is assessed by our guides, is through that of the *Bodies*. The Light has carefully compartmentalized us into five different Bodies:

The Soul, the personality, the physical, emotional, and the mental, interplay and inter-communicate with each other. Of the group, the Soul acts as a "supervising manager."

Whenever the ego can destabilize through one of its ploys, let us take through anger as an example, it would try it on the emotional body one day, and on the physical body the next day, or on both simultaneously. We would manifest that anger differently in each scenario. The Light knows that our perception is flawed, and does not expect us to see clearly on the issue (if we did, we would not have gotten angry in the first place).

The Light can easily pinpoint which body has been afflicted, and monitors the development. So, to safeguard the entire system, it painstakingly tests and builds up the resistance to anger in each of the bodies.

This comprehensive fortification ensures that even when one layer of the self is momentarily compromised, the integrity of the whole remains resilient and supported by Divine oversight. By strengthening these diverse facets of our being, the Light transforms our vulnerabilities into pillars of spiritual endurance.

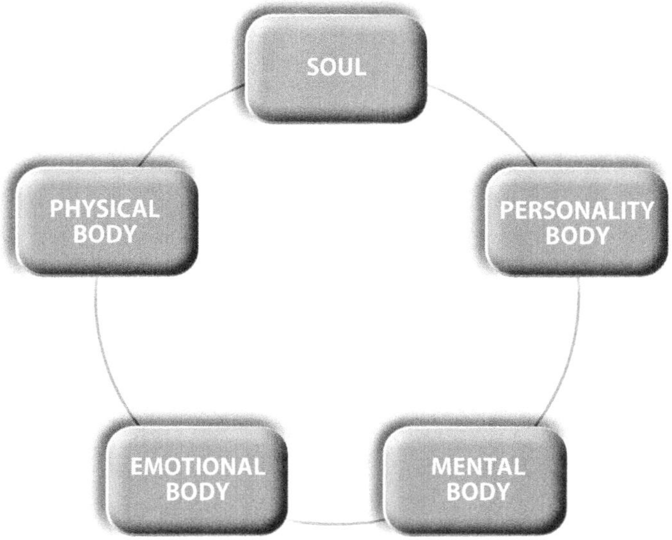

THE RAYS AND THEIR APPLICATIONS

The rays were engineered as fundamental support fields, designed to underpin the evolutionary curriculum required of Souls within the 3rd Density. They represent the primary "course of study" for this stage of our development—a path we embraced with the radiant enthusiasm of those newly graduated from 2nd Density! Together with our guides and teachers, we select five—one for each body—out of the seven rays in each life-between-life experience; this is the required course load. The combination of rays selected is different in each lifetime. The specific rays we agree to focus on in the next incarnation have been chosen after reviewing how we did interact with the selected rays for the past incarnation. Keep in mind that the members and non-members of our Soul group to be active in one life, may have a totally different role in the next life, adding another variable. Here are the seven rays[4], along with a synthesized and abbreviated list of key-words that define them:

1. WILL & POWER: Personal power vs. God's power, God's will over

[4] Sourced from the writings of Annie Bessant, Summit Lighthouse (Ascended Master, Mark Prophet), and LightStreaming (Ananda).

personal will, focus, balance, purpose, synthesis, courage, direction, the masculine energy of the Universe, the Divinity of the God energy. The force of destruction of the old to make way for the new. Ultimately, this ray demands the total alignment of individual intent with divine purpose, channeling the courage to shatter outdated structures so that absolute truth may prevail.

2. **LOVE & WISDOM:** Unconditional love, joy, lightness of being, patience, perception, illumination, understanding, attraction, unity, compassion, empathy, sensitivity, creativity, faith, and trust. It serves as the cohesive force, awakening the soul to radiant understanding, boundless compassion, and the deep realization that all life is fundamentally unified.

3. **ACTIVE INTELLIGENCE:** The power of abstract thought, mental versatility and visualization of concepts, adaptability, and the ability to plan and create strategies, economic structure. This ray embodies the supreme capacity to weave abstract vision into tactical reality, utilizing adaptive intellect to architect the very frameworks of human civilization.

4. **HARMONY THROUGH CONFLICT:** How to handle conflict with graciousness and consideration, reconciliation, human struggle, inner harmony, harmony with self and others, the nexus for change, beauty and artistic expression. Acting as the great crucible of transformation, it refines the turbulence of human struggle into, inner peace, and reconciliation. This ray functions as a battlefield of consciousness, weaponizing the friction of human struggle to smash opposing forces together until they are forced to yield a higher, unbreakable harmony, and artistic truth.

5. **CONCRETE KNOWLEDGE AND SCIENCE:** The skill to analyze, the scientific process, specific detail, scientific perception, ability to discard fact from fiction. Broad knowledge base. It is the piercing lens of absolute clarity, employing rigorous analysis, and empirical truth to dismantle illusion, and illuminate the immutable laws of reality.

6. **DEVOTION & IDEALISM:** Worship, trust, Single-pointed focus and devotion to a chosen goal, loyalty, the feminine energy of the universe, ultimately to live in devotion to our own Higher-Self and Christ consciousness, and the Higher-Self and Christ consciousness of others, inner strength. Fueled by unwavering loyalty, this ray ignites a fierce,

single-pointed devotion that elevates the human spirit to honor the divine spark within both ourselves and humanity.

7. **CEREMONIAL ORDER AND MAGIC:** Organization, manifestation, rhythm, structure, change, transformation and transmutation, magic, the inner change, and transformation versus external change. This ray is all about practical magic—transmuting our inner spiritual shifts into powerful, tangible transformation on the outside.

MEET THE FACULTY!

True spiritual education is a continuous process that far transcends the limitations of our waking reality. While we often view teaching as an activity confined to the conscious plane, profound guidance and initiation occur simultaneously while the physical body rests, unfolding through the vehicle of astral projection. During these hours of slumber, seekers are drawn to higher dimensional spheres to participate in a meticulously organized "night classes" curriculum. This vast, nocturnal school of spiritual transformation is directly overseen, and managed by the enlightened consciousness of Buddha, ensuring that even in darkness, the Soul's awakening remains perfectly guided.

Every subject (ray) taught has a "superintendent," called a "Chohan." It is the Chohan, by default an Ascended Master, who admits qualified "teachers" to his class or his rays, based on their specialization and spirit interest. Not only Ascended Masters are admitted as teachers; Elohim[5] and Cosmic Masters[6] can also teach. Even though teachers are traditionally "boxed" into their dominant area of specialization, their Ray of specialty, they often have several additional teaching skills that can be applied in other rays. Just like in high school: a mathematics teacher could also easily

[5] A primary, high-ranking creator being, ranked a step above the Ascended Masters and even the Archangels, in the hierarchy of Creation. Elohim is a plural form.

[6] Beings who have achieved Ascension—similar to an Ascended Master—but whose evolution, and origin, is often on a cosmic scale. They can be an Ascended Master from Earth who has progressed to a cosmic level of service, or a high-level spiritual being whose origin is extraterrestrial.

teach history classes if that is their forte; maybe they studied mathematics as a major, and history as a minor, or a double major in mathematics and history.

The immense evolutionary distance between humanity and the Cosmic Masters or Elohim underscores the staggering cosmic scale and gravity of Earth's current transition. Because these vast, highly elevated densities are actively directing the process, it becomes clear that humankind's ascension is a synchronized event of profound universal significance rather than a minor planetary shift. This rigorous cosmic hierarchy ensures total alignment, with even the familiar Ascended Masters operating under the precise supervision and wisdom of these higher primordial intelligences to secure the divine blueprint.

A faculty of such deep and varied experience ensures that the Seven Rays of Wisdom are not taught as rigid, isolated theories, but as an integrated web of spiritual application. By drawing on teachers who possess both a dominant specialty, and secondary masteries, the curriculum bridges the gap between esoteric principles, and practical fields like the ones mentioned in the previous two pages.

There is all the necessary flexibility built into in the logistics of teacher assignments. The purpose for having such an elastic model is to be able to pair the most suitable teacher/student duo. Let us look at a sample of a minimized roster of the "faculty:"

1st Ray Teachers:

Archangel:	Michael
Elohim:	Hercules & Amazonia
Ascended Masters:	**El Morya [Chohan]**, Melchizedek, Manu, Moshe, John The Baptist, Chananda
Cosmic Masters:	Metatron, Osiris, Sitatapatra, Vishnu, Mahakala

2ND RAY TEACHERS:

Archangel:	Jophiel & Archeia Christine
Elohim:	Apollo & Lumina
Ascended Masters:	**Lord Lanto [Chohan]**, Yeshua, Kuthumi, Lao Tze, Djwhal Khul
Cosmic Masters:	Amaterasu, Krishna, Helios, Manjushri, Ares

3RD RAY TEACHERS:

Archangel:	Chamuel
Elohim:	Heros & Amora
Ascended Masters:	**Paul The Venitian [Chohan]**, Dom Ignacio, Quan Yin, Mother Mary, Mary Magdalene
Cosmic Masters:	Lakshmi

4TH RAY TEACHERS:

Archangel:	Gabriel
Elohim:	Purity
Ascended Masters:	**Serapis Bey [Chohan]**, Amen Bey
Cosmic Masters:	Inanna

5TH RAY TEACHERS:

Archangel:	Raphael
Elohim:	Cyclopea & Virginia
Ascended Masters:	**Hilarion [Chohan]**, Ptah, St. Athony of Padua, Cha Ara.
Cosmic Masters:	Ganesh, Amaryllis, Susan'oo

6TH RAY TEACHERS:

Archangel:	Uriel & Archeia Aurora
Elohim:	Peace & Aloha
Ascended Masters:	**Lady Master Nada [Chohan]**, Pallas, Athena, Isi, Anubis, Eros, Quetzalcoatl, Portia
Cosmic Masters:	Hathor

7TH RAY TEACHERS:

Archangel:	Archeia Amethyst
Elohim:	Arcturus & Victoria
Ascended Masters:	**St. Germain [Chohan**]
Cosmic Masters:	Ra-Mun, Omri-Tas

HOW THE SYSTEM WORKS

Let us imagine a scenario where our Soul contract includes a focus on the 4th Ray—Harmony Through Conflict—as one of five required rays. Under this contract, all five of our subtle bodies are tested by this specific ray. At the next Life Between Lives (LBL) review, we receive passing grades on four of those bodies: the Soul, the personality, the physical, and the mental. However, we fail the emotional body segment. This failure occurs because we entered a marriage defined by constant, nagging arguments; every time conflict arose, we reacted by crying profusely—unable to bear the friction, and thus failing to find the harmony within the conflict.

During the next LBL review, this dilemma is discussed, and we are advised to re-take that ray, this time with a different partner from our Soul group, and a different Master teacher. In this next life, we retake the 4th Ray, and pass the emotional part with flying colors, but the new partner we chose is not the optimal match (purposely selected by the Light to see how we will navigate in conflict), and we now occasionally react with violence to their behavior! With that, we fail the 4th Ray training on the physical body. It is of no consequence that we had passed it before: *we must pass the ray for all the bodies in the same life-cycle* [7]. There is no rain-check for partial accomplishments in earlier lives. With five bodies, and seven rays with dozens of attributes within them, and dozens of teachers, the combinations are endless.

Remember that each incarnation deals us a new constellation of variables: a different body, a different psyche, a different horoscope, and a landscape of shifting challenges. The ground beneath us is never static. What we once believed fully mastered must now be integrated within unfamiliar conditions, where past understanding becomes a seed tested by

---

[7] We concern ourselves, in this guide, with Ascension through 5th dimension. Final Ascension normally happens at the end of the 6th Dimension. The teachings of the 7 rays are so complete that they carry us until we enter 5th Dimension—Salvation. Once that is achieved, the 7 Rays remain available, not as required curriculum, but as optional support.

new climates, new laws, and new dimensions of experience.

The seven rays—those archetypal streams or learning paths—are explored through many teachers across many incarnations. In one lifetime, we might walk the 2nd Ray of Love and Wisdom under the guidance of the Buddha; in another turn of the wheel, the same recurring curriculum may unfold through the presence of St. Germain or Mother Mary. The hidden intention behind these teachings is to show us how to inhabit each of the seven modes of consciousness without generating new layers of karmic residue.

One may wonder, "How could one possibly release karma by studying the Ray of Knowledge and Science?" Consider, for instance, a life spent as a visionary scientist who designs a technology that inadvertently harms Earth's ecosystems. Such an adverse act, though motivated by curiosity or progress, can still echo through the planetary field. In a future embodiment, one might be drawn once again to the 5th Ray of Knowledge, tempered by the 2nd ray, which cultivates reverence and devotion to the living Earth.

OUR PERSONAL ASCENSION TEAM

It is *expected* that we will have challenges with the seven rays in our incarnations. However, there is a very bright light on the horizon. During the finalization of the Soul contract we are given a dedicated team of ray teachers whose task it is to accompany us, individually, through the upcoming incarnation. For thousands and thousands of years we were not even aware that the Ray-system was playing behind the scenes.

Some of the most critical assistance we can get to handle the issue of the seven rays is to know *who is on our Ascension team, and what Ray each teacher is assigned to*. This would allow us, through Lightstreaming Channeling, to seek counsel with the given entity on how to navigate a given ray issue that we are having in this life.

The teacher will actually pinpoint where we are "going wrong," and how to correct the issue. The purpose for seeking this counsel is to clear as many ray obstacles as feasible, so we can ascend as fast as possible. Now, in place of a daunting, proctored, closed-book examination, the experience has evolved into a collaborative open-book assessment designed for mastery rather than exclusion. That makes a world of difference.

So, anybody who is serious about their Ascension process would be advised to ascertain who is on their personal Ascension team as soon as possible, and in what capacity. The Other Side is waiting for us to contact them so they can give us the answers to the test! Isn't that almost incredible? Having this tool at our disposal is yet another example of why Lightstreaming Channeling is one of the most superior tools available to facilitate Ascension.

WHAT IS IN YOUR SOUL CONTRACT?

It took several decades of living before I (Marc) even remotely heard of the idea of a Soul contract. After that, the concept drifted on the periphery of my awareness, yet never fully entered consciousness. It required several more decades before I realized that I could actually decipher, interpret, and unlock what lay within it. For years, I carried a burning, persistent curiosity, and when I finally uncovered its central theme for this lifetime, the revelation felt like a seminal moment—an internal tectonic shift. I gazed back across the timeline of my life, tracing each milestone, and found confirmation that the framework of *every significant chapter* aligned with that core theme. Even the greatest disappointments, the moments where life fractured and expectations dissolved, were mysteriously synchronized with the deeper blueprint of the Soul contract.

My illusion was complete in believing that once I had identified the purpose of my Soul contract, some new chapter would simply begin, easy and effortless. I was mistaken. The themes of the contract continued and still unfold, perhaps with even greater intensity, and refined precision. Yet, now I see where I have made progress, and where unresolved threads remain, and from that vantage point I can observe with a measure of distance, equanimity, and curiosity rather than confusion.

What has truly reshaped the unfolding of my life is understanding *why* certain events manifested, while others dissolved before materializing. To my astonishment, I learned that some of the entanglements with people around me were not designed solely for my evolution, but served to test *them*—intersections of consciousness where multiple destinies converged.

Pramala and I also discovered in our respective Soul contracts something that has brought us immeasurable joy: the unfolding preparation for our Ascension, and a profound sense that success is not merely possible, but imminent.

Perhaps you stand at the edge of this narrative with a questioning mind, observing from a cautious distance, or with a fierce, unquenchable hunger for inner truth. Do not allow hesitation or procrastination, two of the ego's most elegant mechanisms of delay, to claim yet another quiet victory.

The train has already begun to move. Our system shows you how to board it. We invite you to explore the content of your own Soul contract. Dare to inquire. Dare to initiate the most consequential decision of your existence: a wholehearted commitment to living in unbounded freedom. Dare to take your Higher-Self by the hand, and to step into the victorious journey that patiently awaits your consent!

RESTORE YOUR SELF TO ALIGN
WITH YOUR SOUL CONTRACT!
ALLOW YOUR SOUL TO MERGE
INTO A TRUE PARTNERSHIP
WITH YOUR HIGHER SELF.
COME AS YOU ARE.
NO PRE-REQUIREMENTS,
NO PRE-CONDITIONS,
NO NON-SENSE.
IT IS NOT ABOUT RELIGION.
IT IS ABOUT YOU.
EMBRACE THE OPPORTUNITY
TO CHANGE YOUR LIFE,
AND THE LIVES OF
THOSE WHO SURROUND YOU.
YOU WILL THANK CREATION YOU DID.

CHAPTER HIGHLIGHTS:

- The Life-Between-Lives review is a review period of reflection in which the Soul, identifies unfinished karmic patterns, and **prepares the blueprint for the next life**.
- A Soul contract **is created before incarnation**, establishing the key relationships, challenges, and learning themes intended to accelerate the removal of karma, and support the Soul's progress toward Ascension.
- **These agreements are not rigid fate**; they function like a planned journey with multiple possible routes, leaving room for free will, and different responses to life circumstances.
- The Seven Rays form **the primary curriculum of spiritual evolution**, with lessons in areas like power, love, intelligence, harmony, knowledge, devotion, and transformation.
- **Each incarnation is supported by a spiritual faculty** and guidance team, including Ascended Masters and other higher beings, whose **purpose is to help the individua**l navigate these lessons and progress toward Ascension.

CHAPTER TWENTY

HUMANITY BEYOND THE EGO - THE ROAD AHEAD

Throughout this book, we have explored the structure of consciousness, the role of the ego, and the gradual expansion of awareness. These ideas are not merely philosophical. They point toward a broader possibility for humanity itself.

The movement from ego-centered awareness toward expanded consciousness is not only an individual process. Over long periods of time, it also becomes a collective transformation. Just as individuals gradually grow beyond purely self-centered thinking, civilizations can also evolve beyond structures rooted primarily in fear, competition, and domination.

This evolution does not occur suddenly. It unfolds slowly, through countless individual awakenings that quietly reshape the culture around them. The future of humanity will not be determined solely by technology, economics, or politics. It will ultimately be shaped by the level of consciousness through which human beings perceive reality. When the level of consciousness changes, civilization changes with it.

To bring this into perspective: our home sits halfway between Dallas and the Oklahoma border. For millennia, this land knew only the lazy company of scrub oak, cedar, and rolling pastures. Yet, in just a few short years, an aggressive tide of urbanization has begun to rise, bringing with it the relentless spread of highways and shopping malls. While this expansion hasn't reached our homestead yet, the encroaching "civilization" feels like a looming shadow. One day, as we drove past the advancing concrete, we speculated that within a decade, a carpet of Walmarts, McDonald's, and CVS pharmacies would likely stretch all the way to the border. In that moment of contemplation, Ananda stepped into Pramala's mind with this clarity: *"No, it will not. By that time much of the people where you live will be in 4th and 5th Dimensions, and their hearts will have learned how to respect nature. Development will actually start to recede."*

COOPERATION REPLACING COMPETITION

Much of modern society operates on the assumption that life is fundamentally competitive. From early education to professional life, individuals are encouraged to compare themselves with others, to outperform rivals, and to secure advantage wherever possible.

This pattern is largely a reflection of ego-based awareness. The ego perceives the world as scarce and fragmented. It believes that another person's success somehow diminishes its own.

As consciousness expands, this perception begins to soften. Individuals gradually recognize that human potential is not a fixed quantity to be divided among competitors. It is something that can grow through collaboration.

In a society shaped by higher awareness, cooperation increasingly replaces rivalry as the dominant mode of interaction. Innovation and progress no longer arise from defeating others, but from working together to discover solutions that benefit all participants.

Competition does not entirely disappear. It simply loses its emotional intensity, and *becomes secondary to shared creativity.* It almost evokes how America was one-hundred and twenty years ago, but with heart compassion replacing entrepreneurship. How fantastic is that?

COMMUNICATION BEYOND WORDS

Human communication today relies heavily on language, interpretation, and assumption. Words carry meaning, but they also carry misunderstanding. Much conflict arises not from malicious intent, but from the limitations of symbolic communication.

In 1956, Soviet leader Nikita Khrushchev told Western diplomats: "We will bury you." In Russian, the phrase was closer to a Marxist idiom, meaning: "History will outlast you" or "We will be present when your system ends." However, when translated literally in the West, it sounded like a direct nuclear threat. The statement intensified Cold War fear, and hostility between the Soviet Union and the United States, feeding public perception that the Soviets intended physical destruction of the West.

On September 1, 1983, Korean Air Lines Flight 007, a civilian Boeing 747 traveling from New York City to Seoul, accidentally strayed hundreds of miles off course into Soviet airspace near Sakhalin Island. The Soviet military believed it might be a U.S. reconnaissance aircraft. Several communication failures compounded the situation: The Soviet pilots could not effectively communicate with the airliner. Warning signals were misunderstood or unseen. Ground controllers misinterpreted radar data. A Soviet fighter jet shot down the plane. Result: 269 people killed, and a major escalation in Cold War tensions between the United States and the Soviet Union.

Here is where the archetypal consciousness steps on stage: As individuals become more self-aware, their communication begins to change. Listening deepens. Emotional intelligence grows. People become more sensitive to subtle signals—tone, expression, and intention.

Over time this expanded sensitivity allows for forms of communication that are more intuitive, and less reactive. Understanding begins to arise before disagreement escalates.

It does not take take much imagination to conceive that advanced states of consciousness eventually allow a more direct form of awareness between individuals—an intuitive understanding that requires fewer words, and fewer defenses. Speech is on its way out; purposeful and intentional thought is on its way in. We will share with you that all languages on Earth will eventually be replaced by one language, not one to study at Berlitz, but a Light-language given to us by a very high life form.

Whether expressed through refined emotional intelligence or deeper intuitive perception, the overall effect is the same: communication becomes clearer, calmer, and more truthful and transparent.

THE REDUCTION OF PSYCHOLOGICAL CONFLICT

The majority of human conflict originates in internal psychological tension. Fear, insecurity, resentment, and the need for validation often drive behavior that leads to disagreement and hostility. When individuals begin to observe the workings of their own ego, these patterns gradually lose their unconscious control. The need to constantly defend an identity softens. Emotional reactions become less automatic. As more individuals undergo this inner shift, society itself becomes less psychologically volatile.

Disagreements will always exist. But disagreement does not have to lead to hostility. Diversity of thought and perspective is a natural part of human life.

In a more conscious civilization, *conflict is approached as a problem to understand* rather than an opponent to defeat.

SOCIAL STRUCTURES ORIENTED TOWARD WELL-BEING

Institutions reflect the consciousness of the people who create them. Economic systems, political systems, and social structures all arise from underlying assumptions about human nature. When those assumptions are dominated by fear and scarcity, institutions tend to emphasize control, hierarchy, and competition.

As consciousness evolves, the priorities of society gradually shift. Systems begin to focus less on domination, and more on collective well-being. Education becomes oriented toward developing awareness rather than merely transmitting information. Healthcare focuses not only on treating illness, but also on maintaining physical, emotional, and psychological balance.

Economic systems increasingly recognize that long-term stability arises from *shared prosperity* rather than extreme inequality. This is not an orientation toward socialism or other political models, but a heart-sourced genuineness, born out of kindness and compassion.

None of these changes occur overnight. They emerge slowly as new ideas take root, and older assumptions lose their influence.

CREATIVITY AND EXPLORATION AS CENTRAL HUMAN ACTIVITIES

Much of human energy today is devoted to securing *survival* and navigating social *competition*. While creativity certainly exists, it often occupies a secondary role within structures dominated by economic necessity, and personal ambition. We remind the reader how important creativity is as a conduit for archetypal imprints, as an accelerant to Ascension.

As societies become more stable, and psychologically balanced, human energy can increasingly shift toward exploration and creativity. Creativity is the mother of archetypal consciousness. Science, philosophy, art, and spiritual inquiry begin to flourish in new ways. Curiosity replaces fear as a driving force of discovery. Exploration—whether intellectual, cultural, or cosmic—becomes one of the defining characteristics of human civilization.

In such a world, progress is no longer measured primarily by accumulation of material wealth, but by expansion of understanding, and depth of experience.

THE NATURE OF TRANSFORMATION

To be clear, this vision of transformation is an aspiration, not a guarantee of a perfect world. Human beings will always possess individuality, differing perspectives, and the freedom to make choices that are wise or unwise.

The transformation described here is not about eliminating human complexity. It is about gradually shifting the center of gravity of human consciousness.

As awareness expands, the ego does not disappear. It simply takes its proper place as a useful instrument rather than the dominant authority within the mind. This shift begins very slowly, then accelerating within individuals who become more attentive to their thoughts, their emotions, and their motivations. Each moment of awareness weakens the automatic patterns of ego-driven behavior and strengthens the capacity for clarity and compassion.

Over time, these individual shifts accumulate. Cultures evolve. Institutions adapt. Civilization itself begins to reflect a broader level of awareness.

THE BEGINNING OF A LARGER JOURNEY

To reiterate, the ideas presented in this guide are not intended to project a rigid belief system. They are an *invitation* to explore the nature of consciousness, and the possibility of human evolution *beyond purely ego-centered awareness.*

The transformation described here does not begin in governments or institutions. It begins in the interior life of each of us. Every moment of genuine awareness, every act of compassion, and every step beyond fear contributes to a gradual expansion of human consciousness.

From these small inner changes, larger transformations eventually emerge.

The evolution of humanity is not something that will happen to us. It is something that unfolds *through* us.

And that journey has already begun.

CHAPTER HIGHLIGHTS:

- **Civilization evolves as consciousness evolves**. The long-term direction of humanity is ultimately shaped not by technology or politics, but by the level of awareness through which people perceive reality. When consciousness shifts, the structure of society shifts with it.
- **Cooperation gradually replaces competition.** As ego-centered thinking weakens, the belief in scarcity fades. Progress increasingly emerges from collaboration, and shared creativity rather than rivalry.
- **Communication becomes clearer** and more intuitive. Higher awareness produces deeper listening, emotional intelligence, and eventually forms of understanding that rely less on language, and more on direct perception.
- **Psychological conflict declines** as the ego loses dominance. Fear, insecurity, and identity-defense gradually lose their control over behavior, allowing disagreements to be approached as problems to understand rather than opponents to defeat.
- **Human energy shifts toward creativity**, exploration, and understanding. As societies stabilize and become more conscious, curiosity and discovery replace survival anxiety as the primary drivers of human activity.

CHARTING THE PATH FORWARD

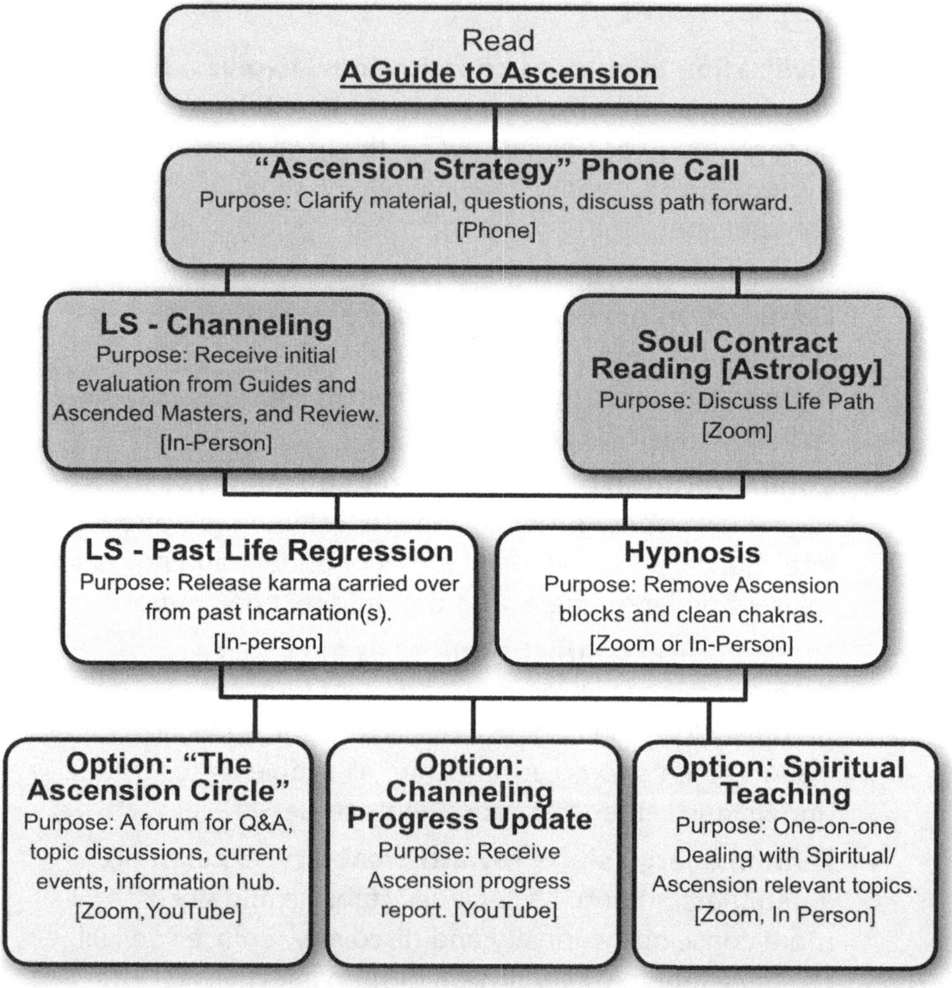

Recommended Reading:

The Law of One
[5 books]
Free online PDFs:
https://www.llresearch.org/books

Jesus: My Autobiography
by Tina Louise Spalding

Living the Wisdom of the Tao
by Wayne Dyer

The Map of Conscious Evolution

A Guide to Ascension

Page 1 – The Human Condition

1 Architecture of Consciousness

We are consciousness expressing itself through many layers.

Universal Consciousness
The source field – infinite, eternal, all-knowing.

Superconscious (Higher Self)
Our true self – wisdom, guidance, higher perspective.

Conscious Mind
Awake awareness – thought, choice, willpower.

Subconscious Mind
Inner storehouse – memory, habits, emotions.

Body / Ego Interface
Physical experience – channel for senses, instincts, survival.

Archetypal Consciousness (The Secret Agent)

Direction
Gives roadmap for spiritual evolution

Mind Link
Bridges Deep Mind w/ Infinite Intelligence

Syncretization
Polarizes Experience Toward Choice

3rd Density History in a Nutshell

Cycle Completion: 3rd Density concluded via three full solar precessions.

Vibrational Limit: Earth's calibration has shifted, ending its role as a 3rd-density vessel.

Sovereign Decision: Mandatory choice between local ascension or incarnation elsewhere.

2 Earth's School of Consciousness

Consciousness expresses itself through many lifetimes and densities.

1st Density – Matter
Consciousness in minerals, crystals and water.

2nd Density – Life (plant, animal)
Consciousness in plants, animals and proto-humans.

3rd Density – Self-Aware
Consciousness in humans.

4th Density – Unity
Consciousness in unity and love.

5th Density – Wisdom
Consciousness in wisdom and love combined.

Two dimensions: 3rd and 4th
3rd: A realm of self-awareness with strong polarity.
4th: A world of collective compassion.

Two dimensions: 5th and 6th
5th: A state of refined wisdom: Salvation
6th: Merging of love and wisdom into a singular, unified consciousness.

3 Our Present Stage

3rd Density – The Density of Challenges

3rd Density – The Density of Challenges
The Great School Of Consciousness and Ego

Free Will
Lesson: Learning to make a conscious spiritual choice.

Polarization
Lesson: Choosing between service to self or others.

Compassion
Lesson: Opening the heart to radiate unconditional love.

Catalyst
Lesson: Using life's challenges to fuel soul growth.

The Journey of Consciousness

Source → Experience → Learning → Balancing → Ascension → Return to Unity

PAGE 2 - THE PATH OF ASCENSION

4 THE EGO ILLUSION

3rd Density consciousness identifies with the limited self.

These illusions distorted perception and create imbalance

SEPARATION
I am separate from others and Source

FEAR
I fear pain, loss and the unknown.

DESIRE
I crave experiences, things, and validation.

ATTACHMENT
I cling to people, ideas, roles, and outcomes.

JUDGMENT
I judge myself and others as wright or wrong.

5 CREATION OF KARMA

Every action sets in motion a chain of energetic consequences.

ACTION
Thoughts, Words, Deeds

TRIAGE
Actions not aligned with the Logos of Creation are furthered for karmic storage.

KARMIC DISTORTION
Energetic imbalance is recorded in the energy body and subconscious.

THE THREE "ENGINES" OF ASCENSION

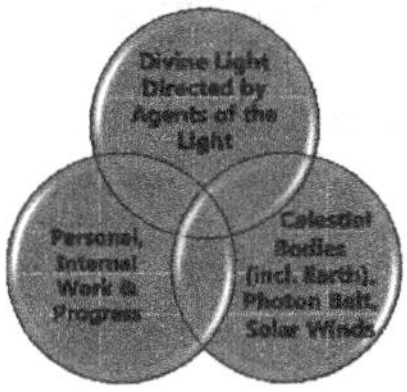

6 MECHANISMS OF KARMA RESOLUTION

Three Divine pathways clear karmic distortion, and restore balance.

DIVINE CLEMENCY
Creation and the Masters have granted "karmic asylum" in one or several chakras.

HARMONIC EQUALIZATION
You have effected positive actions that outweigh the negative karma.

LIGHTSTREAMING
LightStreaming neutralizes specific, targeted karma.

REMOVAL OF KARMA
The negative energy is cleared. Karma is dissolved. Ascension is within reach.

7 THE THREE ROADS TO FORGIVENESS

How we respond determines our path of growth.

LOW ROAD
Ego Reaction
You lied to me, but because I am such a great and kind person, I choose to forgive you.

MIDDLE ROAD
Self-Correction
You lied to me, and my ego reacted to it. I forgive myself for my shortcomings.

HIGH ROAD
The Master's Path.
You lied to me. My ego has been subdued, and I feel for your personal improvement.

♥ *Heart-centered forgiveness is the key that opens the door to Ascension* ♥

8 LIVING IN ALIGNMENT

Daily choices shape our frequency and future.

AWARENESS + INTENTION + ACTION + SERVICE + SURRENDER = ASCENSION

AWARENESS: Observe without judgment. See first the Soul, not the flesh.

INTENTION: Choose love, truth, and compassion with intent.

ACTION: Act in alignment with your highest values.

SERVICE: Serve and help the whole selflessly.

SURRENDER: Release control and trust the Divine Plan.

ASCENSION: You have aligned yourself with Ascension.

THE GREAT TRUTH
You are not your body. You are not your name. You are not your thoughts. You are consciousness using a body, a mind, and experiences to evolve, seek truth, and return to unity.

THE KINGDOM OF GOD IS WITHIN YOU

GLOSSARY

ACIM (A Course in Miracles): A self-study spiritual curriculum designed to help the student shift their perception from fear to love through the practice of forgiveness. The book was channeled by Yeshua from the Father through Helen Schucman, a psychologist, from 1965-1972.

Akashic Records: An energetic "library" or holographic imprint containing the history of every Soul's thoughts, words, and actions throughout all lifetimes, past and future.

Ananda: Sanskrit for *divine bliss* or *joy*; The name of a fluid spiritual memory complex composed of 5-8 members, including Yeshua, St. Germain, Buddha, Melchizedek and others.

Andromeda: Our neighboring galaxy; often seen as a source of high-vibrational wisdom, and home to advanced civilizations assisting Earth. Size and mass are about twice that of the Milky Way.

Angel: A non-physical being of light that serves as a messenger, protector, or guide between the Divine and the physical realm.

Anunnaki: A large ET collective/race (often associated with Sumerian texts) who played a complex role in Earth's early history and human genetic development. Members of the Galactic Federation.

Aquarian Age: The current astrological era, entered into in 2012 and estimated to last about 2150 yrs, It is characterized by a shift toward collective consciousness, innovation, humanitarianism, and the democratization of spiritual knowledge.

Archangel: A high-ranking celestial being who oversees vast aspects of the universe, and provides specialized support for humanity's evolution.

Ascended Master: An individual who has completed the cycle of reincarnation, attained total mastery over the physical plane, and now guides humanity from the higher realms.

Ascension: The process of raising one's vibrational frequency to shift consciousness from a limited, ego-based perspective to a higher state of unity and awareness.

Ascension Team: A group of non-physical guides—including masters, celestial beings—dedicated to supporting an individual's specific spiritual path.

Astral Consciousness: Awareness associated with the astral plane, where perception is shaped by emotions and thought-forms rather than physical matter. (*see also Cosmic Consciousness*)

Astrology: The study of the movements and relative positions of celestial bodies as a map for understanding energy timings and their relationship to cosmos.

Atlantis: A mostly 4th-dimensional civilization located in the Atlantic Ocean, that collapsed around 9600 BCE, due to the misuse of power and spiritual imbalance.

Avatar: A highly evolved being or divine aspect that incarnates into the physical world to initiate major shifts in consciousness.

Chakra: One of the seven primary energetic "wheels" or vortexes in the human body that process and distribute life-force energy.

Channeling: The practice of receiving and transmitting information or energy from non-physical sources through a human "vessel."

Christ consciousness: The state of universal love, wisdom, and oneness that identifies the human consciousness level at its highest level, accessible in the 5th- 6^{th}Dimensions.

Consciousness: The fundamental state of being; the "I Am" presence that precedes all form and is the fabric of reality itself. The building block of Creation.

Council of Light: a collective of highly evolved spiritual beings—often referred to as Ascended Masters, Archangels, and Galactic Elders—who oversee the spiritual evolution of humanity and the Earth.

Cosmic Consciousness: An expanded state of awareness where the individual recognizes a direct connection to the entire universe, or portions of it, and its divine intelligence.

Cosmic Master: An evolved being whose scope of service, and influence extends to the evolution of solar systems, galaxies, or the universe at large. This entity is often a teacher within The Seven Rays.

Crown Chakra: The energy center located at the top of the head; the gateway to connection with higher Spirit beings, and divine inspiration.

Density: A measure of the vibrational "weight" or speed of consciousness; each density represents a specific stage of spiritual evolution. Applies primarily to planetary bodies.

Dimension: A level of vibrational frequency rather than a physical location. Spiritual dimensions describe "how" something is experienced, and are the building blocks of densities. Dimensions are often viewed as different "lenses" through which we perceive reality.

DNA: Beyond its biological function, it is the energetic blueprint that carries "light codes," and dormant spiritual potential waiting to be activated.

Ego: The temporary, 3rd Dimensional identity focused on survival and separation; a necessary tool for navigating the physical world that must be (almost entirely) sidelined for Ascension.

Elohim: Powerful beings of light associated with the original creation of the physical universe and the manifestation of divine will. Mentioned in the Bible (Genesis) as creators of our planet. Ranked a step above the Ascended Masters and even the Archangels, in the hierarchy of Creation. Elohim is a plural form.

Ephemerides: Specialized astrological tables that delineate the precise positions of celestial bodies at any given point in time (since their discovery in recorded history).

Five Bodies, The (as in the 7 Rays): The five domains of the human body that Ascended Masters gauge to prepare us for Ascension: The Soul (the "manager"), the Emotional, the Personality, the Physical, the Mental.

FSS (Forces for Service to Self): Author's term, designating ET civilizations originating from non-ascended sun systems. They are Soul-less, artificially engineered, and believe that taking care of yourself first is more important than thinking collectively. Can be ruthless, cunning, violent, and deceptive.

Galactic Federation: A collective of 53 advanced civilizations in multiple galaxies, spread out on over 500 planetary entities; Think of them as the extra-terrestrial equivalent of NATO on our planet. They are beings from across the galaxy working to support peace and the evolution of worlds. Very positively oriented.

Great Shift: The current planetary transition involving a fundamental upgrade in the frequency of Earth and its inhabitants.

Great Split: The conceptual divergence of timelines where individuals choose to either remain in the lessons of the 3rd Density, or move into higher frequencies.

Harvest: An evaluation of each person's individual spiritual growth is assessed at the end of a precession. The amount of Souls who graduate to move forward is called the Harvest.

Heart Chakra: The body's central energy center; the bridge between the physical and spiritual selves, and the seat of unconditional love.

Higher-Self: The eternal, multidimensional part of your being that resides in the higher realms to guide your physical incarnation. Created at the same time as the Soul, and its constant companion.

Holy Spirit: A 6th Density spirit entity, originally put in place (by the Creator) to assist the return navigation of the ET entities who have later been named "the fallen angels."

Homo Lucis: "Man of Light;" Term coined by the authors as a name for the "new" human emerging with the shift of the Earth in 4th Density.

Hypnosis: A natural state of focused relaxation and heightened suggestibility that allows the conscious mind (the ego) to step aside. In the context of ascension, it is used as a tool to access the subconscious and superconscious minds, facilitating the retrieval of Soul memories, the clearing of karmic blocks, and direct communication with the Higher-Self.

Karma: a spiritual tension mark occurring when words, thoughts or deeds are not entirely governed by love. karma is stored in the chakras when alive, and in the Soul during life-between lives.

Kundalini: Kundalini is the coiled energy (often symbolized as a serpent). It is formed by two energies: one (heading up in the body), originating from the Root chakra, the other (heading down in the body) from the Crown chakra. Their meeting points is where your consciousness currently resides.

Law of One: A body of trance-channeled teachings transmitted through a series of 106 conversations (sessions) between 1981 and 1984 by Don Elkins, Carla Rueckert, and Jim McCarty, and a "social memory complex" from the 6th density residing on Venus, known as Ra.

Law of Reciprocity: "What is given shall be returned." This Law is not only applicable to inter-personal norms, but to spiritual concepts as well.

Life-between-lives: the time-span between two incarnations when the Soul retreats to the Spirit world.

Light: a universal metaphor for the highest state of consciousness, truth, and the origin of existence. It is the the primary intelligence of the Universe.

LightStreaming: An umbrella term for multiple modalities like past life regression, life-between-lives and channeling seeking to clear chakra blockages hindering ascension. LightStreaming only facilitates communication with confirmed agents of the Light.

Lower consciousness: A state of awareness primarily identified with the ego, the physical body, and the illusion of separation. It is characterized by a focus on 3rd-dimensional survival, linear time, and fear-based reactivity, often obscuring the individual's connection to the Higher-Self, and the unified field of existence.

Merkabah (or **Merkaba**): A Hebrew term meaning "chariot" or "to ride." In an esoteric context, it refers to a star-tetrahedron shaped "light vehicle" that surrounds the human body. It is composed of two counter-rotating fields of light, and serves as a multidimensional tool for protection, healing, and traveling between different densities of consciousness.

Metaphysics: Metaphysics is a primary branch of philosophy that explores the fundamental nature of reality, existence, and the universe. While physics deals with the how of the material world (laws of motion, particles, energy), metaphysics asks the what and why (what is existence, why is there something rather than nothing). The three main pillars of metaphysics are Ontology (The Study of Being), Cosmology (The Study of the Universe) and Universal Science (First Principles).

Miracle, The: Within the framework of A Course in Miracles (ACIM), a miracle is a fundamental shift in perception—the moment one chooses to see through the lens of love rather than the ego's lens of fear. It is an internal "correction" of the mind.

Moksha: (See Salvation) A Sanskrit term for liberation; the Soul's release from the cycle of rebirth (samsara) and its return to an eternal state of unity with the Source.

Multidimensional: The reality that consciousness exists on many levels of frequency and density simultaneously. To be multidimensional is to recognize that we are not merely physical beings, but exist across many planes of existence at once.

Nirvana: (See Salvation) A state of transcendent peace and the "extinguishing" of the ego's desires and suffering, leading to a permanent realization of Oneness.

Past Life Regression: A technique—often involving hypnosis—used to access subconscious memories of previous incarnations to heal current karmic patterns or emotional blockages (*see LightStreaming*).

Perception: The subjective lens through which we interpret reality. Ascension is the process of shifting from "egoic perception" (which sees separation) to "unified perception" (which sees connection).

Photon Belt: An astronomical and esoteric band of high-frequency light energy. As Earth passes through this "belt," it acts as a cosmic catalyst for the quickening of human consciousness.

Piscean Age: The astrological era (roughly the last 2,000 years) characterized by hierarchy, religious dogma, sacrifice, and the struggle between belief and doubt.

Plasma: In an esoteric sense, the "fourth state of matter" that serves as the bridge between physical matter and pure energy, often acting as a conductor for higher-dimensional light codes. Plasma is ionized gas particles. It is a state of matter where gas has become electrically conductive.

Prana: The universal life-force energy that sustains all living things. It is absorbed through the breath and circulated through the body's energy meridians. Most equivalent to Chi, the vital life force flowing through meridians.

Religion: A structured system of faith and worship often focused on external rules or deities; in this context, it is contrasted with Spirituality, which is based on direct internal, individual experience.

Root Chakra: The first energy center (Muladhara), located at the base of the spine. It governs physical survival, grounding, and the sense of safety within the physical world.

Sacral Chakra: The 2nd energy center (Svadhisthana), located in the lower abdomen. It governs creativity, emotional flow, and the vital energy of manifestation.

Sacred Consciousness: A state of awareness that recognizes the inherent divinity, holiness, and interconnectedness of every aspect of creation, activated during

5th and 6th Dimensions.

Salvation: In an ascension context, this is the "saving" of the Soul from the limitations of the 3rd-dimensional density and the successful integration with the Higher-Self.

Self: The eternal, unchanging "I AM" presence of a being. While the ego is a temporary mask, the Self is the immortal observer that journeys through all lifetimes.

Social Memory Complex: A collective consciousness formed when a group of Souls reaches a degree of unity where all thoughts and experiences are shared for the evolution of the whole.

Solar Plexus Chakra: The third energy center (Manipura), located above the navel. It is the seat of personal power, will, and the transition from ego-driven desire to spiritual intent.

Soul: The individualized spark of Divine Light that undergoes a journey through various densities to gather experience, wisdom, and self-awareness.

Soul Contract: A pre-incarnation agreement made by the Soul to encounter specific people or challenges for the purpose of spiritual growth and karmic resolution.

Soul Group: A cluster of Souls who share a similar vibrational signature and mission, often incarnating together across many lives to support one another.

Soul Star: The 8th chakra, located approximately six inches above the head. It acts as the gateway through which the Higher-Self filters light and wisdom into the physical vessel.

Soulmate: An individual from one's Soul group, or who interacts with the Soul group as an outlier, who provides a deep mirror for growth. These relationships are designed to provoke awakening, whether they are harmonious or challenging.

Spiritual: Pertaining to the non-physical, eternal aspects of existence and the expansion of awareness toward the Source. An ego-less state.

Star of David: A symbol of the Merkabah, representing the principle of "As Above, So Below"—the perfect integration of Spirit (the upward triangle) and Matter (the downward triangle). Considered an archetype.

Vedic: Vedic relating to the Vedas, the oldest sacred scriptures of Hinduism, or to the ancient Indo-Aryan culture, language, and era in which they were composed: estimated from ~1500 BCE to ~500 BCE. This era was marked by the development of early agrarian societies, and the foundations of classical Indian philosophy, social structures, and spiritual traditions.

INDEX

C

D

E

Q

R

S

U

A Final Reflection

The journey described in this book is not a distant future event.
It is the gradual unfolding of awareness that is already
occurring within humanity.

Each moment of greater understanding, each act of compassion,
and each movement beyond fear represents a small step
in that evolution.

Ascension is not an escape from the human experience.
It is the transformation of that experience
through expanded consciousness.

The purpose of this exploration has not been to provide a belief system,
but to invite a deeper awareness of the nature of mind, reality,
and the living field of consciousness in which all life participates.

The movement from ego-centered awareness to unity consciousness
begins quietly, within the inner life of each individual.

And from that quiet transformation,
the future of humanity gradually unfolds.

**The journey of consciousness
is already underway.**

Made in the USA
Coppell, TX
19 June 2026

81354872R00173